TEAMS THAT LEAD

A MATTER OF MARKET STRATEGY, LEADERSHIP SKILLS, AND EXECUTIVE STRENGTH

TEAMS THAT LEAD

A MATTER OF MARKET STRATEGY, LEADERSHIP SKILLS, AND EXECUTIVE STRENGTH

Theresa J. B. Kline
University of Calgary

LAWRENCE ERLBAUM ASSOCIATES, PUBLISHERS

2003   Mahwah, New Jersey   London

Copyright © 2003 by Lawrence Erlbaum Associates, Inc.

Lawrence Erlbaum Associates, Inc., Publishers
10 Industrial Avenue
Mahwah, NJ 07430

Cover design by Kathryn Houghtaling Lacey

Library of Congress Cataloging-in-Publication Data

Kline, Theresa, 1960–
Teams that lead : a matter of market strategy, leadership skills,
    and executive strength / Theresa J. B. Kline.
    p. cm.
Includes bibliographical references and index.
ISBN 0-8058-4237-3 (cloth : alk. paper)
ISBN 0-8058-4542-9 (pbk. : alk. paper)
1. Leadership. 2. Executives. 3. Organizational effectiveness.
    I. Title.
HD57.7 .K549 2003
658.4'092—dc21

                                                              2002027150
                                                                     CIP
Books published by Lawrence Erlbaum Associates are printed on acid-free paper, and their bindings are chosen for strength and durability.

Printed in the United States of America
10 9 8 7 6 5 4 3 2 1

Contents

Part II   Team Leadership Roles

Part III   Top-Team Actions

List of Tables

List of Figures

Preface

This book was written for individuals whose primary interest in perusing this type of material is to find information that can be turned into useful knowledge for a specific purpose. The focus of this book is on teams and, in particular, the concept of leadership in teams. Thus, those who stand to benefit most from reading this book have an interest in the scholarly literature on teams and leadership insofar as it can be useful. These individuals respect that good practice is based in good science. However, they have neither the time nor the inclination to wade through volumes of journal articles to find something that they can use in their own organizations.

This book does try to strike a balance in providing a summary of much of the current scholarly literature in the three topic areas of market strategy, leadership roles, and executives as they pertain to teams. However, covering the entire waterfront of each of those areas in terms of specific studies would require separate volumes in and of themselves. Thus, although each section begins with an overview of the literature, the focus is to translate that into practical applications for improving team performance—specifically in the three domain areas noted. The chapters that follow in each part do just that.

The first part of the book focuses on how to become a "leading team." The literature on team effectiveness and impact at the organizational level is virtually nonexistent. An important question then is: How can teams be more effective at contributing to the bottom line of the organization? One way to tackle this is by discerning how well teams are structured, populated, and managed, so that they are fully integrated into the marketing focus of the company. Teams are expensive to develop and maintain; to be viewed as an essential asset rather than a liability for an organization, this link to market strategy needs to be made.

The second part of the book turns to leadership activities that need to occur in teams. Who is responsible for what activities has, until now, gone unnoticed by scholars and practitioners. The skills needed to effectively provide leadership to teams are many and varied. How to best develop the skills most essential for a specific leadership role is an effective and efficient way to deal with the fact that individuals have a limited number of resources at their disposal to develop skill sets. They need to hone in on the ones that they either (a) want to develop or (b) need to develop. A framework for how to assist in this process is provided in Part II.

The third part of the book focuses on "leadership teams"—better known as executive teams. Again, the literature on these teams is scarce. I have spent the past few years researching them and have some concrete suggestions about how they can become "leading teams."

Measurement tools, case studies, and examples populate this book. It is my intention to make readers aware of some of the current thinking, introduce new ideas about team leadership, and also provide some direct links to how this might be of value to them in their own work.

✦ ACKNOWLEDGMENTS

Thanks for ensuring that this project was completed go to several individuals. First, much appreciation goes to Anne Duffy, Senior Editor at Lawrence Erlbaum Associates; she was unflinching in her support from the get-go. Second, the reviewers who took the time to carefully read and make excellent comments ensured that this was a much better product in the end than it would have been without their assistance. Finally, I am indebted to all those individuals who willingly provided their time in participating in my research.

CHAPTER

1

Introduction: Defining Leading Teams

The purpose of this book is to provide three perspectives, or lenses, through which to view team leadership and how those various lenses can assist in making teams more effective. The first lens is one that focuses on paying close attention to the market strategy of the organization and how it should drive key decisions. These decisions include creating appropriate cultures, selecting and rewarding members for activities aligned with the strategy, and setting up structures and processes that align team activities with the organization's market focus.

The second lens focuses on the multiple roles of the designated leader of a team. Leaders need to interact with their teams differently depending on the team's needs. Activities that any given leader should focus on should be those most beneficial to their particular team.

The third lens shifts to executive teams. These teams need to be populated by those who have honed their team skills well. To be a highly effective team player in the executive environment poses unique challenges. These three lenses are not meant to exhaust all possible ways to examine or facilitate team leadership. They are, instead, presented as useful ways of thinking about teams and leadership.

1

The book is structured so that the practical implications rest on theoretical and empirical grounds. That is, first relevant theoretical perspectives and results from studies are reviewed. After these introductions, how this information can be useful to practitioners follows using examples, cases, measuring tools, and questions. These are provided to transform the abstract theories and sometimes far-flung, esoteric research findings into practically useful information. This approach should be particularly valuable to those who work with teams and develop team leadership as part of their professional lives and who desire to have their activities grounded in state-of-the-art theory and research.

✦ WHY THE INTEREST IN TEAM LEADERSHIP?

Teams have too often been the wrong solution to an organizational problem. They have been seen as a way to get around the fact that organizations have all but eliminated their middle layers of managers; teams were used to make up for these position deficiencies. They were a way for organizations to adopt aspects of total quality management (TQM) practices without having to bite off the whole TQM philosophy. Teams were seen as a way to increase employee commitment to organizations in the hope that members would feel a sense of loyalty to their teammates that they might not feel toward the organization as a whole. One of the results of these misapplications of teams has been an underestimation of the amount of resources it takes to make teams a viable organizational entity. Another has been a growth in the belief that teams don't work. The latter is an outgrowth of the former.

Some of the concerns associated with the poor realization of what teams were supposed to accomplish have been remedied by several empirical studies accompanied by reports of the practical applications of that research. Most promising have been the findings highlighting the management of the team's context as a primary driving force in team success or failure (e.g., Guzzo & Shea, 1992; Kline, 1999; Mohrman, Cohen, & Mohrman, 1995).

One of the most important contextual variables that keeps cropping up is that of team leadership. However, the complexity of this "leadership" phenomenon has not allowed teams and organizations to capitalize on the opportunities that excellent team leadership can provide. So what do we mean by "team leadership"? Given the high degree of interest by organizations in developing both teams as well as leadership, this phenomenon needs to be systematically understood.

There are many sources on and various perspectives about what constitutes team leadership (e.g., Manz & Sims, 1987; Tjosvold & Tjosvold, 1991; Wellens, Byham, & Wilson, 1991). A major difficulty is wading through this voluminous information and finding out what is relevant for which organizational context and to solve which problem. If the purpose is to increase team leadership capability, then we need to first go back and think through how team leadership is defined. Once defined, the hunt for an appropriate intervention or development strategy can be focused and effective.

This book operationally defines three fundamentally distinguishable, but complementary, aspects of team leadership; these are shown in Fig. 1.1. This model provides one team leadership framework. The various perspectives will assist in developing teams that lead in a particular context.

The model indicates that high-performing teams are the result of (a) the team being in tune with its market environment, (b) the roles of team leaders being allocated and executed appropriately, and (c) the top-management team modeling effective team actions. When these are in alignment, the environment is set for successful team performance.

✦ MARKET ENVIRONMENT

The first perspective focuses attention on the importance of the organization's market environment. Treacy and Wiersema (1995a) argued convincingly that for an organization to be a market leader, it must adhere to primarily one market principle. They noted that market leaders are leaders because they typically have excelled at one value discipline; however, a small handful of companies have mastered two (Treacy & Wiersema, 1993).

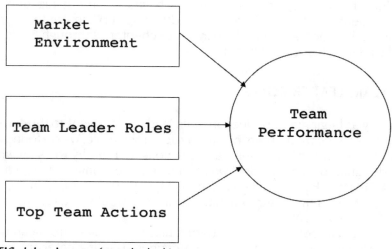

FIG. 1.1.   Aspects of team leadership.

The three options proposed are: (a) product leadership, (b) operational excellence, and (c) customer intimacy (Treacy & Wiersema, 1995a). Treacy and Wiersema (1995b) noted that pursuing a value discipline is not the same thing as choosing a strategic goal. The choice of discipline cannot simply be grafted onto existing operating policies. It is not a marketing campaign ploy or a way to woo stockholders. Choosing a discipline for focus shapes every other act and practice within the organization; it defines what an organization does and therefore what it is.

Product leadership means that a conscious decision has been made to put organizational resources into "doing new things," in other words, being the first to market with a new or innovative product or service. Research and development are areas of high resource consumption in these organizations.

Operational excellence means that a conscious decision has been made by the organization to improve on what is already in place. Efficiency is the hallmark of these organizations. They deliver a product or service at low cost; and they strive to do so in record time and with no errors. The resources of these organizations focus on process innovation.

Customer intimacy means that a conscious decision has been made that the organization will not be all things to all people. The customer niche has been selected and all systems are set up (including the team systems) to enhance the effectiveness of developing, cultivating, and sustaining a select group of customers.

The decision of the organization to focus on a particular market strategy—or discipline—has clear implications for all the systems in the organization. Teams labeled as "high-performance" or "top-performing" are leaders because of an alignment with their organization's market discipline; that is, they are leading teams because the organization has clearly defined its market strategy and has set up the context for its teams to be leaders. Part I, which includes chapters 2 through 5, defines and explains this feature in detail.

✦ TEAM LEADER ROLES

When I was beginning a project on team leadership, I went to the existing literature to see what others had to say about the topic. What I found was a confusing array of no fewer than 71 various and sundry roles for which the designated "team leader" was supposedly responsible (e.g., Parker, 1994; Yeatts & Hyten, 1998; Zaccaro & Marks, 1999). After carrying out these 71 roles, I'm not sure when this individual would actually have time to do their own work!

There did appear to be a way to organize these roles into meaningful and, more important, manageable categories. The first category is that of a *team manager*. The team reports to and is responsible to this individual, and this individual has position authority over the team. The second category includes roles that are primarily operational in nature— getting the tasks done and being mindful of team member needs. I call this category *team coach*. The final category is that of a *team facilitator*. This individual is interested in improving the processes by which the team's work is accomplished.

By grouping the roles into categories, a useful way to assign, monitor, assess, and train team leadership skills becomes apparent. Better yet, you can actually get someone to be pleased to be assigned the position of "team leader." Part II, which includes chapters 6 through 9, expands on this team feature.

✦ TOP TEAM ACTIONS

I interviewed an individual who had recently become a member of his firm's executive team. He pointed out that he was surprised at how little attention executive team members paid to the fact that they were closely watched by the rest of the organization's members. Executive teams have been of interest to scholars and practitioners alike (e.g., Bantel & Jackson, 1989; Carpenter & Fredrickson, 2001; Finkelstein & Hambrick, 1990; Nadler, Spencer, & Associates, 1998). However, their effective functioning as a team has remained elusive.

There do appear to be several ways to enhance the function of these teams. These include: a clear understanding of their role in the organization, definitive accountability for their actions, excellent chairship, a common goal, a sense of personal accomplishment at the individual level, interpersonal skills, functional expertise, and appreciation of diverse perspectives. Executive team actions are carefully monitored by other organizational members as well as members of the public. The degree to which these teams, made up of functional experts, are capable of modeling cohesive team leadership determines to a large extent the degree to which other teams in the organization can be leaders. Part III, which includes chapters 10 through 13, highlights the important functions of executive teams.

✦ BOOK PURPOSE AND OUTLINE

No single perspective, nor single text can do justice to all of the variables associated with the complex, interrelated, and dynamic nature of team leadership within an organizational context. This book is not meant to be a comprehensive review of every current theory and research study associated with teams and leadership. Nor is it meant to examine a model of interpersonal team dynamics. Rather, it is a contribution to the growing need for taking what we know and applying that knowledge to team leadership and team leadership development. Part I focuses on developing "leading teams" by ensuring that the market strategy meshes with organizational systems that impact teams. Part II is devoted to identifying and developing specific team leader roles. Finally, Part III describes how teams of leaders—executive teams—can be most effective.

Each of these parts is divided into sections. The first section sets the stage with existing theory and research that speak directly to the issue under consideration. This may seem somewhat tedious or superfluous for those who want a quick answer on how to use the information. However, a firm understanding of what we actually do know—and the questions still left unanswered—is useful in providing a framework for why team interventions work or don't work. The next sections in each part are devoted to cases, examples, and measuring tools. These are practical tools that will help individuals or organizations develop team leadership in all three domains of market environment, team leadership roles, and executive team actions.

I

Market Environment

B y way of a brief introduction, the focus of the next four chapters is on the market environment faced by all organizations, regardless of sector or industry type. That is, determining the best market focus for the organization must set the stage for all else that occurs in the firm. Teams, of course, are part of the firm and as such are greatly affected by the market strategy of the organization. This book takes the approach that if the organization actively targets a market approach, then the structure, culture, policies, and personnel systems must be aligned closely with such a strategy. In chapter 2, a clearer picture of three market foci is introduced and exemplars of firms that exhibit these characteristics are described. In chapter 3 the market focus is innovation, in chapter 4 the focus is on process effectiveness, and in chapter 5 the focus is on customer service. In each of these chapters, how to set up the organizational features most critical to success is defined.

Market Environment

Organizational Strategy

Ⓗow do organizations create an environment that is conducive to the development of leading teams? By this I mean that others point to these teams as being special; they are able to elicit interest from outsiders as to why they are so good at performing their work; they are the ones that are called "high-performing."

✦ CONTEXT FROM THE ORGANIZATIONAL BEHAVIOR FRAME OF REFERENCE

In most models of team performance, based on organizational behavior perspectives, there has been a conspicuous absence of the important role of the organization's external environment and its influence on team performance. This is the case even in many of the most well-known models of team performance. Table 2.1 summarizes the major work done in this area and highlights the fact that this perspective on "context" has largely meant the internal organizational environment.

There have been a few rhetorical attempts to broaden the contextual perspective to encompass the environment external to the organization. However, they have not been used. For example, models by Salas,

TABLE 2.1
Summary of the Team Context Research From the Organizational Behavior
Frame of Reference in Chronological Order

Citation	Context Variables Measured
McGrath (1964)	Team task assignment Team reward structure Level of environmental stress on the team
Gladstein (1984)	Leadership Structuring of activities Intragroup processes Boundary management
Pearce and Ravlin (1987)	Task conditions Organizational conditions (i.e., appropriate team expectations and managerial support) Personnel conditions
Hackman (1988)	Organizational reward system Organizational educational system Organizational information system
Sundstrom, DeMeuse, and Futrell (1990)	Organizational culture Task design Technology Mission clarity Autonomy Performance feedback Rewards and recognition Training Physical environment
Campion, Medsker, and Higgs (1993)	Training Manager support Communication and cooperation between groups
Cohen (1994)	Employee involvement Supervisory behaviors Group task design Group characteristics
Kline (1999)	Organizational support Supervisory support

Dickinson, Converse, and Tannenbaum (1992) and Tannenbaum, Beard, and Salas (1992) both included environmental uncertainty as part of the organizational/situational characteristics influencing the relationships between a series of input-throughput-output variables of team performance. However, the influence is not directly assessed or evaluated in their research. Also, Mohrman et al. (1995) stated that teams are most useful when they fit with the strategy of the organization. However, they did not detail the various strategies that could be undertaken to carry this through. Instead they divided organizations into two types: those that do "routine work" (programmed, repeated patterns, analyzable, well understood, and static) versus those that do "nonroutine work" (emergent, varied, unique, interdependent, uncertain, dynamic). Yeatts and Hyten (1998) specifically pointed out that environmental factors outside the organization have not been well studied in terms of their effects on team performance. They postulated that overall economic conditions, technological conditions, demographic conditions, societal education levels, political and legal conditions, and societal culture would all have an impact on team performance. Unfortunately, no follow-up work on these variables in terms of their operationalization or of their effects has been forthcoming.

In summarizing much of the research to date on team effectiveness, Guzzo (1995) indicated that the importance of the organizational context is a recurring theme. This "context," though, is primarily made up of variables such as staffing and reward practices, technology use, goal structures, decision-support systems, and management of team stressors. This literature highlighted the importance of organizational context, which has significant practical implications. Indeed, regardless of the specific theory used to drive practice, the context as it is defined from this perspective provides organizations with useful levers for improving team effectiveness. However, it is incomplete.

✦ CONTEXT FROM THE TEAM-TYPE PERSPECTIVE

From a somewhat different perspective, team type has been noted to be an important contextual variable in determining team performance. For example, the work edited by Hackman (1990) proposes that there are different types of teams and they will be successful based on unique variables. These team types are set up based on the type of work in which the team is most typically engaged and include: top-management groups, task forces, professional support teams, performing teams, human service teams, customer service teams, and production teams. Although this team typology may be useful in describing the work of different teams, the case studies presented do not shed any light on whether the organization's strategy or external environment was a factor in determining whether or not the teams worked well.

Using a different typology approach, Scott and Einstein (2001) proposed that different types of teams (e.g., work and service teams, project teams, and networked teams) needed to be appraised and rewarded for different types of activities. I agree with them. However, although they called this a "strategic performance" approach, what was missing in the strategy was the link with the external environment. In Cohen and Bailey's (1997) review of the team literature, teams are divided into four types: work, parallel, project, and management teams. In the end they called for more research into the environmental factors that will influence team effectiveness above and beyond that provided by the team-type approach.

✦ TAKE-HOME MESSAGES FROM THESE PERSPECTIVES

Years of exceptionally well conducted team research using these models can be readily translated into human resource practices. Specifically, for teams to be effective, the type of task the team works on should drive the structure of and processes surrounding the team. That is to say that the task the team has been set to accomplish should drive fundamental team issues such as team size, configuration, and member role. Additionally, the team's task should require a high level of interdependency among members. The literature to date is very clear that teams must have interdependent work or they will not behave like a team. Quite simply, if the team is to perform, it must have the physical, financial, and human resources to execute the work. Teams need to be supported by the organization by having support systems for team training and team performance in place. At the individual member level, the ability to contribute in terms of both technical skills and knowledge as well as inter-personal and communication skills is essential for teams to work well. Teams need to understand how their work fits into the overall organizational goals. Effective feedback systems should be in place to direct the team's activity to align with the desired organizational goals. Accountability for and evaluation of team outputs are also essential for teams to be successful.

Clearly, the road to building a successful team environment is an expensive one and should not be embarked on with the notion that the organization will go from a traditional, individualistic operation to a team-based one overnight. As for the aforementioned team context variables, we are highly confident that managing them effectively will result in good team performance. However, from an overall understanding of why some teams are able to perform exceptionally (are leaders) and some are not, an important aspect has been lacking. Specifically, the broader context in which the organization finds itself has not been included in the research and practice of building effective team environments.

✦ THE PERFORMANCE CONTEXT FROM A STRATEGIC MARKETING FRAME OF REFERENCE

The literature on organizational performance from a strategic perspective has a very lengthy and successful history. Pioneer researchers in this area (e.g., Burns & Stalker, 1961; Lawrence & Lorsch, 1967; Miles & Snow, 1978; Mintzberg, 1979) concluded that organizations that are structured and designed to take advantage of their environment by aligning with it are the most successful. The environmental variables that they have argued are most important include the age and size of the organization, stability and complexity of the market, and degree of technological dependence. Somewhat later, Nadler (1992) too, suggested that variables such as technology, competition, customer expectations, ownership, globalization, and government participation influence organizational effectiveness. Senge's seminal work (1990) reminded us of the need for systemic thinking in order to maximize performance. His contention was that the components of systems thinking, personal mastery, mental models, building shared vision, and team learning combine to create the potential for learning at the organizational level.

It is time to think about teams from a strategic frame of reference. Specifically, the perspective adopted here is that a market strategy should be used as a way to leverage the organization's strategic position (see Fig. 2.1). How teams "fit" into an organization's strategy is the first issue to be dealt with in building leading teams.

There are some excellent examples of strategic market alignment in the extant literature. For example, Walker and Lorsch (1968) suggested that the most fundamental issue facing a manager is whether to group organizational activities primarily around a product or around a function. They went on to describe the repercussions of this initial choice. Alternatively, Porter (1980) suggested that two business strategies exist: low cost and differentiation. The low-cost strategy allows the firm to produce and sell its products or services at the lowest possible cost. The differentiation strategy involves producing products or services that differ markedly from others on the market. Another way to approach strategy uses the product life cycle of growth, sustain, and then harvest as its basis (e.g., Drury, 1994; Sizer, 1989).

Another strategy was proposed by Treacy and Wiersema (1993) and is adopted as the strategic perspective in this book. They contended that to be a market leader, an organization must be excellent at primarily one thing. The premise for excelling at one thing is that an organization can-

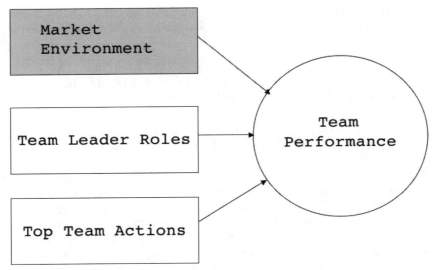

FIG. 2.1. Aspects of team leadership: Market environment.

not be all things to all people. Instead it needs to focus its resources on a specific competitive advantage.

It is worth noting that many researchers in the organizational behavior area typically are not familiar with the work of Treacy and Wiersema (1993, 1995a, 1995b). This is not true, however, in many other disciplines such as sales (e.g., Shepherd, 1999), marketing (e.g., Jacobs, Hyman, & McQuitty, 2001; Srivastava, Shervani, & Fahey, 1999), accounting (e.g., Moore, Rowe, & Widener, 2001), logistics (e.g., Waller, Dabholkar, & Gentry, 2000), and services (e.g., Helman & DeChernatony, 1999). Bringing this model into what has been traditionally the domain of organizational behavior provides a perspective on team performance that is ripe for being taken advantage of in terms of improving team performance.

The three marketing disciplines identified by Treacy and Wiersema (1993) are: product leadership, operational excellence, and customer intimacy. Although these descriptors are helpful in terms of defining the markets, the terms themselves are somewhat limiting. Specifically, "product leadership" excludes innovation in the service sectors, "operational excellence" excludes all other aspects of the process of product or service delivery, and "customer intimacy" would be very difficult to adhere to in some situations, such as in the "dot-com" environment.

Thus, the terms I use throughout this book to more broadly define these segments, and thus to be more inclusive of the review of the literature, are: *product/service innovation, process effectiveness,* and *customer service.* (see Fig. 2.2). All organizational systems—including why and how to use teams—that are supportive of the strategy adopted need to fall into place.

Organizations that don't pay enough attention to all three strategies are not going to survive either. Treacy and Wiersema (1993) rightfully acknowledged that an organization needs to meet industry standards in all three strategy areas, but carve out its specific niche in one. In other words, there is a minimum standard of performance on all three dimensions that customers expect. For example, excellent interactions with customers will not make up for tediously slow delivery or poor quality. However, the decision to focus on one strategy is what will set an organization apart from the others in the industry. This is also what will set an organization's teams on the track to being identified as leaders.

In the next few paragraphs, I attempt to link the market strategies suggested by Treacy and Wiersema (1993) with developing teams that will capitalize on the market strategy adopted by the organization as a whole. In other words, the rhetoric about what the organization needs to do to be a market leader has to be translated to the level of the teams that make up the organization.

If the organization's strategy is to focus on product or service innovation:

1. Teams will need to work on problem-solving and creativity-building skills.
2. Acceptance of novel ideas to pursue must be an organizational and team norm.

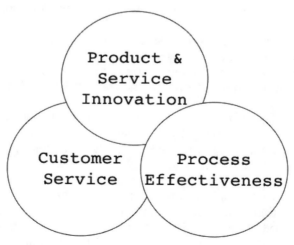

FIG. 2.2.   Market strategies.

3. The ability to tolerate criticism, and the ability to provide constructive critical evaluation will be paramount for team members involved in product innovation strategies.
4. The resource of time to search out the "latest and greatest" will need to become part of the job description for members of these teams.
5. The understanding that those outside the organization will be most likely to shed new light on ways of doing business will ensure that these team members are outwardly focused.
6. Sharing information with team members will be rewarded, and hoarding it from them will not be tolerated.

If the organization's strategy is to focus on process effectiveness:

1. Teams must constantly be looking inward at how to get the same product or service to market faster and more efficiently.
2. Rewards and recognition for these teams comes via acculturating new members quickly, streamlining processes, adapting to the established "organizational ropes," and adherence to company standards.
3. When the organization shifts gears, the most effective teams will be those that are able to adapt current processes to new ones.

If the organization's strategy is to zero in on customer service as its market trademark, then its success will depend on the one-to-one interactions between customers and employees and:

1. The interpersonal skills of teams must be highly developed as the team members' primary purpose is to make sure that customer expectations about being treated as important and unique are exceeded.
2. Teams will need to be empowered to make decisions as they relate to customer needs.
3. This empowerment will need to be accompanied by training and reward systems that reinforce team members for working together to solve customer problems.
4. Teams will need to be cross-trained not necessarily based on tasks but on customers. How to effectively "hand off" a customer to another team member when a shift ends or a project moves to another phase will be critical.

Teams are costly to initiate and maintain. For them to be viewed as an investment rather than a cost, teams must be seen to be consistently contributing to the rapid implementation of the organization's strategy. This means measuring team performance in terms of attainment of the organization's strategic goals.

It is time to shift the spotlight of team performance directly onto the strategic organizational level. When this is done, it becomes clear that leading teams means first and foremost strategic market alignment. In the next section, the three market strategies are described in detail using the work not just of Treacy and Wiersema, but of many other researchers and practitioners who have studied them in depth.

◆ LEADERSHIP VIA A FOCUSED MARKET STRATEGY

Dividing market strategies into three primary areas has some definite advantages. Organizations cannot be all things to all people. Instead they need to decide what they will be known for, that is, what customers will expect from them. The next sections describe in some detail the three strategies as well as some organizations and people who best exemplify the different strategies.

✧ The Product/Service Innovation Strategy

Foxhall (1984) pointed out that effective consumer product innovation (i.e., those products that were considered successful) have three fundamental characteristics. First, they add value by providing something that is not available elsewhere. Second, they are distinctive enough to be considered very different from other competing products. Finally, these products arrived to the marketplace first. The processes in place to assist in this endeavor included: (a) a superior understanding of customer needs, (b) resources put into marketing of the new product, (c) thorough product development work, (d) freely involving external technological expertise and advice, and (e) personal commitment on the part of those involved in the product development to see it be successful. A key finding of Foxhall's was that the ability to increase the effectiveness of new products was more under executive control than environmental control. What he meant by this was that it mattered less what type of environment or industry the organization was in than how the organization responded to that environment. Responding meant designing organizational structures and processes that supported new-product development success and he viewed this as under executive or management control.

Treacy and Wiersema (1995a) argued that customers are not impressed with one-time innovations followed by a series of "improvements." This, they said, is not a product/service innovation strategy. They attributed the formula for success within this market strategy to Thomas Edison, who is credited with more than 1,300 inventions. Some aspects of this formula include getting and keeping highly motivated, talented, and creative people, keeping the organization's goals simple (e.g., how can a building be kept lit?), and understanding that part of the marketing process would include educating in terms of what the new product could do to enhance people's lives. This last part of the formula is consistent with a key ingredient of the product leadership market strategy as described by Treacy and Wiersema, that is, to appeal to people's experience and emotions. They cited Nike as indulging people's hunger to be associated with sports heroes, Revlon as tapping into people's hopes for beauty, and Maxis computer games as playing into people's need for power.

Though Treacy and Wiersema (1995a) cited several companies that have successfully adopted this strategy, they used Intel as a featured exemplar. They did so partly because the microprocessor chip industry is highly competitive. They noted that Intel spends lavishly on its research and development and pushes to the very limits its manufacturing technology. In addition, Intel retains product leadership by "precisely targeting customers, educating them about complex products with missionary zeal, feeding customer ideas back to marketers and designers, operating with a team-based quick-change organization, constantly trying to go one better than competitors, and disciplining people's innovative ideas to meet the demands of new markets" (p. 105).

Christensen (1997) provided another perspective on innovating organizations. He pointed out that organizations wanting to capitalize on technological innovations (defined as "processes by which the organization transforms labor, capital, materials, and information into products or services of greater value" [p. xiii]) should take heed. First, he divided the technological innovations into two types: *sustaining technologies* and *disruptive technologies*. In essence, sustaining technologies are readily integrated into existing organizational systems and improve the performance of existing products or services.

Disruptive technologies, on the other hand, result in worse performance in the near term. These are changes where either the "value added" dimension of the new product or service to the customer is undefined or the market for such value is unknown, is very small, or has yet to be defined. When organizations pursue the marketing of their products that use disruptive technologies in the same way as for their established products, it causes organizational havoc. Primarily, this stems from the traditional customer base not understanding or not being interested in using the new technology. The potential market for such technologies is at the fringe of the traditional customer base. Christensen (1997) went on to counsel organizations interested in taking advantage of such technologies to: (a) disregard the traditional marketplace, as those customers are not the ones most likely to be interested in the new technology, and instead try to come up with new markets, and (b) form a small business unit and provide it with enough resources to give the new technology a try. This way the entire organization and the traditional systems set up to support the traditional products and services are not at risk.

Kuhn (1996), in his discussions about the conditions under which revolutions are created in science, pointed out that, "As in manufacture so in science—retooling is an extravagance to be reserved for the occasion that demands it" (p. 76). Thus, he concurred with Christensen (1997) insofar as dramatic change can be highly disruptive. No longer are the tools of the scientific trade as they presently stand sufficient to cope with the new theory. As in manufacturing, then, revamping an entire operation around a yet-to-be-established market is risky.

Christensen (1997) pointed out that pursuing these disruptive technologies can be dangerous for organizations that are not set up to take advantage of such technologies. His concern is echoed by Berggren and Nacher (2001) in their description of why new-product failure rates are so high. However, some organizations have been very successful at creating an environment that emphasizes taking advantage of disruptive technologies. These are the organizations that have made a concerted effort to develop their structures and processes to be consistent with a market strategy that is product/service innovation oriented.

A book by Kanter, Kao, and Wiersema (1997) highlights five organizations (3M, DuPont, General Electric, Pfizer, and Rubbermaid) recognized for their product innovation. These organizations, though they operate in very different industries, demonstrate a consistent product/service innovation market approach to their organizational design and processes. That is, these five organizations have made innovation systematic and perpetual by building it into their cultures and processes.

The first of the five is 3M. Coyne (1997) described the 3M's product innovation strategy. 3M tries not only to keep up with customer needs but to anticipate them. This means that employees need to know how 3M products are being used on the shop floors. There is strong encouragement for interdepartmental conversations. Forums are held regularly so that the technical people throughout 3M have the opportunity to listen to presentations by speakers from Nobel laureates to 3M managers on all kinds of interesting topics, for example, describing product nightmares so that others don't make the same mistakes. A culture of creative risk taking is adopted. Reward, recognition, and promotion systems are based on adherence to the product innovation strategy.

Miller (1997) wrote that at DuPont there is "an environment that guides and focuses discovery research without stifling it, a structured process that uses multidisciplinary teams to speed and guide our discoveries ... and systems that assure that our technology development speaks to the needs of our customers" (pp. 68–69). He noted that findings of surveys of technical employees show that these individuals take great pleasure in collaborating with their colleagues and peers—both within and outside the organization.

Edelheit (1997) recounted that General Electric used to completely separate the research and development group from the engineering group, who were separate from the design and production group. He noted that in today's environment, focusing on retaining skills, or on being faster than the competition, or on reducing costs is not enough to sustain a company. Instead, GE tries to achieve simultaneous and continuous improvements in performance, speed, cost, and quality. To do this the boundaries between the various parts of the organization needed to be eliminated. Cross-functional innovation teams are continually being set up. Close contact with suppliers and customers is critical.

Steere and Niblack (1997) claimed that Pfizer manages its innovation. To do so, they set up multidisciplinary teams to critically examine potential drug candidates, focus their efforts on applied rather than basic research, manage collaborative relationships with organizations outside Pfizer, communicate effectively with various constituencies, and reward teams for their contributions.

Schmitt (1997) said that Rubbermaid is the master of the mundane—they solve everyday problems that confront all people. He noted that Rubbermaid has been one of the most admired companies by adopting several operating principles. These include:

1. Cross-functional teams are the primary organizational configuration.
2. Oversight teams are drawn from the company's top executives and supervise every business unit.
3. Company-wide business councils are set up to focus on performance and innovation—the business units of marketing and design—not known traditionally as being very innovative.

In addition, the company ensures that resources are made available to stay keenly aware of customer needs and changing demographic trends. Finally, innovation is rewarded and the employees know it is.

Hurley and Hult (1998) found, in their study of 56 research and development groups, that more innovativeness was found in those organizations that emphasized learning and development and used participative decision making. Specifically, when members of work groups were encouraged to learn and develop, as well as able to influence decisions, more innovations were observed. Their findings suggest that organizations need to pay close attention to the type of environment that is being fostered. The structures, processes, and cultural characteristics are important in developing teams with a capacity to be innovative.

From a personal perspective, I have also observed organizations that adopt a product innovation market strategy. One of my colleagues is a piano player. When I asked him for some advice before purchasing a keyboard myself, he indicated that he been a customer of a particular brand for many years. He was completely loyal to this company. The reason was simple: This company had the latest and greatest in technology integrated first into their keyboard systems. The salespeople were very knowledgeable about the new features and this appealed to his personal interest in music. I have also observed, as have many others, the craze to purchase the latest electronic games—often spurred on by children's persistent requests to their parents. These electronic gizmos are very expensive but appeal to people's sense of fun. One company (Company ABC) constantly puts out new electronic products and, as a result, the market knows that Company ABC uses product innovation as a market strategy.

There are some very clear themes that arise from these product or service innovators:

1. They use a cross-functional or multidisciplinary team approach to their work.
2. They are "out in the trenches" with their customers so that the customer's needs can be identified or even anticipated.
3. The reward and recognition systems are set up to foster creativity. Fear of failing just is not part of the culture—fear of not trying is.
4. "Outsiders"—whether these be suppliers, customers, purchasing agents, retailers, universities, or government agencies—are all part of the organization's fabric of doing business.

✧ The Process Effectiveness Strategy

Organizations that adopt the process effectiveness market strategy must keep in mind several aspects of production and delivery. One is that these products or services need to take into account individual differences in customer wants or needs. Anticipating these wants and needs means that close contact with customers to ensure that the production line is prepared to cope with them is an imperative. A second is that speed of delivery is a critical element in securing market share. Customers want the product or service and they want it now. Finally, there is a high degree of reliance on technology. Without it, none of the breakthroughs experienced by the organizations (described later) would have been possible.

Pine (1993) put forward a compelling case for how the process effectiveness strategy can take into account individual customer needs. He argued that organizations need to shift away from mass production, with its focus on operational efficiency, toward mass customization, with its focus on total process efficiency. Mass production is concerned with delivering a product or service manufactured at low cost and provided to a massive and stable consumer market at a low price. To attain this, needs for economies of scale and standardized products emerged. A hierarchical organization with professional management staff using principles of scientific management was the order of the day for mass-production organizations.

The past four decades have seen an erosion in the utility of the mass-production model. Instead, a mass-customization approach seems to be the most effective way to become a market leader based on the process effectiveness strategy. The controlling focus of mass customization is "variety and customization through flexibility and quick responsiveness" (Pine, 1993, p. 44). The goals of organizations that are market leaders in mass customization include "developing, producing, marketing, and delivering, affordable goods and services with enough variety and customization that nearly everyone finds exactly what they want" (Pine, 1993, p. 44).

This approach is well suited to the unstable, fragmented demand for individual products or services that characterizes today's heterogenous marketplace. Organizations pursuing this strategy must continuously recognize the fragmented nature of the market and find niches to fill. They maintain low cost and high quality as a key feature of their strategy. They need to be able to live with short product development and product life cycles. Pine (1993) argued that technology plays a critical role in ensuring that these goals can be met. Mass customization achieves low cost primarily through economies of scope. This is the application of a single process that provides a wide variety of products or services.

Pine (1993) provided several examples of organizations that have successfully shifted from the mass-production to the mass-customization approach. Toyota Motor Company, over a period of 30 or 40 years, has been working toward reducing time-to-delivery as well as shortening the time frame to deliver a variety of car models. At IBM's Rochester business unit, walls that surrounded the programming and engineering developers were removed. Incremental changes based on customer feedback became an integral way to do business. Bally Engineered Structures had been in business since 1933, but by the 1980s was slowly losing market share. A shift in strategy from mass production to better meeting customers' individual demands, delivering faster than the competition, reducing costs, and continually developing new products has revitalized the company.

Whereas the previous three examples are companies that moved relatively slowly, the next examples Pine (1993) described are ones that moved rapidly toward mass customization. In the 1980s Motorola's pager division was in danger of going out of business when Japanese pagers entered the market and sold for half of what the U.S. manufacturers were asking. A 24-member cross-functional team was charged with revamping the entire manufacturing process—and doing it in 18 months. Not only was the manufacturing process revamped (to include 29 million possible variations), the entire business cycle was revised. This resulted in shorter cycles for individual customer orders to be filled (from a month to 1½ hours). The Societe Micromechanique et Horlogere (SMH) manufactures Swatch watches. Sales were initially poor until SMH discovered that increased variety, short product life cycles, and mass-production costs were needed. A perpetual innovation system was adopted to ensure that these needs were able to be met. Computer Products, Inc. (CPI) needed to turn around quickly in 1988—it was losing $27,000 each day. CPI used TQM principles to ensure its success. Specifically, CPI focused its efforts on meeting individual customer needs and delivering its products faster than its competitors. CPI became solution- rather than product-centered.

Finally, Pine (1993) described organizations that have used mass customization as a strategy from the beginning. France Telecom (Minitel) is one. It started in the late 1970s and was designed to provide individualized service over standard phone lines. More than 15,000 different services are available; the source for this inspiring tale was none other than the French government. Azimuth Corporation (founded in 1985) is another company that started out to provide small businesses with high-quality, customized signs, at a low price. Personics Corporation was very successful in producing personalized music cassettes. Customers chose the songs they wanted from a stock of thousands. These individualized cassettes were very inexpensive to produce. Not too surprisingly this organization found itself embroiled in lawsuits with the recording industry over copyright violations, but their initial idea, using principles of mass customization, was a huge success.

Lowson, King, and Hunter (1999) also provided excellent examples of industries that would benefit from the process effectiveness strategy. They called their specific approach the *quick response* (QR). Characteristics include flexibility with rapid response. Importance is placed on providing variety in the product. Thankfully they pointed out that this approach is not a universal panacea—nor is it a "best practice" that applies to every organization within an industry sector. Instead they argued that for some organizations this approach is very useful. Examples they used include the National Bicycle Company of Japan, which delays frame welding until the specific dimensions of the customer are provided. Levi's has implemented a system so that the customer can purchase a "personalized pair" of jeans at relatively low cost. Lenscrafters promises to make to order a pair of prescription glasses in less than an hour. They described several other organizations in the furniture, sheets and towels, footwear, and apparel industries that have benefited from the QR approach.

Treacy and Wiersema (1995a) argued that organizations adopting an operationally excellent strategy primarily devote their energies to providing an acceptable product at the lowest total cost. Low cost means that the organization assures its customers of low prices each and every day of the year—not just during a seasonal sale. Low cost also includes the reliability of the product or service. This appeals to people who want durable, lasting products that are not in need of constant repair. Total cost also includes time. Convenience, fast delivery, and quick and pleasant service are all part of what customers in this market segment value. Treacy and Wiersema noted that Henry Ford's principles of high regimentation, strong policies and procedures, and rule-bound activities of all employees were critical for success. Every Wal-Mart, McDonald's restaurant, Southwest Airlines, and PriceCostco is set up and operated in the same manner.

Treacy and Wiersema (1995a) cited AT&T, with their introduction of the Universal Card, as an example of a company that has used the operational excellence market strategy with great success. This company waded into the highly competitive credit-card business and pushed out the competition. They capitalized on new ways to use changing technology and the AT&T brand-name familiarity. They also kept interest rates low, and provided fast and pleasant customer service for things like stolen-card replacement or change-of-address. The delivery of highly reliable service at low cost was the credo for this company.

One personal example of observing a process-effective organization at work was at Company XYZ when I was purchasing a home-office desk. This no-frills store offers a convenient way to configure a desk using modular components that allowed for the best fit of the desk to the space available. The pieces were ordered online and delivered within a week. Now, the customer is left to put the pieces together, but the low inventory coupled with having the customer do some of the labor allowed me to put together a customized desk and purchase it at a low cost to boot. I left that store feeling that things were set up there—everything from the layout, to the salespeople, to the way shelves were stocked—to be as efficient as possible. Another example of observing process effectiveness in action occurs wherever I go to a well-known fast food restaurant. No matter where in the world you are, you know before you walk in the door what the menu offers, how your order will be taken, that the food will be delivered quickly, that the bill will be comparatively low, and that the place will be clean. When I want to have this type of eating experience, it is helpful to know where to go to obtain it.

❖ The Customer Service Strategy

Although the product/service innovation and the process effectiveness market strategies have customer interactions as an integral part of the process, it is not their primary concern. That is, innovation is best executed when the organization can anticipate customer needs. Similarly, processes become more streamlined and more versatile based on feedback from customers. Both of these approaches view customer interactions as a means to an end. On the other hand, organizations that pursue customer service as their market strategy view customer service as the most important end in itself.

Organizations that focus on customer service as their market strategy provide more than just a product or service. They are there to assist the customer in solving a problem. They must take the time to develop excellent rapport with their customers in order to understand them better. People who interact with the customers must have a high level of expertise. Employees cannot just deliver a product or service that a customer orders. Instead, the employee needs to see what the customer is trying to do and suggest ways to solve the problem. Education and hands-on help are hallmarks of these types of organizations.

Brown noted in 1992 that value is in the minds of the buyers, not in the minds of the makers. He also pointed out that the relationship that is made between the buyer and seller is as important as the product or service being exchanged. This is certainly a distinguishing feature of the customer service strategy. Organizations do not just have to pay lip service to "service"; instead, a service culture needs to be developed in the organization. He went on to cite several studies that support the premise that satisfied customers are repeat customers and losing a customer because of poor service is extremely costly to organizations. He proposed that a *total quality service* (TQS) program should be part of every organization. Though I agree with the assumption that a specific level of service is expected regardless of what organization you are talking about, the strategic approach of customer service is more than just the attainment by all organizations of a minimal level of service. In addition, given the high cost of a customer service strategy, not all organizations should adopt this strategy.

Carr (1990) argued that whereas much of the marketplace is out of the organization's control, how the organization deals with customers is always within its control. In addition, nothing else the organization does will provide the same level of return on investment as does dealing effectively with an unhappy customer. Carr described Scandinavian Air Systems, Micro Center, and a Cooker restaurant as exemplars of taking customer satisfaction very seriously. He said that developing a culture of customer service excellence is something that needs to be done day in, day out. In other words, it is not a quick fix. He pointed out that an organization's front-line people are the key to success in establishing a customer service-oriented organization and they need special training in how to deal with customers—especially dissatisfied ones.

Cottle (1990) examined customer service in the professional client service industry. He noted that ensuring good quality means meeting or exceeding client expectations. The underlying assumption here is that the employee knows what the client's expectations are in the first place. He listed the five dimensions of client service. They are as follows:

- Reliability—deliver the promised service dependably and accurately.
- Assurance—the feeling the client has that their problem is being dealt with appropriately.
- Tangibles—the artifacts of transactions with clients such as letters, facilities, and personnel appearance.
- Responsiveness—timely and prompt service.
- Empathy—individualized, concerned attention to the client.

He went on then in detail to describe how to measure and also how to improve these dimensions.

Davidow and Uttal (1989) proposed that the evolution of most markets goes from features, to cost, to quality, to service. Although this may be true of many products, it does not conform to the strategic model of market focus discussed thus far. The "features" element corresponds to the product/service innovation strategy, the "cost" element roughly corresponds to the process effectiveness strategy—although speed is also a crucial element in the process effectiveness strategy—and the "service" element corresponds to the customer service strategy. However, in all of the Treacy and Wiersema (1995a) strategies, a certain level of quality is needed. They argued, therefore, that to be really market-dominant, an organization needs to stay focused on only one of the strategies, not march through the evolution suggested by Davidow and Uttal.

Despite the differences in why service is important, however, Davidow and Uttal's (1989) suggestions for improving service are worth noting. First, they asserted that, "In all industries, when competitors are roughly matched, those that stress customer service will win" (p. 40). They cited Liz Claiborne, Inc. as a fashion store for women that focuses its attention on customer service. This company does not try to latch on to every new sports/fashion trend. Instead the focus is on service to retailers and customers. Another example they cited is Bugs Burger Bug Killers (BBBK). This exterminating company charges at least four times what the competitors do, but is very successful. BBBK provides added value and service guarantees that make it remarkably healthy financially. Another example was Shelby Williams Industries, which dominates the market in making chairs for hotels and restaurants. This is a low-technology, commodity market. The reason for their continued success is that all operations take a back seat to customer service.

Davidow and Uttal (1989) defined six elements of service. The first is strategy. This involves segmenting the market on the basis of service needs and then deciding which customer service needs the firm will fulfill. The second element is leadership. Because customer service occurs primarily at the interface of the client and front-line staff, staff must have discretion in handling customers. Large numbers of rules, regulations, and operating procedures cannot be relied on to guide the front-line decision making. Instead, it must come from a strong service culture that is espoused and practiced incessantly by organizational leaders. The third element is personnel. Employees treat customers as they are treated. Organizations with a customer strategy must take pains to hire, train, and reward customer-focused employees. Design is the fourth element. Products and services need to be designed to meet or exceed customer expectations. To ensure that this happens, consulting customers in the design phases is imperative. The fifth element is infrastructures. The linkages between organizational systems that serve the customer need to be fast and seamless. Finally, the sixth element is measurements. Customer satisfaction and other variables that impact customer satisfaction must be constantly monitored.

Disend (1991) provided an eminently readable and useful resource for building excellent service into the fabric of any organization. He found some common themes in his studies of customer-focused organizations. Some of these are: Everyone shares a common vision of service; service is more than a happy customer, it is turning a dissatisfied customer into a satisfied customer; the most important people are the customers; customer service is not a program, it is an attitude—a way of life. It occurs when employees take an interest in customers, accept responsibility for their satisfaction, and think about customer needs above everything else. He suggested that there are seven phases to improving customer service: (a) awareness and assessment to determine what the organization doing right and wrong to facilitate customer service, (b) executive commitment to a service strategy, (c) educating employees at all levels, (d) commitment by each organizational member to adopt a customer focus, (e) implementing a redesign of the organization and all of its systems to support a customer service strategy, (f) evaluating how the organization is doing on customer service, and (g) maintenance and periodic review so that the organization does not become complacent.

Harris (1991) also highlighted the need for customer service to first and foremost become an attitude that people throughout the organization eat, sleep, and breathe. Other steps to improve service include:

understanding customer needs, developing a customer service strategy, training employees to be customer-sensitive, support from organizational leaders, recognizing employees for delivering exceptional service, soliciting and using customer feedback for continuous improvement, and promoting the organization's success to the industry as a whole.

A more recent collection of readings edited by Hennig-Thurau and Hansen (2000a) reinforced the importance of customer relationships as a market strategy. They specifically used the term "relationship marketing" as the process by which customer retention is a key outcome. They pointed out that there are substantial differences in dealing with customers in a traditionally transactional manner versus a relational manner. For example, transactional marketing focuses on a single transaction with many customers, acquiring new customers, low-intensity customer contact, quality of output, and mass production. Relational marketing, on the other hand, focuses on multiple transactions with the same customer, maintaining existing customers, high-intensity customer contact, quality of interactions, and mass customization (Hennig-Thurau & Hansen, 2000b).

Diller (2000) spoke to the outcome of customer loyalty as central to the relationship marketing strategy. He claimed that first customers must be satisfied; that is, their expectations need to be met or exceeded. Next, customers need to be involved with the product/service in order to become loyal; that is, there should be some emotional attachment to the product/service beyond that it is simply "useful." Finally, to be truly loyal, customers need to be voluntarily committed to the relationship.

Treacy and Wiersema (1995a) argued that the reason for IBM's market domination in the 1970s was not based on new-fangled gadgets, or on low price. Instead, IBM focused on extraordinary levels of service to its customers. This included guidance and hand-holding when working through changes in information technology. IBM offered assistance in integrating and planning new business applications and provided courses for clients so that they would be better able to take advantage of the new applications. Treacy and Wiersema conceded that IBM's more recent history of nonleadership is due to its inability to adapt to new customer demands.

Airborne Express is the customer service organization highlighted by Treacy and Wiersema (1995a). This organization is set up not to just deliver a package by a specified time. Instead it offers a package delivery system to improve the business of its clients. In other words, they partner with their clients. They offer specialized, tailor-made services to their clients. Instead of focusing on low variety and large volume from a large number of customers, Airborne Express focuses on a smaller number of high-volume corporate accounts. It set out to carve a market niche in a very specific way and it has worked.

Dilts and Prough (2001) argued that the travel service industry is facing a turbulent environmental situation. Cost pressures, changing customer demands, and new information technologies have the potential to re-shape the industry. Agencies that will survive and prosper in such an en-vironment are those that build strong customer relationships. Agents will need to capitalize on their industry knowledge and become travel counselors—not just order takers.

McDougall (2001) noted that customer retention strategies are not for everyone. He cautioned that embarking on a customer retention ap-proach is costly, and the presence of several factors needs to be ascer-tained before embarking on such a course of action. One factor is that the firm needs to be able to tolerate high expenses to obtain a new customer as well as to "enter" them into the firm's administrative system. The firm also must have systems set up to process customer transactions effi-ciently so as to realize reasonable margins on sales. The firm must be able to realize high sales volume per customer. Finally, firms need to encourage and capitalize on using a word-of-mouth referral system.

A personal example of an organization focused on customer service was a floor-covering company. As part of the process of building our house, we had to select every floor covering for every room. Now, we don't know a lot about carpets, linoleum, hardwood, and so on. So, our builder suggested a particular floor company. The salesperson had to spend a lot of time with us. She took the time to learn what type of ambi-ance we were trying to achieve with each room, how much traffic there would be in each room, what our price restrictions were, and the like. To ensure that the correct decisions were made, she also had to have a lot of product knowledge. Durability, quality, variety, and price options were things that she knew about, and we had to trust her to advise us properly. We had an excellent experience there and would definitely return.

✧ Summing Up Strategy

Most of us recall organizations that provide us with something special. Sometimes the something special is a new product or service, some-times it is a familiar product delivered at an exceptionally low cost, and sometimes it is extraordinary customer-specific service. When one of these specialties is the organization's market focus, its characteristics can be found throughout its operating systems. Only then will the orga-nization be highly regarded by its customers for what it does best. Though there are other ways to "carve up" organizational context—for example, by industry type—the market focus is readily understood by customers and employees alike. It has an intuitive appeal. More impor-tant, the market focus drives all of the systems in the organization. For purposes of this book, the market strategy is the backbone on which leading teams rest.

◆ HIGH-PERFORMING TEAMS AS PART OF THE STRATEGIC PLAN

So where do teams fit into this market strategy scheme of things? In all of the writings cited thus far, teams are an integral part of each of the strategies. A key to understanding this piece of the "team performance" puzzle, though, is that the teams are designed and managed differently depending on the organization's market strategy. Teams that are leaders are those that are aligned with the organization's market strategy. Thus, the context is much broader than has been typically defined in the traditional team literature. It is not just manager support, the tasks, and communication systems. The external context of market strategy drives all of these other internal organizational contextual factors. The degree to which they are in alignment will determine whether or not a leading, high-performing team can emerge. The next chapters demonstrate ways and means to effectively leverage teams within the three market strategies described here.

3

Innovation-Focused Organizations

$\mathbf{T}$he premise of the previous chapter was that a firm must adopt a market focus in order to be truly a leading organization. That is, an organization must be recognized for its distinctive competitive edge. The three market strategies described in detail were: product/service innovation, process effectiveness, and customer service. Though all three strategies have to be maintained at the very least to industry standards, what sets an organization apart, and will allow for leading teams to flourish, is the degree to which the organization has fully adopted a specific market focus. Translated into what this will mean for employees in their everyday work is that all of the elements of strategy, structure, and processes are going to be aligned with the market focus.

✦ IMPLEMENTING A PRODUCT OR SERVICE INNOVATION MARKET STRATEGY

This chapter describes how to implement a product/service innovation strategy (see Fig. 3.1). The internal contextual elements of strategy formation, organizational structure, management function, culture, personnel characteristics, personnel systems, and organizational outcomes are covered.

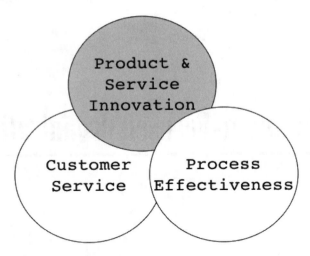

FIG. 3.1.   Market strategies: Product and service innovation.

Although these may not seem to be immediately connected specifically to "teams," this is not at all the case. Recall how important to team performance these internal context variables are. That is, we cannot discuss how a team can become a leading team in a vacuum. The external market strategy drives the internal organizational context, which has been demonstrated over and over again to have substantial impact on teams and how well they perform.

The product or service innovation strategy has been well studied and the findings are clear and coherent. Basically, they support the contention that success in this domain will come not only from leveraging individual employee creativity characteristics, but also by carefully attending to the organizational ambiance (e.g., Amabile, 1998; Amabile, Conti, Coon, Lazenby, & Herron, 1996; Shalley, 1991; Shalley, Gilson, & Blum, 2000).

✦ STRATEGIC FOCUS

The strategy for successful innovating must conform to several criteria. Specifically, the organization must be future-driven. Many innovations must survive a process that, although it varies somewhat between organizations, demands a considerable amount of time and resources. Thus, a long-term planning approach is required. Results will not be realized from the innovation for many months or even for many years. Organizations with no tolerance for these time frames are not likely to be successful at the innovation strategy.

Second, all employees in the organization must constantly scan the environment for new ideas that may be of use in their own organization. This means that not only will employees focus on their own area of expertise and what is happening there, but also they will be cognizant of what is occurring in more tangential industry areas. This wide scanning process provides the opportunity for putting new knowledge to work in a way that will uniquely benefit the organization.

The success of an innovation strategy is based on the organization being the first to fill a new market need. Thus, the planning process must take into account the present marketplace and its ever-changing needs. That is, the innovative product or service must fill a need of the marketplace and those needs may not even be known by the market to exist. There are dozens of examples of new-fangled gadgets that people initially did not adopt such as fax machines, cell phones, cable television, and e-mail systems. Until they started to be used by a significant portion of the market, these innovations were perceived as luxuries that would not really catch on. Therefore, an exceptionally up-to-date and thorough understanding of the marketplace is an essential part of the innovation strategy process.

All of these criteria point to a highly external, industry- and market-focused strategy. To be prepared to take advantage of opportunities, the overriding work strategy of all employees must be that of continually scanning the industry environment, seeing new ideas, making new connections, and selling them to the marketplace as adding value.

✦ ORGANIZATIONAL TEAM STRUCTURE

The organizational structure most likely to support an innovation strategy is based on a flat hierarchy with loosely grouped individuals who form not for structural purposes but for innovation purposes. This particular structuring approach is a rather frightening concept for many managers. The lack of control over information flow and ideas is something with which managers in such organizations must learn to live.

It is critical that these loose groupings (I prefer to call them that rather than teams) are able to form and then re-form as times and conditions change. That is, initially, small groups of individuals with homogeneous backgrounds will likely interact with one another. Our humanness impels us to seek out the company of others who think and act as we do. The result of this is that conversations about new ideas will begin informally within these pockets of individuals. These individuals will have formal job descriptions that require them to be involved in specific activities. However, the topics of conversations they have over lunch or coffee may not center on these formally prescribed duties. Instead, it is more likely that these discussions will be characterized as free flowing and unstructured and will include new ideas in the industry, reports of findings at a conference, or new ideas in tangential industries. The expected outcomes of such loose groupings of individuals are many new ways of thinking about problems and new ideas for products or services. The discussions are not formal, nor are the individuals defensive about an idea.

These loose-grouping teams don't need to be formally part of the organizational chart. In fact, they probably should not be. As their personal interests change and grow over time, it will be healthier for them to interact with other individuals in the organization. Thus, there is a definitive need for loose-grouping teams to be able to flourish in the organization, even if these groups are not formally constituted teams.

The initial innovative ideas of these loose groupings need to survive the test of their professional peers. In this psychologically safe haven, employees freely exchange the glimmers of new ideas, banter, question, and so on, without fear of reprisal and without political agendas taking over. Refinements in thinking about the new ideas occur here in these small, informal, and unrecognized groups.

If the idea does survive the "initial glimmer" stage, then the innovation will take on more shape and structure. The constructive criticism provided by peers will assist in this task. At this point the idea moves on to the next stage. Here a group of individuals who are formally recognized as a team discusses the merits and potential drawbacks of the innovation. This next level of groups is formally recognized in the organization as cross-functional review teams. Part of their work involves evaluating new ideas in a formal manner for potential organizational benefit.

The composition of this team includes individuals who can provide various perspectives on the innovation. The voices of various functional areas such as marketing, operational, procedural, legal, and human resources should all be considered when deciding whether or not the organization should put resources into the innovation. All evidence suggests that successful innovations come from exploiting the strengths of these cross-functional teams.

It is critical that these cross-functional review teams be composed of individuals who are at similar hierarchical positions within the organization. Because new ideas are being formally proposed and evaluated, it is important that people be able to speak their minds freely, which some may be reluctant to do when in the same room as a superior. In addition, political agendas emerge when there is a superior in the room.

This does not mean that there is no one to whom the review team reports. Another layer of management must then be prepared to examine the findings and recommendations of the review teams and pursue next steps. Depending on the organization's size, geographic dispersion, and number of product/service lines, these next steps may vary considerably. For instance, in some very large organizations, secondary or even tertiary cross-functional review teams may be part of the organizational structure. Their mandates would include determining which of the innovations endorsed by lower level review teams should be pursued. At the other end of the continuum, the decision of the first review team may be tantamount to approval for pursuing the innovation.

Regardless of whether there are many cross-functional review teams or just one, their roles and how they interact with one another are of vital importance to the organization. Communications between them are discussed in a later section.

In addition to individuals, loose groupings, and cross-functional teams devoted to idea generation, a set of implementation teams is designed into the structure of effective innovative organizations. The implementation teams must coordinate the efforts of research and development, marketing, operations, and procedural functions. The organization must be prepared to commit to resources for these teams. The literature is clear that even the best idea cannot sell itself (e.g., Frost & Egri, 1992).

These cross-functional implementation teams will spend considerable time and effort discussing where the organization is at, in terms of the innovation, in order to avoid delays either in getting a promised innovation to market or in marketing the innovation so that the marketplace is prepared to receive the idea. Spotting bottlenecks before they start, and ensuring that the way is smooth to get the innovation to the marketplace, is how these teams justify their existence. These teams must exhibit mutual support for each other and use all communication channels to effectively handle potential and existing crises before they get out of hand.

The final stop for the innovation is at the market interface. The individuals who actually deliver the innovation must be constantly in touch with members of the implementation teams regarding the innovation. They can be distributors, store owners, manufacturing centers, or primary caregivers. Because these people actually link the organization to the marketplace, they are designed into the organizational structure. They provide feedback critical to ensure that continual innovations are forthcoming from the organization as well as feedback on how the market is responding to current innovations. Figure 3.2 summarizes the innovative structure.

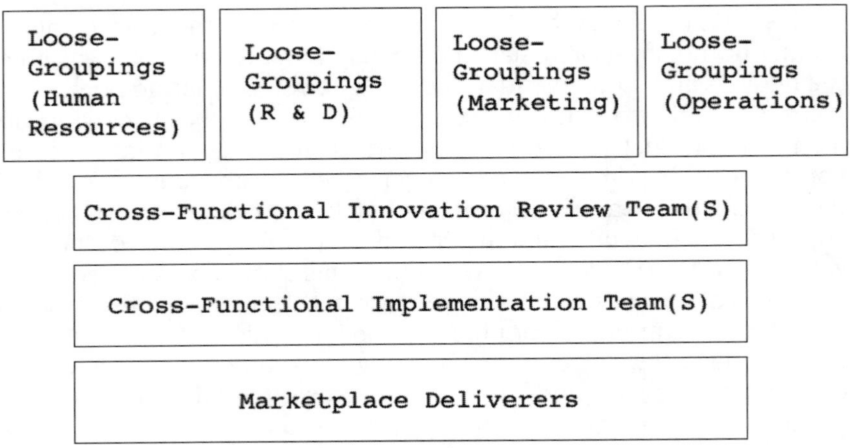

Loose-Groupings (Human Resources)	Loose-Groupings (R & D)	Loose-Groupings (Marketing)	Loose-Groupings (Operations)

Cross-Functional Innovation Review Team(S)

Cross-Functional Implementation Team(S)

Marketplace Deliverers

FIG. 3.2. Product and service innovation structure.

✦ MANAGEMENT FUNCTION

As noted earlier in this section, the activities of the loose groupings and then the cross-functional generation and implementation teams are the heart of the organization. They form the core function. Managing this type of structure means that the role of managers is to support the activities of these groups and teams. Control in these organizations is wielded by the employees in terms of how they spend their creative time and energy. Management's role in "control" here is to be a role model for how to behave and to actively manage the environment in which the employees work. Managers in these organizations are perceived as useful only to the degree that they support the generation and implementation of new ideas.

A management philosophy for innovative organizations is one where innovative results are important but turf-building or status differences are not. Power in the organization comes not from position, but from contributions to innovation. Decisions about innovations must, by definition, be made where there is the most expertise. This is most likely not going to be found in the "management" function.

In terms of everyday tasks, this means that managers need to: (a) pass along information they may run across to individuals who might be able to make some use if it, (b) identify possible links between the ideas of individuals and/or groups within the organization, (c) provide the resources—including time, physical space, equipment, and personnel—to explore innovations, (d) ensure that the environment is such that the incentives are in place to support collaborative group and teamwork, (e) ensure that rewards and recognition for idea generation are allocated to those most responsible for their success, and above all (f) provide constructive feedback and encouragement when an idea is not endorsed. The reason for this is that the key to an innovating organization's success over the long term hinges on employees continually coming up with new ideas. Because most ideas are not ultimately endorsed by the organization, employees need to stay motivated to stay engaged in this process. Most people are willing to accept that an outcome is not in their favor if the process by which the decision is made is transparent and perceived to be fair, and if the bad news is delivered in such a way so as to maintain the dignity and self-esteem of the employee or employee group affected (e.g., Greenberg, 1996).

There are several behaviors that managers must avoid at all costs to maintain innovation. These include: (a) watching over individuals' shoulders or second-guessing the decisions made by employees in pursuing ideas, (b) trying to control people's time, (c) insisting on meetings outside those relevant to the pursuit and implementation of new ideas, (d) chastising ideas and their authors that do not work out as planned, (e) putting excessive time constraints on experimenting with the idea, (f) emphasizing the extrinsic rewards that the employee might receive, (g) setting up competitions between groups of employees, and (h) taking credit for others' ideas.

Individuals in management positions need to be evaluated by their peers and subordinates on these types of dimensions. The results will provide the organization with some insight as to whether the current managers are actually adopting an appropriate management function philosophy to foster innovation.

✦ CULTURE

Culture is discerned by organizational members as they observe the behaviors of those who are successful in a particular environment. To create an environment that will foster the generation and implementation of new ideas means that there has to be concrete evidence that new ideas are supported. The behavior of managers and coworkers, how rewards and recognition are distributed, and how the failure of an idea is dealt with all are critical aspects of the organization that employees will look to in order to determine how they too can be successful in the organization.

The worn-out admonition to "think outside the box" skirts the following issues: (a) Why is there a box in the first place, and (b) of what is the box made? The first question should be understood by noting that organizations are not free to do anything they want. There are parameters that govern how any organization operates. What is important is to understand why those boundary conditions exist. The legal system, and the corresponding rules and regulations that ensue, is one source of these boundary conditions. Another source stems from standards of practice in a profession and/or industry. Finally, individual codes of ethical responsibility place an additional set of constraints on what is acceptable for an organization. After these are taken into account, however, there should not be any other sources of constraint in terms of the ideas that an organization pursues with vigor.

The second question asks of what material the "box" is made. This is a cultural question insofar as it addresses the strength of the unwritten rules about "the way we do things around here." If the box's walls are made of concrete and steel reinforcing bar, then you should not expect employees to readily embrace trying out new ideas. If the box's walls are permeable, then new ideas can freely flow in and out. Organizations should examine their unwritten rules and regulations about new ideas and make sure that they support an innovative culture.

Some of the questions to ask about the organization's culture that provide some insight into the generation and implementation of new ideas include those in Table 3.1.

✦ PERSONNEL CHARACTERISTICS

Individuals who work in innovative organizations must have a very high level of skill in a particular area. This ensures that they have the capacity

TABLE 3.1
Questions for Assessing a Culture of Innovation

1. What are the sources for new ideas in this organization?
2. When someone comes up with a new or unusual idea, what happens to it?
3. How many resources (physical, financial, human, and time) are set aside to specifically foster the generation of new ideas?
4. On what criteria are new ideas evaluated for their organizational utility?
5. Who makes the decisions about what new ideas to pursue?
6. If a new idea does not "fly," how is this information conveyed to those invested in the idea?
7. How is information shared with the express objective of encouraging innovation?
8. How are the rewards and recognition for successful ideas distributed?

through their technical skills and knowledge to contribute to the organization. Amabile (1983) called these domain-relevant skills for the creative process. She argued that they are dependent on innate cognitive, perceptual, and motor abilities, as well as formal and informal education. In addition to these skills, however, other questions remain with regard to whether a particular person will enjoy and fit into an organizational environment that focuses its strategy on innovation.

Some suggestions have been made in the literature reviewed in the previous chapter about the characteristics of individuals who are likely to thrive in an organization that demands and supports innovation. Table 3.2 lists each of those characteristics along with a question that might assist in determining to what extent the individual has exhibited this characteristic. These questions are set in the format of a patterned behavior descriptive interview (PBDI) (Janz, Hellervik, & Gilmore, 1986). The theory behind the development of a PBDI is based on the assumption that past behavior is predictive of future behavior.

If a PBDI is used as part of a decision-making process for individual selection, there are several steps to be taken throughout the process. First, a thorough job analysis is conducted so that the interviewer is very clear on the job expectations in that particular organization. Follow-up probe questions are created in the PBDI to facilitate a complete response by the interviewee. The interview questions need to be administered in a standard and structured format so that all applicants are responding to the same questions in similar circumstances. The applicant should be interviewed by more than one person so as to ensure that all information is

TABLE 3.2
Characteristics and Accompanying Possible Questions
for Assessment of Individual Innovation Potential

Consider how you would rate each of the responses to the following items (note that you can use a scale of 1 = poor response and 5 = excellent response).

1. *Enjoys challenge.*
   Describe a challenging circumstance that you have recently faced.

2. *Intrinsically motivated.*
   Describe a situation where you were highly motivated to create something new.

3. *Desires freedom and autonomy in their work.*
   Describe how you dealt with and felt about being given an ambiguous task to perform.

4. *Experimentation and tolerance of failure.*
   Describe a situation when you have been frustrated in accomplishing a goal.

5. *Tolerance for open and constructive conflict.*
   Describe the circumstances and outcomes of when you disagreed with another person about a fundamental issue.

recorded. Interviewee responses need to be carefully recorded so that the information can be reviewed. Scoring of the responses should not be conducted until after the interview is fully completed. Once the interview is completed then the responses of the applicants can be scored with regard to the expectations of the organization.

✦ PERSONNEL SYSTEMS

Once you get the right people into the organization, the personnel policies need to be consistent with promoting innovation. In an innovative organization new ideas must constantly be moving into the organization. This means that employees have to be encouraged to find and use information from a variety of sources.

Opportunities for professional interactions with members of the organization need to be provided through in-house seminars or debriefing meetings. Experts in the field should be brought in to make presentations on a regular basis. Developing links with the world outside the organization is important and can be accomplished in several ways, as follows. Establish formal ties with research institutions, as often the findings from these institutions are nonproprietary and as such can be used by the industry. Send employees to attend and present material at professional conferences and then have them present what they learned to others in the organization. Subscribe to professional journals and set up a library to house the information. Invite, and thereby reward, customers (or potential customers) into the organization to talk about their needs in the industry. And do the same with suppliers (or potential suppliers). Design an automated system so that employees can alert one another to information that may be relevant to them.

The activities of expertise sharing—coming up with new ideas, providing input into the viability of new ideas, and suggesting the most effective ways to implement ideas—require team members to spend a lot of time together. All members must be expected to participate in a constructively critical manner. To ensure that communication lines remain open, member input then must be respected.

One way to obtain a sense of the degree to which team discussions are productive was suggested by Lovelace, Shapiro, and Weingart (2001) in a study of cross-functional new-product teams. They found that the more collaborative versus contentious statements made between team members, the more productive the creative teams were. Specifically, how the task disagreement was communicated, how free team members felt to express task-related doubts, and how effective the team leader was perceived to be, all had an effect on team performance. Table 3.3

provides some protocols to adhere to in ensuring that the teams have constructive meetings and discussions.

Employees have to be encouraged to use these communication systems not only to stay current, but more important, to project into the future those innovations that are most likely to succeed. Taking advantage of these opportunities to share expertise must be part of employees' job descriptions, and appropriate time has to be allotted to them to do so. This will foster individual learning of information that has the potential to become organizational knowledge, which knowledge in turn can be used to lead the market.

The number of ideas generated for new products or new services is the most valued aspect of the employees' work. Reward, recognition, and performance management systems in innovating organizations must be con-

TABLE 3.3
Protocols for Ensuring Collaborative Meetings

Consider how you would rate the meeting with the following items (note that you can use a scale of 1 = rarely adhered to and 5 = almost always adhered to).

1. Ensure that all materials relevant to the meeting have been circulated ahead of time.

2. Establish areas of congruence or agreement first. These include (a) the overarching team goals, (b) the specific goal of the meeting and how it fits into the overall team goals, (c) the outcomes expected at the meeting, and (d) reaffirming that all members' contributions are expected and important.

3. Keep the focus of the conversation on solving the task-related problem.

4. Refrain from making comments about a particular individual.

5. Listen to other team members. This includes allowing each member to finish speaking, and then paraphrasing what that person said. Even if all members don't agree with the statement, the speaker will appreciate that the rest of the team understands what they are trying to convey.

6. The person who responds to the speaker must build on the previous speaker's statement. This assists in moving the conversation forward, and yet keeps it from becoming disjointed.

7. Assign one person to record the major points of concern brought up by members so that the points are not forgotten. What this process does is slow down any escalating conflict situations.

8. Periodically assess the progress made and highlight that movement has occurred. If it has not, then take a moment to determine why the conversation is going nowhere and change the conversational strategy.

9. Insert summary comments that encourage the team.

10. Remain calm during the discussions. When the situation seems to be becoming emotionally charged, something needs to be done to calm down again, which may include taking a short break.

sistent with this strategy. In addition, there needs to be a high level of energy and enthusiasm for trying out new ideas. Our North American societal values place emphasis on getting it right the first time. This tendency needs to be combated on a regular basis in innovating organizations. The reason is simple—most ideas don't work. Thus, the organization and its employees need to have some resilience with regard to things not working out as planned. That an idea did not come to fruition has to be perceived as a learning opportunity and a challenge—not as a "failure" to be hidden from view.

With this in mind then, Table 3.4 presents several areas of employee performance at the individual level that will contribute to a workplace that fosters innovation.

Reward systems clearly need to be tied to staying true to the innovation process. Some excellent examples of individual and team rewards have been provided in other sources (e.g., Jones & Schilling, 2000; Lawler, 2000; Parker, McAdams, & Zielinski, 2000; Rynes & Gerhart, 2000). All of them note that the strategy is clearly understood by all parties. This means that new ideas must be central to the reward system. In addition, a clear "line of sight" between what the individuals and teams do on a day-to-day basis and how well the organization performs at a more general level needs to be visible. Those who participate in all of the expected behaviors (includ-

TABLE 3.4
Individual Performance Areas for Fostering Innovation

Consider how you would rate the person on the following items (note that you can use a scale of 1 = rarely and 5 = almost always).

1. Independently seeks out information sources within the organization to create new ideas.

2. Independently seeks out information sources from outside the organization to create new ideas.

3. Provides information to other employees so that new ideas can be generated.

4. Provides constructive criticism to self-generated ideas.

5. Provides constructive criticism to ideas generated by others.

6. Persistently pursues new ideas.

7. When presented with negative information about an idea, moves on to the next challenge.

8. Actively shares both positive and negative experiences with new ideas.

9. Actively listens to others' positive and negative experiences with new ideas.

10. Articulates what are the "lessons learned" in the development of new ideas.

ing interpersonal and management skills) need to be recognized. Finally, sharing in the success of the organization with tangible rewards is a delightful bonus.

✦ ORGANIZATIONAL OUTCOMES

The outcomes of the process of having employees cognizant at the individual and team levels that new ideas are valued will result in tangible organizational outcomes. The first is that many ideas—not just one or two but dozens or hundreds—will be generated. There should be a noticeable upswing in the number of new ideas generated for new products or services when the structure, management philosophy, culture, and personnel systems combine to focus on fostering, rewarding, and recognizing ideas.

Another outcome will be the number of successful ideas. Most ideas do not work in the form in which they were originally conceived. They often need to be refined or modified after initially trying them out and finding them flawed. This trial-and-error process is encouraged and valued. By having more ideas to work with, more are bound to survive the weeding-out process. If you only have one idea, then you are not likely to be successful in innovating. If you have a hundred ideas, you have a lot more ideas to choose from so that you can separate those that will most likely survive the process from those less likely to do so.

More and better ideas will result in the organization being recognized as a leader by its peers in the industry. This will spiral into even more success because those individuals who thrive in an environment of innovation will be attracted to the organization, resulting in turn in higher work satisfaction and lower turnover. The final reward will be higher market share.

4

Process-Effective-Focused Organizations

$\mathbf{F}$igure 4.1 highlights that our focus is shifting to developing process-effective teams. As was noted in chapter 2, the traditional marketing and operational philosophies consistent with the assumptions of mass production have been changed to be consistent with those of mass customization. A process-effective organization will be judged on its ability to deliver customized products or services to large numbers of customers at a low price. All aspects of the organization's delivery system have to be scrutinized continuously to ensure that no "slack" exists. The environment must be continually scanned for new technologies that can assist in delivering products or services faster and cheaper.

✦ STRATEGIC FOCUS

The strategic focus of a process-effective organization is to quickly and dependably deliver mass-customized products or services at the lowest possible price. These organizations pride themselves on being the most efficient deliverers of a product or service. They are not noted for their new-product or service innovation, nor are they known for extraordinary customer service. Consumers purchase the product or service because it

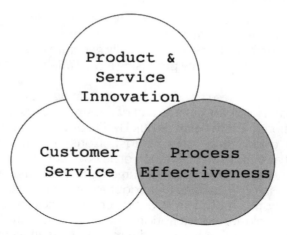

FIG. 4.1. Market strategies: Process effectiveness.

costs the least and is delivered quickly. When this combination of characteristics is the primary reason for customers to choose your organization over another, you need to make sure that you are able to maintain this edge.

Thus, the strategy that needs to be engaged in is a constant review of the environment for new technologies that can be incorporated into the delivery system to (a) make the product available to more people, or (b) make the product cheaper to deliver, or (c) get the product into the hands of the customer faster. This means that those individuals scanning the environment must completely know their business and industry, as well as see connections between markets, products, and technologies, so that when an opportunity comes along, the organization is prepared to take full advantage of it.

Some writers suggest that process efficiency is not a market strategy at all. However, the writers cited in chapter 2 disagree. Not only is process efficiency a viable market strategy, it is making a real comeback as mass-customization principles replace mass-production principles. These mass customization principles have had to be adopted for several reasons. For example, many sources have cited that over the past 20 years, major economic trends have put tremendous stress on organizations. One of the most prominent of these trends is increased competition (Nadler, 1992). There are more competitors and they come from around the globe as well as via the Internet.

Another important trend is technological change. The first organization that spots a technological innovation that can be used to deliver their product or service more quickly or at a lower cost than the "other guys" wins more market share. Higher-than-ever customer expectations for quality and speed of delivery is another trend that has forced process-efficient organizations to continually generate new customers and to keep existing customers by promising more variety, faster delivery, or lower price.

The upshot of all these trends is that maintaining the process-efficient edge demands a lot of work on the part of the strategic team in the organization. Decisions have to be made quickly and often with limited information, or an opportunity may be lost. Constant checking on the environment and constant integration of new systems into old so that the edge is maintained fosters a sense of urgency in these organizations that is not present in organizations that adopt a different market strategy.

Interestingly, much of the rest of this chapter tries to convince you, the reader, that old-fashioned notions such as long-tenured employees, bureaucratic rules and policies, and a traditional management style of control and coordination are keys to success with the process-effective strategy. This may seem to stand in stark contrast to the speed and risk-taking actions in which these organizations must continually be engaged to stay at the front of the pack. A resolution to this paradox should become clearer as you read on. Luckily, Jaques (1990) did an excellent job in paving the way with his treatise "In Praise of Hierarchy."

◆ ORGANIZATIONAL STRUCTURE

The organizational structure that will best meet the strategy of process effectiveness is one where those individuals who are involved in delivering the product or service are grouped together up and down the hierarchy. These groups start out as small, basic building blocks and are ad hoc/project teams populated by members with different skill sets who are geographically located in close proximity. The members come together to deliver a product or service and then re-form into new teams to deliver the product or service to another customer.

Thus, team members must have the ability to change work teams on a frequent basis. A particular employee may come to know all of the other employees in the organization by virtue of having been on many different teams over a period of time. On the other hand, some teams may be made up of the same individuals for long periods of time—particularly if the organization is small or geographically widely dispersed. A segmented organizational structure with teams designed to carry out one part of the system is an optimal approach for process-efficient organizations.

It is not important for these delivery teams to maintain their contact with the customers once the product or service has been delivered. Different teams take over the process efficiency after delivery. These new teams may carry out roles such as customer training, product maintenance, or service upgrading.

All teams must have clear understandings of what the product or service is, and how best to deliver it. There is very little variation in the day-to-day work of these teams. For the process to be effective there needs to be a lot of communication between the various teams involved in the product or service delivery. This means manager roles are going to be focused on the smooth integration of the system as a whole. (Fig. 4.2 illustrates the process-effectiveness structure.)

All members of the team must be depended on to carry out their portion of the delivery or the delivery won't occur. Clearly, there is a risk for organizations that set themselves up to be process effective. Teams have to have exceptional ability to anticipate problems in delivery before they occur and then take appropriate steps to ensure that (a) the problem is avoided, or (b) the product or service is delivered as soon as possible and the customer is made aware of and understands the reasons for the delay. If Item a or b is not done, then customers are lost—perhaps for good—to another organization that can meet their needs.

✦ MANAGEMENT FUNCTION

The management functions of most importance for process-effective organizations are: (a) to ensure excellent communication between groups/teams who deliver the product or service, and (b) to anticipate blockages in the systems before they occur and fix them. Nothing can come before these roles. These are the roles for which these managers are responsible and for which they should be compensated.

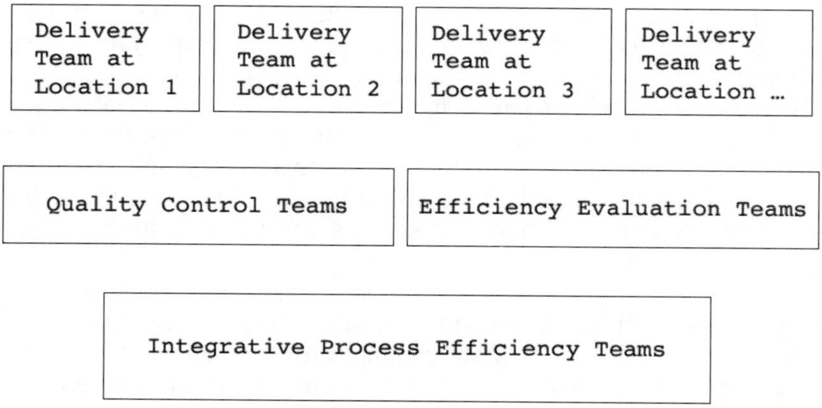

Delivery Team at Location 1	Delivery Team at Location 2	Delivery Team at Location 3	Delivery Team at Location ...

Quality Control Teams	Efficiency Evaluation Teams

Integrative Process Efficiency Teams

FIG. 4.2.   Process effectiveness structure.

Management must know the business inside and out. Managers who really know what happens "on the shop floor," have "worked their way up," or have "paid their dues" are far more likely to be effective in their roles than those who have not. They are highly skilled in their specialized area and know how the business as a whole works. Managers have to be able to pitch in where and when needed. As such, they have to be trained in the various functions of the organizational delivery system. In some organizations it is possible to transfer individuals from one industry specialty to another successfully. However, this is not usually the case in process-effective organizations because of the intimate knowledge needed about how the industry and the organization work.

The process-effective type of promotional structure gives rise to a command, coordinate, control type of management style. These organizations appreciate employees who have similar values to those of the broader organization. Thus, managers in process-effective organizations are constantly monitoring all employee work and procedures to determine how to deliver the product or service faster or at a lower cost. Most managers, then, have a very hands-on style and are involved in the daily activities of the employees. They have to be or they become out of touch with where the processes can be improved upon.

Some employees resent this approach. To a large degree, however, whether or not it works comes down to how individual managers perceive their role and how they carry out their mandate. If, for instance, they berate their employees, then they are not carrying out their roles properly and of course employees are going to be resentful of management "watching over their shoulders." If managers, though, indicate clearly that they are involved in daily work tasks because they want to directly observe the process, a much more welcome reception will be given by employees. Excellent process-effective managers are able to engender respect for their exceptional knowledge of the business and their ability to solve problems. They are perceived by the employees as being "in it with them" and as one of the crew.

Thus, managers need to make it clear that their job is to know how to make the business run more smoothly and effectively. They are there to remove bureaucratic rules that don't support the strategy and to put into place procedures that facilitate the strategy. Instead of managers being seen as interfering, they should be seen as collaborators in the game of process effectiveness.

Thus, managers in process-effective organizations should have at least some of their compensation tied to the speed and cost of delivering the firm's product/service. As they are ultimately responsible for the decisions of the organization, their compensation should be directly influenced by these variables. It demonstrates to all stakeholders that managers are keenly aware of their actions and the effects on the organization as a whole.

✦ CULTURE

Process-effective organizations have a sense of urgency about them. For these organizations, there is always a sense that the competition is ready to snatch their market share out from under them. Constant evaluation of the environment to determine what the competition is charging and for what product or service is a must. Decision making is highly centralized in these organizations because changes in one area almost always affect another area. Managers have to be able to be in on these decisions and communicate the changes to their direct reports, and so on down the line. Ad hoc rules made up for a single situation will wreak havoc in process-effective organizations.

Policies and procedures must be well articulated and published in volumes that are accessible to all employees. Standard operating procedures must be enforced and employees should be expected to toe the line. The process-effective culture approves of behaviors that conform to how things have always been done as these have been proved to be effective. As suggested by Christensen (1997), process-effective organizations that adopt disruptive technologies without careful consideration about the market and the process of delivery are doomed to failure. Instead, deviations from the norm are allowed only under certain controlled conditions. New markets can be cultivated and new processes tried out, but not at the expense of losing the current customer base.

Process-effective organizations value longtime employees because of the wisdom they have about how to do things most efficiently. There is a security in these organizations in terms of what employees are expected to do. Boundaries for acceptable behavior are clear and made explicit.

These organizations may sound harsh in many ways and somehow alien to the present zeitgeist culture of participation and empowerment. However, they have some excellent qualities. Job roles are usually clearly defined—a rarity in many organizations. Expectations for performance are also very clear. Rewards for conformity are plentiful. In these organizations people know where they stand and what the organization stands for. For some, this culture, rather than being problematic, is refreshing in its clarity.

Table 4.1 provides a series of questions about process-effective organizations. To assess how well your organization's culture fosters this strategy, determine how many of these questions you can respond "yes" to.

✦ PERSONNEL CHARACTERISTICS

Valuable members of process-effective organizations are disciplined to carry out their roles as other members expect them to, and are dedi-

TABLE 4.1
Questions for Assessing a Culture of Process Effectiveness

1. Does your organization convey a sense of urgency to all of its members to dependably deliver your product or service fast and at low cost?

2. Do members of the organization spontaneously suggest ways to capitalize on opportunity that would improve on procedural effectiveness?

3. Are organizational members rewarded for providing suggestions for procedural improvements?

4. Is a system for implementing procedural improvements in place?

5. Do members feel proud to be associated with the organization?

6. Do members feel that they have a duty to maintain high standards when delivering a product or service?

7. Is conformity to rules and regulations considered an asset to be rewarded and recognized?

8. Are members aware of all aspects of the business?

cated to the values of delivery speed and low cost for the customer. People who like working in process-effective organizations enjoy orderliness and clarity in their work. They like to know what is expected of them and they want to be recognized for performing to clearly defined standards. They can be counted on to pull their weight even when the work becomes tedious. They do not thrive well in environments that constantly change—where the rules and regulations are fluid and decision making is arbitrary. Table 4.2 provides a list of questions for individuals who are most likely to succeed in an organization that values process effectiveness.

✦ PERSONNEL SYSTEMS

Supporting process effectiveness strategies begins with training newcomers when they come into the organization. Some organizations have mastered this socialization process to the extent where they have their own "universities" or "boot camps." There, new employees are inducted into the organization by learning about its beginnings, hearing stories about its heroes, and learning what is expected of them. Though many organizations do not have such formalized systems, procedurally effective organizations must have some way to convey this information to new members in a structured manner.

TABLE 4.2
Characteristics and Accompanying Possible Questions for Assessment
of Individual Process Effectiveness Potential

*Consider how you would rate each of the responses to the following items
(note that you can use a scale of 1 = poor response and 5 = excellent response).*

1. *Dedicated.*
   Describe a situation where you were persistent in keeping after a goal.

2. *Motivated by contributing to the organization.*
   Describe a situation where you have been proud to be part of an organization.

3. *Works well in a structured environment.*
   Describe how you have responded to work situations where the task is very
   structured; for example, there are rules and procedures to follow and the performance
   outcomes are clear.

4. *Dependable.*
   Describe a situation where others depended on you to do something.

5. *Likes to be part of a team.*
   Describe a situation where you been part of a group that has accomplished a goal that
   none of the individuals themselves would have been able to accomplish on their own.

6. *Follows instructions.*
   Describe a situation where you have followed instructions without knowing why they
   had been given or even when you disagreed with them.

Training systems include at a minimum some sort of orientation program for new employees. Unfortunately, most of these programs are set up so that new employees are overloaded with policies-and-procedures manuals that make no sense to them. Care needs to be taken to provide new employees only what they need to know to start with. They'll have enough trouble just figuring out how to work the photocopier. Periodically, new information should be systematically introduced to new employees. For example, touring other functional units within the organization should occur sooner rather than later so that the newer employees can see how the organization as a whole operates.

Effective training systems include job pairings, where a new person learns their job from a specific senior employee. This is not likely to be a full-blown mentoring process as the new employee may not make it past the usual probationary period and formal mentoring programs are expensive to operate. On the other hand, the more seasoned employees can be hand-picked to help newcomers figure out the way things are done in the organization. The newcomers are much less likely to make mistakes of overstepping their boundaries if someone tells them where the boundaries are in the first place.

To be contributing members of the organization, employees need to be experts in their given areas. Initially, members may not need specific skills, just the motivation to work hard and to learn. However, this cannot be the status quo. Members have to continually learn about first their own area of the delivery system, then other areas of the delivery system, and then upgrade their skills with perhaps formal training or course work that will lead to certification. Process-effective organizations lose heavily when long-tenured employees depart and their expertise is lost. These organizations need to invest in providing upgrade training to all employees. In this way, the expertise is built and maintained within the organization.

Organizational members must know what the other members of their team as well as other teams do in terms of delivering the product or service. This means that time must be set aside for understanding the interconnectedness of the organization's product or service delivery systems. Cross-training opportunities are of great value to process-effective organizations as they provide for depth of expertise to be called on when a gap needs to be filled.

A formal mentoring program for more senior employees, despite its expense, can be a very valuable tool for retaining the best employees. Those who participate in these programs develop a depth of expertise about the business that is not possible by just taking formal education courses. These programs also foster loyalty to the organization insofar as employees who view the organization as committed to them are more likely to be committed to the organization. Table 4.3 lists the individual performance areas that mentoring programs and the like help to promote.

As part of the training system, ongoing assessments of the utility of all training programs must be part of the organizational effectiveness equation. Those programs that do not provide a good return on investment should be modified or dropped, whereas those programs that work should be expanded on.

Table 4.4 provides a set of user-friendly suggestions about how to carry out an assessment for a training program. Although there is some reservation about using a full-blown utility analysis for such programs (e.g., Skarlicki, Latham, & Whyte, 1996), this should not preclude the underlying principles of such analyses from being carried out. Quite simply, the more criteria that are evaluated the better.

Opportunities for promotion and advancement are important motivators for members of process-effective organizations. Finely layered hierarchical structures provide opportunities for promotion that can be used as an incentive. In the past 20 years, North American organizations have engaged in a frenzy to de-layer and flatten organizational structures. This has had some very adverse consequences for process-effective organizations. Several of these have been documented elsewhere. For purposes here, however, one problem with this approach was

TABLE 4.3
Individual Performance Areas for Fostering Process Effectiveness

Consider how you would rate the person on the following items (note that you can use a scale of 1 = rarely and 5 = almost always).

1. Knows their own job.
2. Knows the tasks of all their team members.
3. Is ready to "pitch in" to assist wherever needed.
4. Follows procedures correctly.
5. Mentors new organizational members to "learn the ropes."
6. Articulates the firm's market position.
7. Knows how well the firm is doing in relation to its competition.
8. Takes pride in doing things the right way—no errors.
9. Recognizes the contributions of other organizational members.
10. Contributes to organization by submitting ideas for improving procedures.

TABLE 4.4
Sample Evaluation for a Safety-Training Program

Both formative and summative evaluation procedures are useful for quite different reasons. A formative process generally answers the question: "Why is the program successful or unsuccessful?" A formative evaluation sheds light on where the program might best be modified in the future while retaining the current program strengths. A summative evaluation provides the "hard numbers" required by stakeholders and generally answers the question: "How effective is the program in terms of the bottom line?"

Kirkpatrick's model (1959, 1960) suggests that there are four levels of evaluation: (a) reaction, (b) learning, (c) behavioral, and (d) impact. The former two levels are relevant for formative evaluation, whereas the latter two form the basis for the summative evaluation.

Reaction. The first formative evaluation criterion focuses on participant reactions where participants provide feedback on a number of program dimensions. These "Reaction Measures" are highly subjective and are meant to be so as the program participants are the "closest" to it in regard to its execution. Typical questions might include:

a. Was the information on the safety program presented in an organized manner?
b. Was it made clear why safety is important to the organization?
c. Was your interest in acting safely increased?
d. What was the quality of the support materials (videos, booklets, etc.)?
e. Did the program live up to your expectations?
f. Would you recommend the program to others?
g. What did you like best about the program?
h. What would you suggest for changes to the program?

(continued on next page)

TABLE 4.4   *(continued)*

Learning. The next formative evaluation criterion is learning. This is usually carried out by having participants take pretests before the instruction and then posttests upon completion of the training. Essentially, this evaluative component is concerned with whether and the extent to which knowledge has been imparted by the program. It is important that the criteria for learning be specified in advance so that the program content can adequately cover the topics of interest. Excellent ways to evaluate learning in the workplace context is using simulations or role-play exercises as these are appropriate for adult learning styles.

For example, participants are presented with scenarios involving safety violations and are asked to indicate where the violations have occurred. Another example would be to show an accident on videotape and have the participants complete an accident investigation form. Another way to assess learning would be to identify hazardous materials using symbols. All of these would assess learning involved in the various aspects of a safety-training program. Follow-up assessments each year would provide an index of when refresher courses should be implemented.

Behavioral. Turning now to the summative evaluation criteria, the first is behavioral. This level is evaluated by examining how the program has changed participant behavior. A safety program would be expected to decrease some types of behaviors and increase others. This means that before the training takes place, baseline information on safety criteria must be gathered. This can be done at the individual or group level. Examples of such behaviors would include: violations of safety procedures, exhibiting safe lifting procedures, carrying out vehicle checks prior to delivering something.

Behavioral change then can be assessed in using a "before and after" within the same group, or the behaviors of one group that has gone through the training can be compared to that of another group that has not yet received the training.

Impact. The final evaluative level is impact. That is, what is the impact of the program? With respect to a work safety program, some relevant criteria to track would include the number of accidents, the number of accident claims filed and the costs associated with those claims, employee absenteeism, and replacement worker costs.

Clearly, there are substantial costs to the organization in assessing training programs—particularly at the behavioral and impact levels. However, it is only at these levels that the organization sees the benefits of the program. Thus, to make an argument to maintain or cut a program, these data are necessary.

that the reorganizations frequently took out the communication mechanisms without replacing them with anything else. It also removed the ability for the organization to reward employees by promoting them. It is time to rethink the value of promotional systems and set up mechanisms and structures to allow this to happen.

Communication systems are an absolutely integral part of the process-effective organizational strategic advantage. Tracking systems that show where in the delivery process a particular product is, or where a maintenance crew is presently working, have to be set up, maintained, and upgraded. Communication links between teams are essential. If one team needs assistance, it needs to be able to contact other teams for help and the help has to get there as soon as possible. If not, a customer might be lost.

At any time, any member should know how the firm is doing in relation to its competition. This means that communication systems must be set up to take advantage of technologies that convey this information. This information can be sent to workers' e-mail at periodic times during the day. Public "billboards" or screens that post this information might be an option for smaller organizations. A more passive system where members can log on to a site that conveys this information is also possible.

Customers of process-effective organizations are likely to take advantage of computer-based purchasing. Systems have to be set up so that transactions can be dealt with electronically. These systems have to be highly reliable and easy to fix if they do break down. The more dependent the organization is on a particular technological system, the worse off they will be when something goes wrong (note that I did not say "if"; I said "when" because all machinery is not 100% reliable). Backups must be built in from the start because more than any other market strategy, the process effectiveness strategy relies heavily on computerized and electronic systems.

✦ ORGANIZATIONAL OUTCOMES

As noted earlier, process-effective organizations should have information about the delivery of their product or service readily available to all organizational members. For example, the success of the organization might be based on the volume of sales made. The outcomes that members should be taking note of, then, include the volume of sales made during a particular time frame in relation to previous similar time frames.

The speed with which a product or service is delivered to a customer is another source of continual feedback that should be monitored. Decreasing the length of time a customer has to wait for their product or service is another positive organizational outcome. The number of products or services customers have had to return or complain about is another source of valuable information. Members should be vigilant about how to decrease these errors.

Increasing the number or types of options available for product customization is also an indicator of procedural effectiveness. This means that the organization has used feedback from its customers to provide products or services that match their unique needs.

"Less is more" if measuring the length of time of customer contact for procedurally effective organizations. That is, the less time customers interact with members of the organization, the better. Take the fast-food restaurant business. The longer customers wait in line to place their order or wait for the food to reach them the more unhappy they become. The longer customers are "on hold" waiting to have a customer service representative take and place an order—whether it be for a discount airline ticket, a book order, or a stock trade order—the more unhappy they become. The more customers have to contact an organization to find out where an order is or when the maintenance people are going to arrive the more unhappy they become. Customers unhappy with an organization that has promised "process effectiveness" will move rapidly to take their dollars to another organization that will deliver on such a promise.

The cost of the product or service—particularly as compared to that of other organizations delivering similar products or services—must be monitored. Costs to produce and deliver the product or service should go down on a regular basis.

All of these indicators should be updated—in real time if possible. The data should then be graphically represented to all organizational stakeholders. These are incredibly useful and motivating feedback mechanisms, particularly for organizational members. They reinforce the values that the organization stands for and they are at the fingertips of employees.

5

Customer Service-Focused Organizations

F igure 5.1 indicates our next stop on the road map to creating an environment that fosters the development of teams that lead the way in customer service. It is useful to be aware of a couple of things before embarking on a service strategy. First, a "service product" is often intangible. For example, at the end of the day, there is no new car in your garage—only a repair job to the car you already owned. After your holiday, you don't have anything tangible except some photographs. Instead, the service provided by the hotel staff on your holiday is part of the "customer service product" you should have enjoyed. Thus, the customer tends to view the entire delivery system as the product. Therefore, the customer service strategy has to include all aspects of the service delivery—not just one or two components.

Second, be mindful that if you diversify your products or services, your service needs will increase exponentially. This is because now you will need to ensure that the linkages between the operational systems are smooth—which is no easy task.

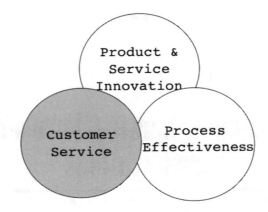

FIG. 5.1. Market strategies: Customer service.

✦ STRATEGIC FOCUS

With these considerations in mind, the first component of developing an effective customer service strategy is to tightly narrow the scope of the market to be served. This approach allows for the optimal amount of resources to be expended on specifically targeted areas of customer service. If you spend too little or spend on developing the wrong things for your customers, then you run the risk of losing the customers. If you spend too much too quickly, then you run the risk of going out of business before being able to establish or retain your market share. Inherent in these statements is that the organization cannot be all things to all people. It must choose its market carefully and go after it with tenacity.

Customer service segmenting differs from traditional market segmenting. Traditional market segmentation is based on "purchase/no purchase" data or some other binary decision made by a potential customer. At best it can define your market in terms of its demographic characteristics. Customer service segmenting means you go beyond the market identification stage. Instead, you need to understand what your market wants—before they purchase, at the purchase, and after the purchase. This means that you must come to know your customers' expectations at all points as they come into contact with your product or service.

So, the first task is to find out who exactly are your customers. This task is often easily, but deceptively, answered through examining archival information. You can take a look at the sales sheet or service record to get some idea of your market's demographic characteristics. However, the customer may be the distributor for your product, or a purchasing agent, or the end user, or all of them. Make sure you know! Ask your front-line staff who it is that they sell to, or who it is that they come into contact with, or look at your service calls and see who makes them. This is your best source of information when it comes to knowing who the customer is.

The next task is to find out what those customers expect based on sound research. Do not rely on guesswork and/or the experience of your managers. Davidow and Uttal (1989) said that the way *not* to determine customer service expectations is by: having a staff meeting, brainstorming possible areas of service expectations, creating a survey based on the brainstorming session, sending out the survey to all your customers, and tabulating the results. What this process ensures is that the theory of customer service needs provided by the staff at its initial meeting will be confirmed. Studies show that there is a difference between what organizations believe their customers expect and what they actually expect (e.g., Lambert & Lewis, 1983; Marr, 1980).

Instead, customer expectations need to be gleaned from open-ended questions, in-depth interviews, and focus groups made up of customers. Although these methods of qualitative data gathering are expensive to set up, run, tabulate, and understand, the information gained from them is worth the resources expended. It tells you much more about what the customer wants before, during, and after their purchase. It is the beginning of understanding your market.

Next, you will need to flesh out the differences between what you and the competition can offer to these individuals. Find out what your competitors are providing and see where your organization can fulfill an expectation that has not yet been met. By using your marketing information and your customer expectations you can fill gaps in service excellence that will ensure that your organization is the market's choice.

✦ ORGANIZATIONAL STRUCTURE

An important aspect of customer service strategy is the recognition that it can't be stored in a warehouse. It involves a high degree of human interaction. This "high touch" approach is what your market values. By definition this means you can't be laying off staff and rehiring new people.

An example of organizational structures facilitating this thinking include an upside-down pyramid with customers at the top followed by front-line employees, with the president at the bottom point (see Fig. 5.2). Another is a concentric circle with customers in the bull's-eye and employees in the next ring. Executives are at the outermost ring (see Fig. 5.3). Figures 5.2 and 5.3 highlight that the most valued interaction is between the front-line staff and the customer.

These figures are used to demonstrate the importance of the customer focus of the organization. Missing in these depictions, however, is

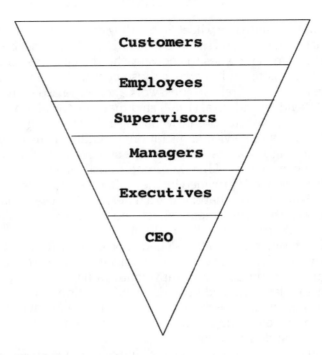

FIG. 5.2. Upside-down pyramid.

FIG. 5.3. Concentric circles.

some notion of teams. The literature is adamant that teams provide an essential ingredient for effectively managing a customer service strategy.

Examining the workings of customer-focused organizations, there are clearly two sets of teams that should be formed. One set is made up of individuals with similar capabilities—they are called "expertise teams." This provides the organization with the depth needed for expertise in a particular area. If one individual is not at work on a particular day or leaves the organization altogether, the organization cannot be crippled by the absence. Thus, these expertise team members may not even be at the same geographic location. They are set up to provide support for each other in terms of expertise and backup. For example, in a financial service company, many individuals may have expertise in investment banking. They need to have colleagues within the organization who they can call on for advice, for assistance if they are overly busy, and so on. These teams of investment experts should know each other well. They should be held accountable for maintaining their level of expertise so that they can be active contributors to the cross-functional teams described next.

In addition to being part of an expertise team, all organizational members are part of cross-functional customer service teams. These teams are made up of individuals from the different organizational units that deliver an entire product or service to the customer. Continuing with the financial institution example, a cross-functional customer service team would be made up of individuals from expertise teams in basic banking functions (such as checking or savings accounts operations), Web-based financial interactions, loans and lines of credit, international banking, investment banking, and so forth. These teams are each responsible for a set of individual customer accounts. Customers would come to know the names, faces, and voices of each of the team members as well as their area of expertise.

Finally, one member of each of the expertise units also participates in the cross-functional planning team. Their role here is to make sure that strategic and tactical decisions are made that customers will appreciate and that those delivering the service have the expertise to support. Figure 5.4 shows how an organization can structure its human resources to capitalize on customer service teams.

One industry example for this type of structure is in the hotel business. Expertise teams from various locations of the hotel chain ensure that service is delivered. For example, if more housekeeping staff are needed at one location, the housekeeping expertise team knows to send more people to that location. The cross-functional service teams are made up of members from the expertise teams of housekeeping, front desk, maintenance, bellhop, food service, and so on. These teams ensure that the customers in their particular units at their particular loca-

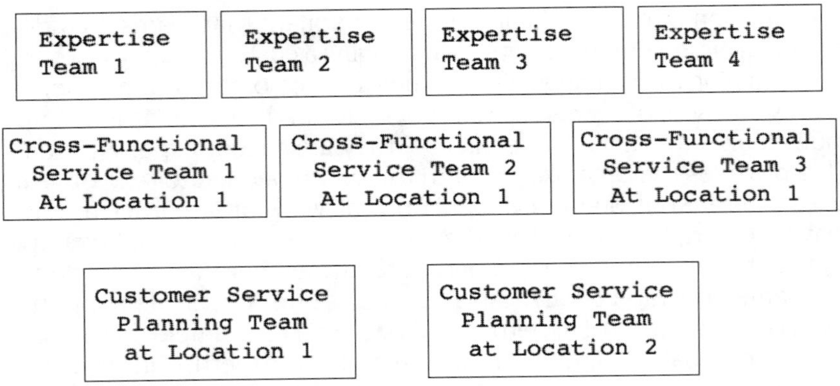

Expertise Team 1	Expertise Team 2	Expertise Team 3	Expertise Team 4

Cross-Functional Service Team 1 At Location 1	Cross-Functional Service Team 2 At Location 1	Cross-Functional Service Team 3 At Location 1

Customer Service Planning Team at Location 1	Customer Service Planning Team at Location 2

FIG. 5.4. Customer service structure.

tions are delighted with their stay. The customer service planning teams ensure that policies and procedures are in place that facilitate customer service, identify bottlenecks in the service delivery process that have to be overcome, and ensure that customer service audits are continually carried out and acted on.

Notice that a customer service department is not in the structure. This is a deliberate omission. A customer who is having difficulty does not want to be shunted to the customer service department (which really means the complaint department) where there is not the expertise to deal with the problem. Instead, any member of the organization, when confronted with a customer concern, must be able to either solve the problem themselves, or take it to the member of their team who can solve the problem. These days it seems that most organizations use the fiscally prudent approach to staffing their "call centers," using only part-time, new employees who they don't have to pay very much. This approach runs counter to the strategy of customer service. You need your most senior people handing calls from frustrated customers. Members of organizations who have been around for a long time and understand all the systems and how best to solve the customers' problems are the ones you need staffing these centers—not junior people who don't have the background or expertise to make a decision.

If this approach sounds like it takes time and effort, it does. A customer service strategy requires the organization to develop relationships with each and every customer. It also requires much time and effort devoted to ensuring that customers are linked into the organizational decision-making process. It requires organizational members to work together—in teams made up of people within their area of expertise as well in teams where other areas of expertise are present. If the organization is not willing to do so, then it should adopt a strategy more in keeping with where it believes it has the best market opportunity.

✦ MANAGEMENT FUNCTION

The management function for customer service-focused organizations requires that their activities assist teams in delivering service. Like the other market strategies, power in the customer-focused organization does not come from position. Instead, it comes from customer satisfaction. Decisions have to be made quickly to solve a customer's problem. The authority and expertise needed to make the decisions comes from those who have contact with the customer. Thus, there is a very minimal chain of command in customer-focused organizations.

As a result, the day-to-day tasks of managers are to:

1. Ensure that there is enough staff to deliver high-quality service.
2. Listen to the customer service teams from across the organization and determine where to initiate changes so as to better serve customers.
3. Shield staff from customers who harass.
4. Regularly initiate, review, and take action on customer service audits.
5. Ensure that staff have adequate training in their area of expertise.
6. Ensure that staff have adequate training in customer service.
7. Ensure that backup systems are in place so as to minimize any downtime customers experience.
8. Value most highly those individuals in the organization who interact with the customers.
9. Recognize and reward incidents of exceptional customer service.

High staff turnover is going to harm business, as customers want continuity in their relationship with the organization. This means that stopping the usual high turnover in service industries is going to be critical to the success of a customer service organization. This issue falls squarely into management's bailiwick. Many times employees in these organizations look for role models about how to deal with customer problems. They will look to managers for expected behaviors and ideas about customer relationship building. It is imperative that managers behave in a manner that the employees should be modeling.

To be avoided at all costs are rules, regulations, policies, and procedures that stop those in contact with customers from being able to solve their problems. Of course, there are laws, statues, and industry standards to which all organizations must comply. At issue are rules that make sense only from the perspective that they make the job of the organization easier, whereas from the customer perspective the rule makes no sense. Another of management's functions, then, is to frequently reassess the overlay of organization-specific rules and polices and get rid of any that impede customer satisfaction.

All of these management functions shift the performance focus of the organization and individual employees away from "pleasing the boss" to "pleasing the customer." Managers who behave in a manner consistent with this philosophy should be recognized and rewarded. Those who insist on pleasing the organization should not remain.

◆ CULTURE

On their first contact with the organization, individuals will notice a "customer-first" strategy. This is because the organization is populated by employees who have adopted this strategy and it shows even in how potential customers are greeted. Employees who appear pleasant, act in a professional manner, and initiate a helping conversation are those who customers like to have assisting them. If employees look unhappy or anxious, this will stand out to customers and scare them off. So, if your employees are unhappy, the organization needs to find out why and remedy the problem.

Impressions are made in seconds. The impression you want to convey is that the customer is all-important. Some questions provided in Table 5.1 will uncover the extent to which your organization is a customer-focused one.

A culture that fosters customer service depends on customer input into efforts toward continual improvement in service. This means that you have to have partnership-type relationships with customers. It is important to recognize that customers may include those external to the organization—including suppliers and distributors—or those internal to the organization, such as another business unit, or both. Regardless of who the customer is, or who the customers are, they are an integral part of the constant improvement process.

Interestingly, by getting customers to take more of a role in the organizational functioning, they actually learn more about the organization and its capabilities. If customers can see how their input influences decisions, they will feel not only more in control about what the organization does, but also that they have a personal investment in its success. The end goal is to establish a culture that has customers wanting you to succeed.

TABLE 5.1
Questions for Assessing a Culture of Service

1. How does our organization differ from competitors in adding customer service?
2. When a policy impedes solving customer problems, what happens?
3. How many resources (physical, financial, human, and time) are set aside to specifically foster customer service?
4. How does our organization solicit and use information from customers to improve service?
5. Who makes decisions in dealing with a customer's problem?
6. If a customer problem is particularly difficult to solve, who takes the blame and how does it get used as part of organization learning?
7. How does our organization deal with negative reactions from customers?
8. How are the rewards and recognition for customer service allocated?

✦ PERSONNEL CHARACTERISTICS

Individuals who thrive in organizations where the primary activity is dealing with the public are the ones you want to attract and retain. These folks like solving problems and they actually get a kick out of seeing a customer smile. They are the ones who don't view customers simply as a source of income, but as individuals. They empathize with customers who are experiencing difficulty. In addition to treating customers well, they treat other workers around them in a similar interpersonally skilled manner. These individuals are patient, are good listeners, and have excellent communication skills. Using the PBDI approach described in chapter 3, some characteristics of these individuals and questions to assess them are shown in Table 5.2.

✦ PERSONNEL SYSTEMS

One of the most underutilized personnel systems for customer service is the training system. It is common to see organizations spend a perfunctory amount of time orienting new employees to their place in the organizational chart. Their roles and responsibilities are outlined for them and that is about it. Little to no attention is paid to the fact that customer satisfaction is a highly valued outcome. Most individuals don't feel part of a team whose mission is to make the customer happy. To help combat this problem, training programs should focus on ensuring that

TABLE 5.2
Characteristics and Accompanying Possible Questions for Assessment
of Individual Customer Service Potential

Consider how you would rate each of the responses to the following items (note that you can use a scale of 1 = poor response and 5 = excellent response).

1. *Enjoys solving problems.*
   Describe a situation where you confronted with someone else's problem. What did you do?

2. *Motivated by helping others.*
   Describe a situation where you were highly motivated by assisting someone in achieving their goals.

3. *Desires a high degree of social contact in their work.*
   Describe a situation where you were required to work with a group of people to carry out a task.

4. *Interpersonally skilled.*
   Describe a situation when you have had to call on your interpersonal skills to solve a problem.

5. *Calm.*
   Describe a situation when you have calmed down others who were highly anxious.

6. *Patient.*
   Describe a situation where you have had to be extraordinarily patient.

all front-line people have the information, skill, and authority to solve customer problems.

So exactly what should a training system look like for developing customer service? Knowing how the business works is a critical first step because it provides the employee with a framework for problem identification and problem solving. Every employee from the CEO down should have at least a rudimentary idea of the specific steps involved in how the product or service is delivered. Second, training should include ways to meet and greet customers that demonstrate their importance to the organization. This includes showing them keen attention and treating them as individuals. Third, assume that the customer is there to have a problem addressed. Even if the "problem" is simply to purchase an off-the-shelf product, this act is one that requires service. This service includes making eye contact, smiling, checking to see if there is anything else that can be done, checking to ensure that the customer feels good about the contact with the organization, and ending the contact gracefully.

Be prepared. Not all products or services will be delivered without a hitch. If a design defect is noted, gear up your people to be trained to deal with the fallout. On such occasions, the "problem" to solve is much more complicated and the customer may very well be upset. In this problem-solving situation, the first step is to correctly identify the issue. Get the customer to tell you what the problem is. Note that if they are upset, you will first have to get them to calm down. Let the customer speak his or her mind before attempting to start to resolve the problem. Use techniques such as speaking slowly and calmly, smiling, taking a deep breath, and reiterating what you have heard so that the customer knows that you have correctly identified the issue of concern. Use phrases such as: "What happened?" and "What would you like to see our organization do?" These phrases initiate the resolution to the problem. Do not use phrases like "Why did you do that?" or "Why should our organization take responsibility for that?" These immediately put the customer on the defensive and will not engage them in assisting you to solve the problem to their satisfaction.

Don't allow employees to politely refuse to respond to a request for service. All employees need to know how they can find a way to deal with a problem. Statements such as the following are not acceptable: "That is not my department"; "I'll have to get authorization from my boss"; "That is against company policy"; "I'm sorry it happened but it is not our fault"; "It is not something we can control"; "What you were told was wrong." If the employees are saying these types of things, then something is very wrong.

Identify your best employees in terms of how they deal with customers. Pair up new people with these "old hands" so that newcomers have a role model from whom to learn. Provide role-playing sessions where customers call or come into the organization presenting a problem. Employees should have the opportunity to play the role of the irate customer and the employee. Observing others in these roles provides more ideas about how to problem solve.

The training should include how to follow up with a customer in terms of their satisfaction with the product or service. As part of this approach, have teams keep track of their customers. Information about what types of products or services customers frequently purchase will assist the team in alerting their customers to new products, new services, or new information that will benefit the customer. For example, your organization may send out newsletters or newspaper or magazine articles to customers. Team members should make periodic phone calls or send out personal letters to customers regarding new information that may be of interest to them.

Cross-train your employees. Although they will all be part of their expertise team, there are times when the organization will be short-staffed and will need to call on employees to fill in where needed. This means that all employees should have some training not only in their own area but in one or two others as well. Remember that dealing with customers and customer complaints requires a high degree of emotional outlay by your employees. Have employees take frequent breaks if necessary so that they are fresh and ready to deal with the next problem. Cross-training will ensure that you have enough depth or expertise in your organization to provide breaks to your employees who have a high degree of customer contact.

Follow up the training sessions by interviewing the employees and finding out what was most useful. Interview the employees' coworkers and supervisor to see if the employee is demonstrating the new behaviors on the job.

Train your customers as well. Educate them about how to use a new product or service that you have introduced. You might do this in formal, free-of-charge sessions (such as providing a workshop on "how to restore your wooden furniture") or informally as part of the delivery package (such as walking a new customer through the process of online banking).

Finally, it should be noted that not just your front-line employees need interpersonal skills training. Make sure you train the managers as well. Managers sometimes have to take over front-line worker positions. This means they need to know how to work with customer problems. In addition, and perhaps most important, employees treat customers the way they themselves are treated. Therefore, management staff must value the contributions of their employees, and periodic training programs should serve as a reminder of this. Table 5.3 summarizes the primary areas of training for developing a customer service-oriented workforce.

Reward and recognition systems in many customer service industries are notoriously poor. You need to remedy this. Identify heroic acts by your employees and publicly praise them. Tell the employee ahead of time you will be doing this and do it as soon as possible. In your praise tell the story of exactly what the employee did right—be specific. Make sure in your story to tell how what the employee did links to the organizational strategy and encourage the employee and others to do more of the same.

Send a personal note of thanks to the employee—don't just send a quick e-mail. This provides a record of your thanks and tells the employee that you thought enough of them to take time to write. Provide the opportunity for a visible career path for your employees. By developing their cross-trained expertise skill sets and their interpersonal skill repertoire the employees will be more valuable to your organization.

Provide skill-based pay increases for employees who do develop new and useful skills that will contribute to the organization. Link part of employees' pay to overall organizational performance, and part to overall customer satisfaction (this is particularly true for managers and executives).

TABLE 5.3
Training Programs for Great Customer Service

1. Inform all employees about what the organization provides and how this is delivered from start to finish. This provides a framework for understanding where a problem might have started and points in the direction of where to go about solving the problem.

2. Practice "meeting and greeting" customers. This includes not only those customers experiencing problems, but also those who have come for simple assistance.

3. Practice identifying why the customer is there and how the organization can assist in solving their problem.

4. Assume that problems will arise. No matter how much advance planning occurs, it is safer to assume that things will not run smoothly. Make sure your employees can convey a sense of preparedness to your customers.

5. Practice calming down irate customers by using phrases that demonstrate to the customer that (a) the problem is important to solve, (b) the problem is shared by both the customer and organization, and (c) the organization will solve their problem.

6. Provide opportunities for employees to work with individuals who are highly skilled at dealing with customers who have problems.

7. Demonstrate techniques for following up with customers that show the organization takes a special interest in the customers' unique circumstances.

8. Cross-train your employees. The more they know about the inner workings of other units the better prepared they will be to address customer concerns.

9. Evaluate the effectiveness of your training program by observing your employees as they interact with customers. In addition, ask the employees to provide constructive criticism about what was most useful in the training program and what was not.

10. Train your employees to train your customers. How to best use a product or service is not always known by your customers. They will appreciate your organization taking the initiative in making sure that your product or service is utilized most effectively.

11. Train your managers. Management staff are not exempt from dealing with customers. They should be able to step in at a moment's notice to cover the work of their direct reports.

Material rewards can include such things as pins, travel, vacation time, and providing new training or educational opportunities. Encourage employees to catch another employee in an act of good service and report it to that employee's supervisor. This promotes an atmosphere of collaboration and appreciation by all organizational members. Make sure that stories about an employee get retold so that the person becomes a service hero or service legend. (Table 5.4 outlines the individual performance areas in the customer service arena.)

TABLE 5.4
Individual Performance Areas for Fostering Service

Consider how you would rate the person on the following items (note that you can use a scale of 1 = rarely and 5 = almost always).
1. Knows who their internal customers are.
2. Knows who their external customers are.
3. Helps identify customer problems.
4. Solves customer problems quickly.
5. Goes above and beyond customer requests.
6. Shows courtesy to customers.
7. Provides assistance to other members of their team.
8. Shows respect for other employees.
9. Follows up with customers to determine satisfaction levels.
10. Contributes to organization by submitting ideas for improving customer service.

Not all employees deserve reward and recognition. If you need to give negative feedback, do so in the most constructive way possible. This means telling the employee (a) what the event was, recounting exactly what happened, (b) what the effect of the employee's behavior was on them, on other employees, and on the organization, (c) what the employee needs to do now to remedy the situation, (d) what should be done in future situations like the one encountered, and (e) that they are a valued member of the organization.

At rare times you will need to protect your front-line people from abusive customers. Not all customers are ones that you want to have return. If you encounter these individuals, their abuse of your staff cannot be tolerated. All you are required to do with these customers is ensure that you protect yourself from them legally.

Communication and information flow systems need to be examined in terms of the extent to which they support customer service. Customer databases provide invaluable information about which customers use which products or services. Though many organizations have set up these systems, they have not actually used the data gathered to improve customer service. Check your system to ensure that it is streamlined as much as possible. This minimizes frustrating wait times that all too often occur in the initial stages of getting the customer into the database.

Despite the fact that customer service organizations by definition rely on personal relationships, this does not mean that technological advances should not be exploited to the fullest. Some of your customers will really like being able to link up and order things on the Internet. Many customers enjoy having the degree of control and flexibility that using the Internet provides. Your organization has to be ready to respond to this customer capability.

As part of your customer service information flow, do a service map. This means auditing requests or queries that come in from a customer. What happens to the request? How is it handed off? How many links does it go through before it reaches the one that can solve the problem? What is the response time to get back to the customer? Remove anything in this service map that compromises customer satisfaction.

Examine the communication systems between team members. Make sure that they have the information they need to be active and contributing members of their expertise as well as cross-functional customer service teams. Remember that the goal is to serve the customer when creating communication systems. Frequently, communication systems are set up to make communication efficient for the users of the system rather than the customers they are supposed to serve.

Regular and informal contact between customer service teams and managers (including top-management teams) are a must in these organizations. There is no other way for the feedback from customers to get to managers in a timely manner. Part of the role of managers is to be informed about customers and their needs.

✦ ORGANIZATIONAL OUTCOMES

So how will the organization know that it has created a successful customer service organization? One criterion is the number of customers who return. It will be very important to track your frequent customers. These are the ones who will provide you with the best information about what you are doing right and where you need to improve. Another criterion is the number of word-of-mouth referrals. Track where your new customers come from. If they come from other customers you are doing a good customer service job.

Other indicators include the number of new advertising gimmicks you have to use. The less often you have to employ this as a tactic for survival, the better. You don't want new customers all the time—what you want are customers who are loyal to you. In addition, customers being willing to be contacted by you for input and being willing to take the time to provide you with feedback suggests that they want to help you. This is a good sign. Regular assessments on how responsive the organization is to customers must be part of the organizational feedback loop system.

Put into place a constant evaluation system where assessments are accompanied by action and review.

Employees who are proud to say that they work for your organization in industries where employee satisfaction is notoriously low is an important criterion to monitor. Related to this is the turnover level. Low levels suggest that employees want to stay with the organization. Because an effective customer service strategy depends on a high degree of interpersonal contact and relationship building, low turnover is a prerequisite.

II

Team Leadership Roles

The focus of the next four chapters is on the roles taken on by team leaders. The premise of these chapters is that the expectations of team leaders are presently in a state of chaos and are also unrealistic. In a review of the literature as well as a description of some of my own research, I have come to the conclusion that there are three primary roles of team leaders. The expectations of each are organized in a systematic manner and are also capable of being executed appropriately. In addition, each of the three primary roles falls nicely into the three market strategies described in the previous chapters. In chapter 6, the rationale for the roles of manager, coach, and facilitator is set out. In chapter 7 the role of team facilitator as a primary driver of innovative organizations is expanded upon. The role of team manager as a primary driver of process-effective organizations is described in chapter 8, and in chapter 9, the role of team coach as one of primary importance in customer service organizations is highlighted.

6

Team Leadership Roles: An Overview

As stated earlier, Part II of this book examines the roles of the team leader (see Fig. 6.1). The degree to which these roles are carried out plays an integral part in ensuring that team performance occurs.

The role of the team leader has been described in many ways in the extant literature. However, there is no consensus in terms of whether all team leaders should possess all of the listed qualities. There is not even consensus on what is meant by the term "team leader." The existing literature on team leader roles is briefly reviewed, with various theorists' and researchers' perspectives highlighted. First covered is the literature on self-managed work teams followed by leadership within more traditional team contexts. The discussions in these sections amply demonstrate that there is a broad array of team leader roles that are not consistent across studies.

◆ LEADERSHIP IN SELF-MANAGED WORK TEAMS

Several studies talk in very general terms about team leadership from the perspective of self-managed work teams. These researchers report that the role of the team leader is important but fail to articulate the role fully

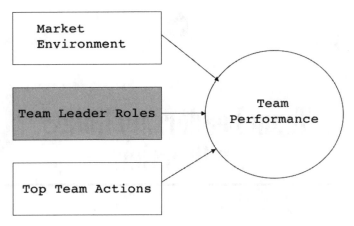

FIG. 6.1.   Aspects of team leadership: Team leader roles.

or to discuss the how these leaders should be developed. Table 6.1 lists the researchers involved and the roles defined in each work cited.

For example, Pearce and Ravlin (1987) argued that traditional managerial responsibilities should be voluntarily accepted by self-regulated work groups (SRWGs). They concluded that an informal "captain" should emerge in SRWGs. However, what this "captain" is supposed to do above and beyond the typical group member remains unexplained.

Manz and Sims (1987) divided the leadership of self-managed work teams into "external versus internal" responsibilities. They asked: "if self-managing teams are truly self-managing, then why should an external leader by required?" (p. 106). Although this study represented a start in the differentiation of leader roles, and possibly assigning them to different individuals, how to do this was left unresolved.

Goodman, Rukmini, and Griffith-Hughson (1988) were more hesitant to advocate the use of self-managing groups. They pointed out that although these types of groups tend to positively affect productivity, the magnitude of the effect is not known. In their discussion, they noted that self-managed teams do need to have in place several traditional management functions. How these functions are to be accomplished within the self-managed group was not made clear.

Despite the cautionary note by Goodman et al. (1988), Barry's (1991) work led him to conclude that the use of self-managed work teams will continue to grow for three reasons: (a) the technological information explosion, resulting in employees knowing more than their bosses; (b) the use of automated, expensive equipment in the workplace, requiring employees to make decisions that were once under the control of manag-

TABLE 6.1
Examples of Team Leaders' Duties in Self-Managed Teams

Citation	Team Leader Duties
Pearce and Ravlin (1987)	Collective responsibility by the SRWG for a substantial and manageable piece of the business. Work arrangements that facilitate social relationships and cooperative interaction. Opportunities for employees to learn all jobs involved within the SRWG's area of responsibility. Enough authority, resources, and performance feedback to carry out the tasks.
Manz and Sims (1987)	External leader roles: facilitate the teams' own self-management through self-observation, self-evaluation, and self-reinforcement. Internal leader roles: facilitate the group's organizing of itself, coordinate job assignments, and make sure materials were available to do the work.
Goodman, Rukmini, and Griffith-Hughson (1988)	Planning, directing, organizing, staffing, and monitoring.
Barry (1991)	Leadership roles should frequently shift from individual to individual, and at any one time multiple leaders can exist in a team. Envisioning, which focuses on creating new and compelling visions. Organizing, which focuses on bringing together the various group tasks. Spanning, which focuses on linking the team's efforts with others. Social, which focuses on the sociopsychological aspects of the team.
Wellens, Byham, and Wilson (1991)	Leader tasks: acting as a spokesperson for the team, coordinating work tasks and activities, training new members, and dividing tasks between members. Coordinator tasks: business planning, communication, developing talent, and setting work standards.
Gordon (1992)	Setting work schedules, dealing directly with outside clients, setting production quotas or performance targets, doing necessary training, purchasing equipment or services as needed, dealing with vendors and/or suppliers directly, carrying out performance appraisals, budgeting, and hiring and firing personnel.
Yeatts and Hyten (1998)	Administrating, facilitating meetings, serving as a spokesperson, helping the team make decisions, facilitating coordination between team members, and facilitating coordination between the team and those outside the team.

ers; and (c) competition, both global and domestic, increasing the need for organizations to be rapidly innovative. These factors have reduced the utility of middle-level managers and increased the need for decisions to be made at the employee level. Hopefully these will be well-informed decisions that can be best dealt with by self-managed work teams. Barry suggested that a distributed leadership model is most effective in such an environment. Who decides who has what role at what time as well as when and how the leader roles are passed along, however, needs more description.

Wellens et al. (1991) noted that self-managed work teams are responsible not only for accomplishing work tasks, but also for managing themselves. They noted that within the team there is a leader (or coordinator) position, which can be permanent or rotating, and also a group leader who is responsible for several teams and acts as a coordinator/facilitator. Again, however, decisions about who takes on the roles and/or how to develop skills in all team members so that they can be active contributors at the leader level remained unstated.

Gordon (1992) found that at least 80% of organizations with 100 or more employees used some form of teams. However, fewer than half of these were characterized as self-managing. These self-managed teams were expected to take on several possible roles. One interesting aspect of this study was the wide variety of tasks and levels of autonomy the teams had, depending on their organizational home. The article concluded by stating that although teams seemed to be used extensively, there was a high degree of variability in terms of which leadership roles they were responsible for carrying out.

Yeatts and Hyten (1998) argued that in self-managed work teams, the leader should be selected by the team with the approval of management, with the proviso that the position can rotate. The leader is expected to carry out leadership functions as well as their own share of the technical work. They noted that there is very little consensus in the literature regarding the specific roles and responsibilities that should be turned over to the team leader. They also reported that managers who clearly understood their new roles and responsibilities, and were provided new decision-making responsibilities to replace those taken over by self-managed work teams, were able to overcome obstacles to managing these types of teams. Again, assistance in terms of how to develop these types of skills and make the transition to new skills was not part of this book.

In an interesting counterexample to the usual findings, Cohen, Ledford, and Spreitzer (1996) examined several variables as they related to self-managing work team effectiveness. They found that encouraging supervisory behaviors was actually *negatively* related to manager ratings of team performance. In this study they also found that, in the more traditional teams, encouraging supervisory behaviors was not related to manager ratings of team performance. They argued that their findings call into question the efficacy of using self-managed work teams. Levi (2001) echoed this sentiment, saying that "developing self-managing teams can be a difficult process, and this type of team is not suited for all situations" (p. 184).

Fisher (2000) and his colleagues (Fisher, Rayner, & Belgard, 1995) concluded that as a result of the common use of self-directed work teams in organizations, the traditional supervisor is an endangered species. They claimed that making the change from a traditional hierarchy to self-directed teams is at least as difficult for supervisors as for team members. One of the most problematic aspects in this transition is the lack of role clarity for supervisors. They noted that the roles of the leader fall into seven competency clusters: leader, living example, coach, business analyzer, barrier buster, facilitator, and customer advocate. Specific behaviors associated with each of the seven competencies are listed in their work. Which, if any, roles are still within the purview of the traditional supervisor is not clear. How to effect the transition is also in need of more description.

Fisher (2000) placed his findings into a five-stage model of self-directed team development. He noted that at the early stages (Stages 1–3) of self-directed team development the roles of the leader are different than at later stages (Stages 4–5). He indicated that no other variable is as important in determining the team's leadership needs than their stage of development. He also assumed that the same individual is the leader throughout the process. That leader must engage in varying tasks (associated with the cultural, operations, and manager roles), depending on the maturity level of the team.

There has been some more recent discussion about self-managed work teams, extending the concept to include empowered teams. Kirkman and Rosen (1999, 2000) noted that autonomy is a necessary and sufficient condition for teams to be self-managing. However, teams need to also exhibit potency, engage in meaningful work, and have an impact on the organization in order for them to be empowered. They found (Kirkman & Rosen, 1999) that when the external team leader allowed the team a high degree of autonomy, the team had higher levels of empowerment and effectiveness. These researchers pointed out the need for training directed at team leaders as well as for teams in order for the potential of teams to be realized.

✦ LEADERSHIP IN TRADITIONAL TEAMS

Other researchers have used more traditional teams as their framework for discussing team leadership. Table 6.2 indicates the researchers involved and the roles defined in each of the works cited.

TABLE 6.2
Examples of Team Leaders' Duties in Traditional Teams

Citation	Team Leader Duties
Hackman (1990)	Selection of effective members; clearly defining the boundaries for the team; establishing and maintaining group norms for work; delegation and accountability; establishing relationships with external stakeholders; setting deadlines and timelines; shifting leaders as expertise needs shift; integrating the team into the organization; handing off reports; providing recognition for work; showing value of the team to the organization; and making roles explicit.
Tjosvold and Tjosvold (1991)	Gather the courage and understanding to confront the competitive-independent milieus of most organizations; work with employees so that they are convinced that teamwork is to their advantage; and put teamwork to work to achieve synergy up and down and across the organization.
Ford and Randolph (1992)	Communication, organization, team building, leadership, coping, technological expertise, providing knowledge updates, task manager, technical administrator, employee developer, and organizational developer.
Parker (1994)	Setting goals, celebrating milestones, establishing a positive atmosphere, executing meetings effectively, and using recognition to motivate the team.
Katzenbach and Smith (1993)	Keep the purpose, goals, and approach relevant and meaningful; build commitment and confidence; strengthen the mix and level of skills; manage relationships with outsiders including removing obstacles; create opportunities for others; and do real work, which means being engaged in the team's work.
Kouzes and Posner (1995)	Challenge the process, inspire a shared vision, enable others to act, model the way, and encourage the heart.
Teal (1998)	Being responsible, communicating clearly, keeping promises, and knowing oneself.
Mohrman, Cohen, and Mohrman (1995)	Task management, boundary management, team leadership, and performance management.
Riechmann (1998)	Modeling high standards; integrity; full and open communication; providing and communicating a clear vision; setting performance expectations as well as monitoring and rewarding that performance; involving team members in decisions that affect them; and publicly supporting the team.
Zenger, Musselwhite, Hurson, and Perrin (1994)	Trust, empowerment, growth, creating team identity, conflict resolution, innovation, and support.
Zaccaro and Marks (1999)	Link the team to the outside environment; establish the strategic and operational directions for team action; and facilitate team operations.

Kline (1999)	Coach/facilitator and controller/planner.
LaFasto and Larson (2001)	Focusing on the goal, ensuring a collaborative environment, building confidence, demonstrating sufficient technical know-how, setting priorities, and managing performance.

For example, Hackman (1990) postulated that team leadership varies along a continuum, with manager-led teams at the left end, self-managing teams in the center, and self-governing teams at the far-right end. Depending on the type of team that is discussed (e.g., tasks forces, performing groups, customer service teams), different conditions need to be present for effective teamwork. One of those conditions is effective leadership. Who takes on the tasks is not made readily apparent.

Tjosvold and Tjosvold (1991) and Ford and Randolph (1992) listed many leader capabilities. However, both sources neglected to mention who is best able to take on these roles or skills and/or how to best develop them. Parker (1994) discussed leadership needs from a cross-functional team perspective. He noted that cross-functional teams are often led by individuals with no formal position authority. As a result, group process skills are very important for these leaders. His work is somewhat at odds with the previously cited literature that speaks to many of the traditional supervisory roles being taken on the by the team.

Katzenbach and Smith (1993) discussed six things they believed necessary for good team leadership to exist. Engaging effectively in all six is a tall order. A result of Kouzes and Posner's (1995) work was the Leadership Practices Inventory (LPI) (1997). In it they extended their work on general leadership to team leadership. A result of this was the Team Leadership Practices Inventory (TLPI) (1992). The same five leadership dimensions are captured with the TLPI as with the LPI. Why they assume that there is no difference between the roles of traditional leadership and that of team leadership was not addressed. In a similar vein, Teal (1998) said that managing is not a series of mechanical tasks but a set of human interactions. His list includes tasks that are highly personal.

Mohrman et al. (1995) argued that teams need different types of leadership depending on their stage of maturity. Regardless of the stage, however, they cited several managerial responsibilities that will need to be dealt with. Riechmann (1998) created the Team Performance Questionnaire, which includes team leadership as one aspect. Within the team leadership construct are several tasks.

Zaccaro and Marks (1999) argued that teams need leaders to carry out specific roles first. Eventually these roles may be delegated to team members. Kline (1999) suggested that team supervision is one aspect of the broader construct of organizational support. She indicated that team supervision can be divided into two dimensions. The degree to which the needs of the team match those of the supervision provided affects team work process effectiveness. Although this provides a start in differentiating what teams expect of their leaders, it does not go far enough.

More recently, LaFasto and Larson (2001) described six dimensions of team leadership. Rees (2001) argued that team leadership is a primarily facilitative exercise, which differs from traditional hierarchical leadership, which is a primarily controlling exercise. However, her model is one in which the team leader is a member of the team—this is not necessarily always the case.

Taggar (2002) hypothesiezed that intragroup processes would moderate the relationship between individual creativity and team creativity. It is worth noting that these processes were: (a) inspirational motivation, (b) organizing and coordinating, and (c) individualized consideration. These three correspond nicely to my three-dimensional theory of team leadership (manager, coach, facilitator) introduced later in this chapter.

As a counterpoint to the primary importance of team leadership, Littlepage, Jones, Moffett, Cherry, and Senovich (1999) as well as Kirkman and Rosen (1999) found that the effects of leadership on team performance were mediated by group processes and group potency. That is, leaders' actions do not directly affect performance. Instead, how well the team processes were set up and how potent the team felt itself to be mediated any effect that the leader may have had on team performance.

◆ SUMMARY OF THE EXISTING RESEARCH

Despite the vast number of chapters, books, and articles written about team leadership, there are still many unanswered questions that could benefit from some empirical studies:

1. Can the multitude of roles outlined by the many researchers mentioned earlier be grouped in such a way as to "make sense"?
2. Do these roles or responsibilities need to be adopted by a single individual?
3. What is the best way to work with team leaders to ensure that they are providing what is needed to their teams?
4. How do organizations select individuals who are most likely to be successful team leaders?
5. What is the relationship between team leadership and team performance?
6. Are some roles more important than others for effective teamwork?
7. What contextual variables enhance or stifle team leadership growth?
8. How should organizations go about developing team leaders?

These are just some of the questions that are not yet fully answered. In fact, they are just beginning to be examined.

What is clearest from this review, however, is that there is a dizzying array of skills, knowledge, behaviors, roles, and so on, associated with the individual who is the team leader. Depending on the type of team, the team's stage of maturity, and the specific author, one has the option to adopt any number of approaches to team leadership. One concern with the extant literature is that many of the models are generally based on experience and practice rather than on empirical findings. Though this is not always the case, clear links between the model proposed and outcomes associated with the roles are not evident. In addition, how to develop the skills or roles is often not described. Another concern is the sheer number of roles associated with the team leader. To try and begin to make sense of this literature, I made a list of all the tasks expected of the team leader based on this previous work. I came up with 71 different roles.

Now, 71 different roles and responsibilities seem to be a bit too much to ask of any one individual. Just who would be willing to take up the challenge of being competent at all of them is not clear. The conclusion that there is too much here for any one person to do well was the impetus for a series of studies I conducted culminating in the Manager-Coach-Facilitator model of team leadership. This model is discussed next.

✦ THE MANAGER-COACH-FACILITATOR MODEL OF TEAM LEADERSHIP

As noted previously, the lack of clarity around team leadership tempted me to embark on a series of studies to gain a better understanding of the construct. In reading through all of this literature, there did seem to be some common themes that emerged. Specifically, I found that some roles were more appropriate for an individual with position power over the team to be carrying out, roles were most appropriately grouped into day-to-day operational monitoring, and several roles would be most effectively carried out by someone who was not personally invested in the team's outcomes but whose focus would be on team process issues. These three role groupings I called team manager, coach, and facilitator, respectively. Figure 6.2 shows these three primary roles of team leaders. Note that there is overlap between the roles. This is deliberate insofar as the roles are not considered to be completely separate. Clearly there are some tasks that may fall into more than one of the roles. The primary benefit of this model that it organizes a very muddled literature into a schema that is useful.

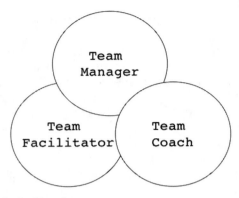

FIG. 6.2. Team leadership roles.

Over the next several pages I describe in detail the findings of three studies I conducted. Although the results are not definitively conclusive, they are quite promising. These studies included an exploratory quantitative study to see if there was convergence on the roles of team leaders, a more confirmatory quantitative study grouping the roles of team leaders, and a qualitative study using interviews of team facilitators to identify pertinent roles for team leaders.

✧ Study 1: A Quantitative, Exploratory Approach

A total of 21 participants from 11 different organizations completed a survey on team managers, leaders, and facilitators. They had been on work teams that had been in existence for an average of 6.4 years (range 4 months to 21 years). They themselves had been on their present teams for an average of 4.3 years (range 4 months to 21 years). The type of team they presently worked on included standing (70%), project (25%), and crews (5%). Their work teams ranged in size from 3 to 13 members (M = 6.0). Participants ranged in age from 24 to 59 years (M = 43.7). The majority (62%) were women.

The survey consisted of a list of different skills/behaviors/competencies (SBCs) exhibited by or possessed by individuals that have been called "Team Leaders" in the extant literature. This list of 71 different SBCs was generated by compiling all the unique roles cited by the various researchers. Participants were asked to read each of them and then to rate each of them three different times. The three separate ratings for each SBC reflected a rating for each of three types of "leaders" (focusing on ideal rather than actual leaders). The rating scale used was a 7-point Likert-type scale, with 1 indicating that the SBC was "very unimportant" to the type of leader, and 7 indicating that the SBC was "very important" to the type of leader.

One leader type was labeled "team manager," defined as the individual who is in a supervisory capacity over the team, having position authority over the team. Another was termed the "team coach," defined as the individual who is a member of the team with no position authority over the team but who is the nominal contact person for the team. The third leader type was the "team facilitator," defined as an individual who is not part of the team and has no authority over the team. Facilitators may or may not be members of the organization to which the team belongs, and are often brought in to assist the team with various aspects of their work and/or development.

In analyzing these data, a cutoff of the 10 most highly rated SBCs in terms of mean importance was used. For team managers, the cutoff score was 6.50 (M = 6.65, SD = 0.41), for team Coaches it was 6.48 (M = 6.63, SD = 0.38), and for team facilitators it was 5.95 (M = 6.22, SD = 1.34). An ANOVA (analysis of variance) carried out on the average of these 10 importance ratings showed that they did not differ significantly across leader type.

The SBCs rated as most important for team managers and their mean average ratings are shown in Table 6.3; for team coaches in Table 6.4; and for team facilitators in Table 6.5. Note that the findings do not necessarily mean that the SBCs were unimportant for the other two leader roles. It simply means that these were the most important SBCs as rated within a leader role.

The SBCs rated most important distinguish between the roles. However, there was some overlap. Specifically, there was overlap for all three leader roles on the SBCs of "encourage the team to celebrate its successes" and "make the team feel it can succeed." There was overlap between team managers and team coaches on the SBC of "trust the team." There was overlap between team coaches and team facilitators on the SBCs of "encourage team members to respect one another," "encourage the team that it can perform well," and "provide an 'optimistic' atmosphere for the team." Thus, there was more overlap in the roles of team coaches and team facilitators than in the roles of team managers and team facilitators.

It is clear that positive "strokes" such as celebrating successes and making the team feel it can succeed cross all three leadership-type boundaries. More "contextual" leadership SBCs, such as helping with team goals and providing needed resources, were ascribed to the role of team manager. Team coaches on the other hand were credited with more "task-related" leadership SBCs, such as ensuring the work quality is high and being clear about member roles. Finally, more "learning/process" leadership SBCs, such as learning from successes and failures as well as thinking about how the team can be innovative, were ascribed to the role of the team facilitator.

TABLE 6.3
Ten Most Highly Rated Skills, Behaviors, or Competencies for Team Managers

Skill/Behavior/Competency	Mean
Trust the team	6.90
Set up the context so that the team can succeed	6.81
Ensure team goals are consistent with organizational goals	6.76
Create a budget or business plan for the team's work	6.62
Ensure that any technical support is available to the team	6.62
Ensure a safe team working environment	6.57
Empower the team	6.57
Make the team feel it can succeed	6.57
Encourage the team to celebrate its successes	6.52
Provide a shared vision among team members	6.52

TABLE 6.4
Ten Most Highly Rated Skills, Behaviors, or Competencies for Team Coaches

Skill/Behavior/Competency	Mean
Model the way the team should act	6.81
Encourage team members to respect one another	6.76
Encourage the team that it can perform well	6.71
Provide an "optimistic" atmosphere for the team	6.71
Trust the team	6.67
Ensure that work quality is high	6.62
Inspire the team to "go above and beyond the call of duty"	6.52
Ensure that team members are clear about their respective roles	6.52
Encourage the team to celebrate its successes	6.52
Make the team feel it can succeed	6.48

✧ Study 2: Evidence for a Three-Dimensional Model

In the next study, a pared-down version of the roles of team manager, coach, and facilitator was created based on the findings of Study 1. Specifically, a list of 39 SBCs was created and these are grouped according to

TABLE 6.5
Ten Most Highly Rated Skills, Behaviors, or Competencies for Team Facilitators

Skill/Behavior/Competency	Mean
Encourage team members to respect one another	6.43
Make the team feel it can succeed	6.33
Encourage the team to celebrate its successes	6.33
Encourage the team that it can perform well	6.28
Assist the team to learn from its successes	6.24
Encourage the team members to provide each other feedback	6.24
Help the team determine how well it is doing	6.24
Provide an "optimistic" atmosphere for the team	6.19
Assist the team to learn from its failures	5.95
Provide assistance in getting the team to be innovative	5.95

leader role in Table 6.6. Fourteen SBCs were associated with the team manager, 11 with the team coach, and 9 with the team facilitator. The other five items crossed all three team leader types—all were associated with providing those "positive strokes" noted from Study 1—and so were subsequently dropped from further analyses. These were distributed and completed by 43 team members who came from 28 different organizations. These were not the same individuals as those from Study 1.

The participants were asked to rate on a scale of 1 "strongly disagree" to 5 "strongly agree," the extent to which the SBC is carried out by an individual in a leadership capacity for their team.

Participants had been on work teams that had been in existence for an average of 4 years (range 6 months to 12.7 years). They themselves had been on their present teams for an average of 3.5 years. The type of team they presently worked on included standing (44%), project (19%), and crews (30%) with three participants not responding to the item. Their work teams ranged in size from 4 to 75 members (M = 14). Participants ranged in age from 28 to 63 years (M = 44). Women made up 58% of the sample, men 37%, with two individuals not indicating their gender.

Internal consistency analyses using Cronbach's alpha were carried out on each of the sets of items for the three separate roles with good results: manager (0.90), coach (0.82), and facilitator (0.84). It should be noted that Cronbach's alpha is affected by the number of items in the scale, and as such the pattern of lower internal consistency when the scales have fewer items is statistically expected.

TABLE 6.6
Items From the Team Leadership Questionnaire

Team Manager Roles

The team knows that there are high expectations about its work quality.
The team is rewarded for a job well done.
Barriers to the team's work are dismantled.
Team members are made clear about the standards of performance.
Members are held accountable for their roles.
A shared vision for the team has been created.
The team receives accurate and timely feedback about its performance.
Resources are made available so the team can carry out its work.
The team is trusted to make the right decisions.
The team's goals are ensured to be aligned with the organization's goals.
The team's successes are publicized to others outside the team.
The team is made to feel it can be innovative without fear of reprisal.
The team is made to be responsible for its actions.
The team feels it is "protected" by a champion.

Team Coach Roles

Team members are made clear about their own individual roles.
Team members are made clear about the roles of other team members.
Team members are encouraged to "go above and beyond the call of duty."
Team members are encouraged to respect one another.
Members are encouraged to "have a say" in the team's work.
Team communication is ensured to be open and honest.
Responsibility within the team is earned.
The team has a budget/business plan.
The team has role models for behavior to look to.
Team timelines and milestones are set.
Member needs for skill training are met.

Team Facilitator Roles

Time to learn from the team's successes is made.
Time to learn from the team's failures is made.
The team takes time to suggest improvements in work processes.
The team is encouraged to be innovative.
The team is encouraged to determine for itself how well it is doing.
Team members provide each other feedback.
An objective "voice" is available to the team.
The team has diagnostic/intervention tools available to help performance.
Expertise on team processes is available to the team.

In addition to the Cronbach's alpha calculations, three principal components analyses were conducted on the separate sets of SBC items for each leader role. Though it would have been preferable to examine the fit of a three-factor versus a one-factor model, the small sample size made that impossible.

It was anticipated that one component would underpin each of the scales. Thus, a single-factor solution was requested in the analyses. For the manager SBCs the eigenvalue associated with the first component was 6.29, accounting for 45% of the variance in the items. Item loadings for the component are reported in Table 6.7 and ranged from 0.31 to 0.83. For the coach SBCs the eigenvalue associated with the first component was 4.35, accounting for 40% of the variance in the items. Item loadings for the component are also reported in Table 6.7 and ranged from 0.30 to 0.83. For the facilitator SBCs the eigenvalue associated with the first component was 4.13, accounting for 46% of the variance in the items. Item loadings for the component are also reported in Table 6.7, ranging from 0.28 to 0.84.

These analyses suggest that the items making up the three roles have good internal consistency. In addition to these analyses, factor-based scores were created for each role subscale. This was done by averaging the ratings for each set of SBC items. Then the correlations among the subscales were calculated as well as correlations between the subscale scores and two criterion variables that made up part of the questionnaire. The two criterion items were: "Overall my team performs well" and "I like being a member of this team." Participants again used a 5-point scale ranging from 1 "strongly disagree" to 5 "strongly agree" in responding to these questions. These correlations are shown in Table 6.8 and all are statistically significant.

There is clearly overlap in terms of how participants rated the roles of those in team leadership positions. Also, the more each of these roles is present, the better the participants rated their overall performance as well as how much they liked being part of the team.

The findings from the questionnaires provide some insights into the roles of the team leader. The small sample and lower than 0.40 component loadings for four of the items highlighted the need for continued modification of the constructs. Study 3 used a qualitative approach to triangulate the findings from Studies 1 and 2. This approach helped to refine the final conclusions on the team leadership roles model.

✧ Study 3: A Qualitative Approach

A total of 12 participants from 11 different organizations were interviewed about the roles of team managers, coaches, and facilitators.

TABLE 6.7
Component Loadings for the Three Principal Components Analyses on the Team
Leadership Questionnaire Items

Team Manager Roles	Item Loading
The team knows that there are high expectations about its work quality.	0.75
The team is rewarded for a job well done.	0.48
Barriers to the team's work are dismantled.	0.69
Team members are made clear about the standards of performance.	0.69
Members are held accountable for their roles.	0.80
A shared vision for the team has been created.	0.78
The team receives accurate and timely feedback about its performance.	0.81
Resources are made available so the team can carry out its work.	0.32
The team is trusted to make the right decisions.	0.65
The team's goals are ensured to be aligned with the organization's goals.	0.49
The team's successes are publicized to others outside the team.	0.46
The team is made to feel it can be innovative without fear of reprisal.	0.73
The team is made to be responsible for its actions.	0.83
The team feels it is "protected" by a champion.	0.65

Team Coach Roles	Item Loading
Team members are made clear about their own individual roles.	0.83
Team members are made clear about the roles of other team members.	0.78
Team members are encouraged to "go above and beyond the call of duty."	0.48
Team members are encouraged to respect one another.	0.64
Members are encouraged to "have a say" in the team's work.	0.78
Team communication is ensured to be open and honest.	0.76
Responsibility within the team is earned.	0.65
The team has a budget/business plan.	0.30
The team has role models for behavior to look to.	0.53
Team timelines and milestones are set.	0.59
Member needs for skill training are met.	0.31

Team Facilitator Roles	Item Loading
Time to learn from the team's successes is made.	0.84
Time to learn from the team's failures is made.	0.81
The team takes time to suggest improvements in work processes.	0.77
The team is encouraged to be innovative.	0.81
The team is encouraged to determine for itself how well it is doing.	0.72
Team members provide each other feedback.	0.60
An objective "voice" is available to the team.	0.62
The team has diagnostic/intervention tools available to help performance.	0.28
Expertise on team processes is available to the team.	0.43

TABLE 6.8
Correlations Between the Different Leadership Role Scores
and Between the Leadership Role Scores and Criterion Measures

	Manager	Coach	Facilitator
Manager	***		
Coach	0.92	***	
Facilitator	0.80	0.78	***

	Overall Performance	Like Being Team Member
Manager	0.60	0.62
Coach	0.61	0.63
Facilitator	0.48	0.54

These individuals had not participated in either Study 1 or 2. They had been in various work team roles (member, supervisor, instructor, facilitator), and had been working with teams for 5 to 30 years.

Participants were asked to respond to the following open-ended question regarding each of the roles: What do you think are the SBCs needed to be an effective (a) team manager, (b) team coach, and (c) team facilitator?

Content analysis was used to examine the data. Table 6.9 shows the SBCs noted by the respondents and the frequency with which an SBC was mentioned for team managers. Table 6.10 does the same for team coaches and Table 6.11 for team facilitators. In these tables, only the top five most frequently cited SBCs are reported. Note that the numbers in the tables represent the number of times the issue was mentioned by one of the respondents. Because there are several similarly related statements in each of the issues, the numbers sometimes total to more than 12, the number of participants in the study.

For team managers, the most frequently cited SBCs included: (a) being a champion/lobbying for the team, (b) helping set the strategic direction for the team, (c) determining how well the team does and rewarding the team for doing well, (d) securing needed resources for the team, and (e) setting standards for work practice. The SBCs cited most frequently for team coaches were: (a) managing day-to-day operations for the team (coordinating tasks, delegating, providing feedback, evaluating the team), (b) ensuring that members have a sense of inclusiveness (e.g., having a "say" in decisions, taking member feelings into account), (c) setting the culture for the team including norms for work, (d) assigning roles

TABLE 6.9
Five Most Frequently Mentioned Skills, Behaviors, or Competencies for Team Managers

Skill/Behavior/Competency	Frequency
Lobbyist/champion/intermediary between the rest of the organization and team/get team recognition in the broader organization/be alert for impact of the team on the organization/validate the team/visible success for the team/celebrate successes publicly/the big cheerleader/show the team that their results have an impact/play up positive aspects of the team/go to bat for the team	21
Ensure all team members understand the team's direction/clarify goals/expectations/ensure team members understand their roles in relation to the overall purpose/ensure team's work is consistent with the strategic direction of the organization/ensure norms and culture of the team is consistent with that of the organization/ensure team knows where management wants it to go	13
Provide feedback/assessment/define rewards for performance	11
Procure needed resources/mechanisms set up so the team can work/be a resource/get rid of organizational barriers to teams	9
Set standards for practice/set high expectations/performance expectations/accountabilities	9

TABLE 6.10
Five Most Frequently Mentioned Skills, Behaviors, or Competencies for Team Coaches

Skill/Behavior/Competency	Frequency
Coordinate roles/work/ensure tasks get completed/deadlines are met/work gets to the right client/reporting to clients/accountable to ensure work gets done/plan tasks/keep the team on track to reach goals/guide them back on track/framework established (timelines, stakeholders, outcomes, measures)/evaluate the team/provide feedback to the team	20
Ensure team member needs are met/all members have a "say"/be aware that different individuals respond differently/ensure all people understand why decisions are made/achieve consensus/provide some support and interpersonal focus not just task focus/know team members' needs/empathize with members	9
Set up a culture of trust/integrity/open communication/challenge/noncompetitiveness/establish norms/operating principles/structure/follow norms	9
Assign roles/leverage team members' skill, knowledge, and ability/delegate as much as possible/ensure team member autonomy as much as possible/ensure team members are as equal as possible	8
Understand that the need for expertise or interpersonal skills or political connections will shift this role around/operate from influence not authority/responsibility is going to fall to someone/earned right/takes on disproportionate share of workload to validate their role	7

TABLE 6.11
Five Most Frequently Mentioned Skills, Behaviors, or Competencies
for Team Facilitators

Skill/Behavior/Competency	Frequency
Get the team to think about how they can work differently/work process thinking/help team with process not outcomes/help team with outcomes not output/help the team learn/go through critical incidents with the team/mediate conflicts/handle misunderstandings/deal with resistance/help establish group norms	13
Be an outside or objective source of information/expertise/understanding of team dynamics/putting their knowledge to work with teams	12
Provide diagnostic and make recommendations on intervention options (decision making, problem solving, conflict management)	11
Act as a good communicator (listener, reflective, mirroring, sounding board, organize what people tell you in a new way, ask relevant and clarifying questions, provide feedback on what people have said, sensitive to nonverbal cues, notice if the team is "not engaged")	11
Maintain objectivity/have no ownership of team outcomes	8

and leveraging member skills, and (e) understanding their own role as team leader. For team facilitators, the most frequently cited SBCs were: (a) scrutinizing work process issues with the team, (b) being an "expert" resource on team issues, (c) providing diagnostic information and intervention ideas, (d) being an excellent communicator, and (e) providing an objective perspective for the team.

✦ CONCLUSIONS

These studies suggest that there indeed are various team leadership roles. This is consistent with a source to which I usually do not subscribe, that is, the sports analogy metaphor when talking about work teams. The rules of the game in sports versus the work world are too different to make the analogy; however, Krzyzewski and Phillips (2000) put together a compelling way of thinking about the roles of the team leader. They pointed out that the coach of the team is just that—the coach. There are certain expectations of the coach. There are other leadership duties associated with creating an environment for a successful college basketball team, though, and these fall to different individuals. Some of them fall on the members of the team and some do not. Keep in mind that the sole job for Krzyzewski is to be the basketball coach. In work settings most managers and team members do not have the luxury of coach being their only task. Still, Krzyzewski and Phillips argued that Krzyzewski can't do it all.

In the model of team leadership I propose, managers, coaches, and facilitators are the three primary categories of leadership roles. They are perceived as having somewhat unique responsibilities for different aspects of team functioning, albeit with some overlap. If the results from all three studies are taken together, a picture emerges that seems quite logical, intuitive, and workable.

Team managers are expected to help champion the team to the rest of the organization and also act as its protector. They are also expected to ensure that resources and the context enable the team to work effectively, as well as link the work of one team with that of another. Finally, they are the conveyors of the strategic vision of the organization, and are charged with ensuring that the team's work is consistent with that vision.

Team coaches are largely expected to ensure that the day-to-day functions of the team are carried out. They coordinate the work, assign the roles, and are accountable for the team's work. The coaches are also there to ensure that a culture of trust and optimism pervades the team, and that norms are established and followed. They are responsible for ensuring that member skills are developed as needed and used appropriately.

Team facilitators are expected to work on process issues. Questions they should be most concerned with include the following: How is the team working? What better ways are there to work? How can the team be more innovative? What worked for the team, what did not, and why?

These roles seem reasonable. They also seem manageable. When teams are introduced into an organization and team leaders are appointed, there may be role confusion for team leaders: What should they be doing? What should they leave to someone else to do? If they are expected to take on all three roles, what does this mean for those individuals? What roles will they be good at executing and what will be best left to someone else with different areas of skill or expertise? These questions should be negotiated, understood, and clarified for those in team leadership roles to enhance their effectiveness. In addition, team leadership-training programs should be clear on what aspects of team leadership are being taught and to whom they should be targeted.

The findings of these studies suggest it is possible to group team leadership roles into compartments around which training and development can effectively occur. Several lines of research have concluded that there are two primary clusters of leader focus (Bass, 1990). The leader- or task-focused cluster includes behaviors or personality characteristics such as autocratic, initiator of structure, task focused, and authoritarian. The follower-focused cluster is characterized by employee consideration, a democratic style, participative decision-making, and a relations orientation. This finding has resulted after years of leadership research, but it has limited applicability to the present work for two reasons. The first is that the concept of team leadership and its operationalization are different from that developed using individual leader–follower dyads as the unit of analysis. The second is that whereas I am reporting three primary roles for leaders (manager, coach, facilitator), they do not have direct parallels in the two-cluster model in the more traditional leadership literature summarized by Bass. For example, the manager role is not the same as the leader-focused cluster nor is the facilitator the same as the follower-focused cluster.

The findings and implications of this work are also somewhat different from that using Fisher's (2000) model. It was, however, supporting to find that his conclusions using his own data and observations arrived at a similar taxonomy of role categories. He called his the manager leader, operations leader, and cultural leader. Many of the same competencies (although certainly not all) he described for these roles are aligned with the roles I have called manager, coach, and facilitator. As noted earlier, however, his focus is on self-directed work teams, whereas the model proposed here is not applicable just to self-directed teams. In addition, Fisher supposed that the roles are all carried out by one individual. I believe strongly that there are simply too many leadership tasks to carry out to have them all assigned to a single individual. Rather, shared responsibility for these roles is most effective. Finally, another difference is that the roles prescribed by Fisher are placed squarely into a staged model of team development. This puts an additional burden on the leader to figure out what stage the team is at and then to tailor their leadership activities to the team. I focus instead on the external environment as the primary variable that determines what leadership competencies will be most relevant. I also do not assume that teams go through clearly identifiable stages of maturity.

The next chapters focus on ways and means to develop all three aspects of team leadership roles: manager, coach, and facilitator. I take a somewhat unique tack insofar as I link a team leadership role to a particular market strategy. This is done not to preclude other ways to link the different leader roles to an organization. It does, however, amply demonstrate how a process such as leadership development needs to be aligned with the strategy of the organization.

Specifically, product/service-innovative organizations need team leaders who act primarily as facilitators. Process-effective-focused organizations work best with team leadership that is primarily managerial. Customer service-focused organizations are suited for team leaders who act primarily as coaches (see Fig. 6.3). Again, I am not asserting that these three roles necessarily line up neatly with the three market strategies with no overlap or possible other strategies, although data is currently being collected to assess this research question. This approach does, though, highlight that team leadership expectations should be thoughtfully developed within a larger framework of the organization's overall goals rather than in a vacuum.

In the next three chapters, each of the team leadership roles is expanded upon. Examples of how to improve these skills and ideas from real teams show how important these roles are. The take-home message from these chapters is that skill development within these team leadership roles is a long process, something that cannot be taught in a 3-day workshop. These skills develop by dealing with problems that range from the mundane to crises. No one would make the argument that you can learn to drive or play the piano in a 3-day workshop (or even over a month if your organization has that many resources to spend on leadership training). This is no less the case for developing leadership skills. And I believe that is what leadership is about—skill development.

The notion that leadership is an all-or-nothing phenomenon possessed by the few—whether right or wrong—is simply unworkable from an organizational standpoint. Organizations need leadership skills at all levels in the organization and of all types. Developing the leadership skills of all employees seems to be a much more attractive approach. The material provided in the next chapter highlights this approach and assumes that all members of the organization should be trying to hone their leadership skills.

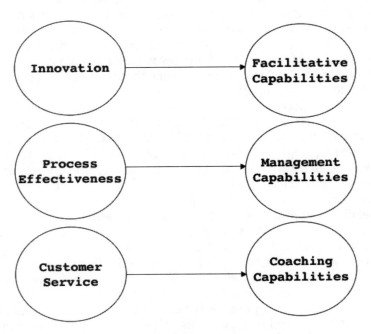

FIG. 6.3. Team leadership using the market strategy approach.

7

The Facilitator

The individuals who make up the best teams in innovation-focused organizations are often highly self-motivated, intelligent, confident in their abilities, usually creative, achievement oriented, and quite often "loners." The organizational structure in which they operate is fluid, dynamic, and flat from a hierarchical perspective. Given these kinds of individuals and the type of environment in which they operate, the type of leadership these teams will likely benefit most from is that of a facilitator. Figure 7.1 highlights that the rest of this chapter focuses on the role of the leader as facilitator.

No one has to tell these teams what to do—they already know. Because of their high level of self-motivation, they don't often need anyone to push them along. These team members get a kick out of their task of constantly innovating, constantly being on the leading edge of technological advances. However, they do not necessarily come to the organization equipped with good team-player skills. Not only would they not have learned these skills while obtaining their educational credentials, but in fact, their educational experiences have more than likely fostered a dislike for teamwork.

So, the most important role of the leader is likely to be that of facilitating the team into performing at its highest level. The leader is not going to be able to coerce or cajole team performance out of these folks. Instead these leaders will have to hone their finest facilitative leadership

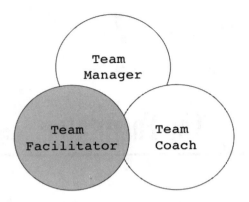

FIG. 7.1.   Team leadership roles: Team facilitator.

skills to get these people to perform as a team. Some recent research speaks directly to this issue, although not within the framework as presented in this book. It is included to justify the importance of the facilitative leadership roles within work teams.

Specifically, Druskat and Wolff (2001) highlighted the importance of developing emotional intelligence in work teams. They pointed out that even if a group of individuals comes together with each member having high levels of emotional intelligence (as described by Goleman, 1995), this does not mean that the team will have high emotional intelligence. This logic also flows in a similar manner regarding intelligent and creative individuals. Just because you bring them together as a group does not necessarily mean that they will perform optimally as a team. The model for group emotional intelligence put forward by Druskat and Wolff maps almost directly onto the facilitating leadership capacities I described in the previous chapter. This is not a coincidence. Nor is it a coincidence that the organization Druskat and Wolff pointed to as being closest to the ideal in terms of emotional intelligence is an industrial design firm noted for its innovation.

Gretz and Drozdeck (1992) described the unique leadership needs in an organization that thrives on innovation. Because the individuals that populate these organizations are often expected to be highly creative, some special management skills are needed. These include being tactful and insightful, respecting individual differences, and appreciating the creative problem-solving process. Facilitative leaders need to be excellent communicators and lead by suggestion, not by fiat. They are able to criticize tactfully and are ready to give recognition to the person who suggested the ideas. When the team is feeling demoralized or at a standstill, these leaders are able to get the team out of their funk and inspire it to keep trying. They also bolster the self-confidence of the team when it needs a boost.

Rickards and Moger (1999) have found that four aspects of leadership are critical to creative teams' success: a mutual "win-win" situation so that the team as well as the organization share in the teams' outcomes, a style that is empowering, encouragement of teams to learn and solve problems on their own, and alignment of team and individual needs.

Clearly, the literature has converged around the notion that innovative teams are going to benefit most from high levels of facilitative leadership that develops emotional intelligence, as their tasks require them to continually interact with each other, test out each other's ideas, criticize constructively, define their tasks, and stay motivated. Not many of us work on teams that are equipped from the beginning with high levels of emotional intelligence. The role of the facilitative leader in fostering, cultivating, and developing that intelligence is crucial.

I am not suggesting that a designated individual must be attached to these teams as a facilitator. However, doing so would be a good idea in many cases. Regardless of where these roles are embodied, the capacity of innovative teams to either be facilitated or facilitate themselves is critical to their success. To not do so will allow the members of these teams to easily drift off to pursue their own agendas.

Table 7.1 asks eight questions that provide some insight about the extent to which the facilitative leadership role is being carried out in a team. These questions are based on the studies discussed in chapter 6. The next section of this chapter describes each of the facilitative roles in more detail and provides ideas about how to strengthen those roles within your teams.

A common thread that runs through all of these facilitative leadership roles is a strong ability to communicate. In fact, Ray (1999) went so far as to say that respectful communication is the foundation of facilitative leadership. He then argued that the single most important communication skill is that of listening.

✦ THE FACILITATIVE ROLES

✧ Taking Time to Learn

Learning cannot be done successfully without reflection. Our action-oriented society does not tolerate well the idea of kicking back and taking time to think. Facilitative leaders challenge their teams to take time to learn from successes and failures, and then to document the lessons learned. This living documentation system assists the team by providing templates and examples of what has worked in the past and stops them from going down "blind alleys" more than once.

✧ Fostering New Ideas

Brainstorming sessions can be tedious. To be useful they have to be structured. Focus groups provide useful information only to the degree that they are focused. Creativity follows a fairly well known pattern. Individuals have to have time to think, to assimilate, and to try out their ideas on each

TABLE 7.1
Facilitator Capabilities

Rate these items on a scale of 1 to 5 with 1 meaning they are not carried out at all, 3 meaning they are carried out somewhat, and 5 meaning they are carried out regularly. Scores range from 8 to 40, with 8–16 indicating low, 17–28 indicating average, and 29–40 indicating high levels of the facilitative role being executed in the team.

1. Our team takes time to learn from our successes and failures.
2. Our team fosters innovation and new ideas.
3. Team members provide each other with constructive feedback.
4. Our team assesses how well it is doing on a regular basis.
5. Our team feels it can be successful.
6. Our team holds effective meetings.
7. Our team uses our facilitator to provide us diagnostic information and ideas for interventions to help improve our performance.
8. Our team uses the facilitator as an objective "voice" to determine how we are making decisions.

other. Creating an environment where constructive criticism can operate is an important part of the facilitator's role. A facilitator will ensure there are no such things as failures—only ideas that need work.

✧ Providing Constructive Feedback to Members

It is easy to say that an idea is a good one. However, most of us are not born with the skill to deliver negative feedback. Some people shy away from the task altogether; others may be too aggressive in how they provide the feedback. Both approaches result in negative consequences—either an idea is pursued that should not be or someone's feelings are hurt to the point where they won't interact with the team anymore. Make sure that the focus is on the idea not the person. When a deficiency in the idea is pointed out, work to provide an alternative solution.

✧ Self-Assessments

Teams have to know how well they are doing. Facilitators help to identify who the team's stakeholders are and make sure that these stakeholders are canvassed as to their perceptions about the team's performance. Facilitators collate and assist the team in interpreting the performance data. Ideas about how to improve come from these assessments. Facilitators ensure that time is taken to engage meaningfully in such a task. Finally, facilitators track the performance data for the team so that they can see how well they are doing over time.

✧ Feeling Successful

Facilitators ensure that teams take the time to reflect back on their accomplishments. Celebrations, rewards, and recognition for these accomplishments are sorely lacking in today's hectic work environments. Too soon teams are pushed on to the next task without visiting what they have accomplished. Over time, this neglect will start to show. People will feel unappreciated and your best talent will leave for an organization where their contributions are recognized. Reviewing accomplishments also serves to help team members keep working even when they are tired or disheartened. By recalling successes from the past, the team will be more likely to rally and put forth the effort to complete the task.

✧ Effective Meetings

Facilitators can be most effective by helping the team to have effective meetings. A common complaint of team members is that they spend too much time in meetings. Now, if the meetings were productive, members would not complain so much. Several sources are available that speak to holding and assessing meetings (e.g., Kline, 1999). Tools provided ensure that the team is conscious about what is happening during meeting times.

✧ Facilitator as a Source of Expertise

Facilitators must have excellent communication skills. They are expected to know a lot about teams and how teams can be more effective. The facilitation expertise most usually needed by teams includes conflict resolution, decision-making strategies, and interpersonal communication skills. Team facilitators have at their disposal resources such as books or articles that discuss and describe facilitative leadership so that they can pass it along to other team members. Facilitators should have measurement tools for team process and outcome effectiveness. If they don't have them, then they should have the skills necessary to create them.

✧ Facilitator as an Objective Voice

Facilitators perform their roles best when they can divest their interest in the team's outcomes and focus instead on the team's processes to achieve those outcomes. Why a team was successful or not is far more important than whether they were. This is perhaps the most compelling reason for disentangling the roles of the facilitator from that of the manager or coach. Facilitators' primary interest is in the health of the team itself. When they act in manner consistent with this objective, it gains them credibility with the team. This is very important, as a facilitator often has no position authority over the team and thus must lead through their interpersonal skills.

CASE STUDY EXAMPLES

The next section of this chapter describes several cases of when a facilitative leader was reported to be an important figure in the success or nonsuccess of a team. These are cases based on actual teams facing real problems.

Successful Examples

Case 1.   This example comes from a team that worked in a large, multidepartmental public organization.

Specifically, a group of professionals from different backgrounds had been placed on a new "team." They were not used to working in a team, and were much more accustomed to the traditional style of manage- ment. They were isolationist in their problem-solving styles, preferring to "go it alone" rather than work together. No team training had been pro- vided to the team. This fairly isolationist approach to their work func- tioned well in that the members could do their part of the team task and then hand it off to the next member. As long as things went smoothly this approach was fine.

However, one day a client came along and started to put pressure on the team to fast-track the approval of a proposed project. The team mem- bers resisted at the individual level, indicating that a process was in place that needed to be adhered to. In fact, at first glance, there were several problems that team members identified, any of which would stop the ap- proval process. To circumvent the process the client arranged to meet with each team member individually. The client put pressure on each member to approve the project. To add fuel to the fire, team members were getting pressure from politicians to approve the client's request. Thus, there was intense pressure on the team to approve the proposal and each member knew his or her own job was at risk by not approving it. The members were feeling very stressed about the entire situation.

A facilitator was available to the team to be used whenever they wanted. Up to this point, the team had considered this individual to be "fluff." They had been able to get by just fine without any assistance what- soever. Now, in crisis, the team asked for assistance. The facilitator worked with the members to create an awareness of what they could do collectively. The facilitator provided the team with a concrete example of how another team that had faced a similar crisis had turned the situation into a success. The example demonstrated that by working in isolation, the team had allowed an individual with strong financial and political clout to disrupt their work. The facilitator worked with them, helping them to articulate what their diverse professional contributions were to the whole enterprise. They could see that there was value in working together as a team, despite their differences in education, training, and philosophy.

The team made a conscious decision that it had to change how it worked. There were some specific issues regarding this particular client that they took action on immediately. They agreed among themselves never to meet with the client except as a group, and never to speak with the politicians alone. It was imperative that they showed that their decisions were based on adherence to professional standards and procedures—both to the client and to the organization more generally. More important from a team perspective was that they needed to show a united front in their actions.

It worked. The client's request was not approved. In the end this turned out to be the best decision for the organization as well. Several legal issues were raised eventually about the project and, had the organization approved it, it would likely have ended up in a legal battle. From a longer-term perspective, the process provided the team with the ability to appreciate the contributions the different members made to the work. With this appreciation came a new sense of being part of a team.

Case 2.   This team was part of a spin-off business from a parent company. It was in the early stages of development and thus resources were conserved in order to ensure that the pilot product being produced had the best chance of success. The pilot firm was geographically located away from the parent organization.

The team members at the spin-off firm observed the parent organization's employees. They were perceived as having far better facilities and perquisites than those of the spin-off team. The team members all wanted the glitter on the "other side of the fence." They became resentful and the issue began to take them off their tasks. The morale of the spin-off team was low, and discussions at the water cooler and at lunch no longer focused on getting the product out but on how much better it was back in the parent organization.

The leader of the spin-off team put on his facilitator hat. He knew that he would be unable to get the best creative work from the spin-off team members if they could not get past this issue. The facilitator worked with the team to create a renewed reason for being. They were not seen as simply a spin-off, but an entity in and of themselves with something unique to contribute to the organization. They worked as a team to set their vision for the new pilot product. They designed their mission and values statements, which were made into plaques that were put on all team members' office walls. The level of pride in the team and surrounding the product on which they were working went up exponentially. Twenty years later, that culture of pride, responsibility, working together, trust, and openness still remains in that team.

Case 3.   This task force team was created to restructure an entire teaching unit at a postsecondary educational institution. The members knew they were not going to be together for very long, which caused some problems immediately as the members really did not have a sense of ownership of the process, outcome, or other team members' feelings.

The individual who was named the "leader" (chair in reality) clearly knew that she had no authority over the team members. In addition, she also knew that she had no authority over those who would be affected by the team's design. This is certainly a precarious position in which to find oneself. Unfortunately, many leaders find themselves in exactly the same boat—all the flack comes to them and they have no authority or resources to deflect it. Individuals most likely to be successful in these leadership situations are those with exceptional facilitative skills. If someone is put into this position without the prerequisite skills, the team is doomed to failure.

The leader recognized the need for facilitative leadership and was able to act on that recognition. Her first task was to bring together all the team members for a meeting explicitly devoted to nontask work. Before launching directly into the restructuring project, the facilitator knew that time was going to need to be spent to collectively develop common goals, or problems would inevitably surface down the road. So, the first team meeting was spent getting all members to agree on those common goals. She focused the discussion, asking, "What is the unit trying to accomplish?" It is not uncommon for such task forces to stray off the main question, and she viewed her role as one of ensuring that the team came back to the original issue on a regular basis.

After the goals had been set, a timeline for delivery of the new unit design was set and tasks to get there were assigned. As part of the task work, several focus groups needed to be run—mostly by team members. Now, most of the team members did not have any experience running focus groups. The facilitator knew that putting team members in situations where they are likely to feel incompetent was not a good idea. So, she set training time aside to show them how to run the focus groups. That way the members would feel much more confident about carrying out their share of the focus-group task.

Once the tasks were set, the team members were able to work semiautonomously gathering their information and presenting it to the rest of the team. The facilitator's role now shifted as she allowed the team members to work. She provided guidance and direction to the team members on an "as needed" basis. In the end, the redesign was a success. Everyone who was affected by it, including the student "customers," was pleased about the outcome. Unlike many such task forces, the work that was generated by this team was valued and implemented. Clearly, the task force leader was very much in tune with what the team needed as they progressed through the task. Her facilitative skills proved to be an important part of the success of this team.

Case 4.   A team of eight senior human resources personnel formed a task force team. Each of them had their own teams working for them. The task force's mandate was to respond to a specific question posed by senior management: Should we amalgamate two divisions in a politically charged environment? Emotions surrounding this issue ran very high. The reason was that the two divisions had very distinctive, strong cultures and identities. The members of the divisions felt a strong bond with one another and felt that a "superdivision" would submerge their cultures. The successful completion of this task was viewed by everyone as very important because the decision would have a substantial impact on the organization.

The leadership necessary in this team was facilitative for a variety of reasons. The primary ones were that all issues were very sensitive and that the task force leader had no authoritative power over any of the other members. The facilitator had to cope with political roadblocks, anticipating them and dealing with them constantly. Adequate and consistent reporting methods for the data collection and analysis had to be determined and agreed to ahead of time. The conclusions of the task force would rest on the perceived validity of the data analyses. The facilitator ensured that all the technological and personnel systems were set up to support the work. Meetings were held when necessary and were carried out effectively and efficiently so that task force members could get back to the work at hand.

Over the next year the team diligently carried out its data collection. Members met with individuals and groups that would be affected should such an amalgamation occur. The team carefully crafted a report of which all members were proud. Despite the fact that the experience could have been very negative, given the particular context, everyone involved said it was one of the best team experiences they'd had. It was a "process" success.

As a sidebar, in the end the task force's recommendation was not followed by senior management. It was scuttled because of company politics. This, of course, was very frustrating for the team members. Members of the team still have respect for the facilitator but not for senior management in that organization.

Unsuccessful Examples

Case 5.   This team of 12 had been brought together a year in advance to plan and execute an international professional conference. These "operational team" members either were appointed to their various roles or volunteered for them. They were all employees at different organizations, but were also part of this professional body. Given the commitment of the members and the amount of lead time to prepare, the team was anticipating an exciting and rewarding year of working together.

The chair of this operations team needed to possess excellent facilitation skills. Many decisions were going to have to be made, and because everyone on the team was a volunteer and a professional, they were not going to be receptive to being told what a decision was—they were going to need to be part of the process. In addition, many diverse tasks would need to be assigned and looked after by various subcommittees chaired by members of the operations committee. Thus, a sense of what the conference was supposed to convey had to come from this team and filter through the rest of the committees as they made their decisions about speakers, criteria for presenters, facilities, and so forth.

The facilitator was a disaster. To prepare appropriately for operations meetings, an agenda with clearly stated summaries of subcommittee reports along with the decisions that were going to be made should have been provided. Instead, the chair would send out reams of paperwork that were much too detailed for the operations team to adequately cover the material and make an informed decision or provide the right direction to the subcommittees. Then, all too frequently, the chair would not bother to show up at the meetings or would arrive late. This left the co-chair in the awkward position of having to carry out the chair's job without a clear mandate to do so.

The chair clearly had her own personal agenda to pursue in putting on the conference. If the operations team was pursuing an idea that was contrary to what the chair wanted to do, she would change the direction of the meeting. For example, the idea of having a "theme day" on a professional interest area outside of the chair's area of expertise was quickly sidelined. The chair acted in a way so as to do things for personal glory. Decisions that the team would make and pursue one week had to be changed the next.

As a result, people had to keep backtracking and starting over again. Team members began to quit. Work that had been started by these individuals was dropped. Other team members had to pick up the slack. From meeting to meeting there was no comprehensive, collective memory of what had been accomplished at previous meetings. Team members spoke to the leader of the conference to indicate their concerns over the operations team chair. The conference leader had no authority to control the operations team chair and refused to tamper with the workings of the team.

As a result, many team members were lost over the year, the direction of the conference was never really clear, the meetings were poorly run, and there was lots of disagreement and conflict at meetings that was never worked out. In spite of all these problems the conference did come together. However, all members of the operations team felt that many things could and should have been better. Quite simply, the potential of this team—members' enthusiasm, professionalism, and time—was not realized by the chair. From a long-term perspective the chair burned many bridges during this exercise. The team members all felt that they would never want to be involved in such an activity in the future.

Case 6.   A medium-sized oil company had recently restructured and decided that it would be a good idea to implement cross-functional teams. This case focuses on one of these teams—the one that was responsible for exploration.

The team was made up of highly educated and experienced professionals. These members were used to working hard and being right. The members thought they were a great team in that there was a high degree of expertise within the team. However, their team skills were lacking. No help, though, was provided to them or their manager to develop skills that would help them coalesce as a team. Conflict within the team was typically handled by either stony silences between members or fiery battles—neither of which resulted in meaningful decision making.

The team was supposed to be autonomous, and self-managing, but because of their inability to work as a team, they always sought approval or an arbitration decision from a senior manager who was not even part of the team. The individual who was previously the "manager" of the team members, who should have been the person to whom the team members turned for assistance, now found himself in a very confusing role. He did not know how he was to interact with the team and what he was supposed to do. One area in which he had particular difficulty was dealing with conflict. Although this former manager knew there was a problem, he refused to deal with it. He had none of his former managerial clout to deal with the issues and did not know how to operate differently.

The team was able to be successful early on because of the work they had done as individuals prior to the team's being implemented. Thus, they could rest on their laurels for a time. However, when their interactions and team processes were closely examined, it was obvious that the team was headed for failure eventually. It was not until a year later when the failures started to come that anyone admitted there was a problem.

Case 7. This small high-technology firm ran into financial difficulty. A five-member team was formed whose sole objective was to look at the books to find places to cut costs. One unusual line item was spotted in a team meeting. The coffee bill for the organization was way out of line with what it should have been. This organization provided coffee and tea for its employees as part of its normal routine.

The team, as a whole, made a presumption that employees were taking the coffee home to stock their personal larders. This knowledge claim was relayed to one of the senior managers. This manager then made the pronouncement that coffee was no longer free to the employees. There was so much anger and resentment by the employees that they were suspicious of everything else the team did. The team lost all credibility with the organization.

Now, one might think that coffee and tea should not be big issues. But the incorrect assumption that employees were pilfering the coffee cost the organization dearly in lost time and high suspicion between employees and managers. Not only did the pronouncement take away what had been an entitlement, but employees felt as though they were all tarred with the brush of stealing from the office.

This issue caused so much chaos that the manager rescinded the decision. However, it took the cost-cutting team 3 months to get on a good footing again with the employees. This time a different tack was used. The team asked for the employees' help in finding a solution to the coffee problem instead of making decisions by fiat. The team also asked for employee assistance in finding other ways to cut costs. They recognized that their actions had destroyed relationships that now had to be repaired.

Lessons From the Cases

1. Facilitation skills include the ability to get the team to act and feel as though they are a team as opposed to a collection of individuals.

2. Communication skills that include assisting the team to make decisions in a fair and expeditious manner are critical to a facilitator.

3. Communication between the team and its stakeholders is necessary for the team to be viewed as legitimate. Facilitators should assist the team with this activity.

4. Techniques for bringing together diverse sets of expectations, experiences, and backgrounds into a coherent whole are hallmarks of a good facilitator.

5. Setting a team loose without providing any facilitative leadership to develop their team skills is likely to backfire.

6. Teams need access to facilitative skills. If they are part of the team's makeup all the better. To assume that these skills will be present because you have a group of highly competent, highly trained, highly motivated individuals is a mistake.

7. Make sure that in a restructuring, the roles and responsibilities of the former manager—who finds him or herself a facilitator—are clear. If the new manager does not have the requisite skills to carry out this role, then training is essential for them to be able to help their teams.

8. Team facilitation skills extend beyond the team itself. Teams usually don't exist in a vacuum. They have to use their facilitation skills when dealing with others within and outside the organization.

8

The Manager

The individuals who make up excellent teams in process-effective organizations typically enjoy working in environments where the expectations for performance are clear and are stable. They expect that if they carry out their designated tasks and stay true to the organization's culture, they will be rewarded. The organizational structure in which they operate is traditional insofar as a hierarchical structure is present and promotional opportunities exist. Clearly, teams comprised of these kinds of individuals, and the process-effective environment in which they operate, will likely benefit most from a manager type of leadership. Figure 8.1 highlights that the rest of this chapter focuses on the role of the leader as manager.

◆ THE LEADER AS MANAGER

Our society has tended to want to downplay the importance of process-effective organizations. The rallying cry to have more empowerment and participative decision making does not play well in process-effective organizations. Despite the present zeitgeist, examples exist where the lack of a strong management culture has damaged the firm. Hoffman, Kinlaw, and Kinlaw (1998) found evidence that the project manager plays an extremely important role in project management team development. Their

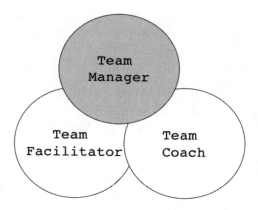

FIG. 8.1. Team leadership roles: Team manager.

study included several project teams at NASA. They found that the three most important roles of project managers in developing their teams were: (a) planning team development by allocating time and resources for team development, (b) initiating team development by communicating team development expectations and a vision for the project, and (c) integrating project team development and project performance by involving the team in all key project tasks, making decisions by consensus, and including team development as part of the project review.

Perhaps one of the most celebrated examples of what can happen when there is a lack of team management was recounted by Levy (2001). He called the lack of team management the "Nut Island effect," wherein five stages of team ineffectiveness lead to the ultimate failure of the team. The team's failure at Nut Island resulted in a catastrophic failure of a sewage treatment plant near Boston. At the heart of this failure spiral was the lack of manager intervention with the team.

The five stages are summarized here briefly:

1. Stage 1: Management perceives there to be a highly visible problem, assigns a behind-the-scenes team to deal with the issue, and grants them almost complete autonomy in dealing with the problem.
2. Stage 2: Management gets some signals that the team is having difficulty, but assumes that the team is self-sufficient and can take care of the problem.
3. Stage 3: The team begins to develop an isolationist and "us against the world" mentality. Team members stop asking for help and management assumes that because no assistance is asked for, none is needed.

4. Stage 4: Management does not provide the team with any feedback from the outside, and as a result the team begins to make up its own rules and norms for behaviors.
5. Stage 5: The stalemate between management and team continues with no communication between them. Outsiders who see there are problems try to intervene with no success. Finally an external source provides information (perhaps a disaster) that demonstrates beyond a shadow of a doubt that the team has failed.

The moral of the story is that management needs to have some input into the actions of those teams who report to them. To not do so is an abdication of the manager's responsibility. Interestingly, I discovered in my interviews with individuals who have worked with teams for many years that they shied away from the term "leaderless teams." They each had run into the phenomenon described by Levy (2001). Although the consequences may not have been as disastrous as that recounted by Levy, clearly teams' performance levels were compromised by having no one present in the manager role.

Team members' roles and responsibilities in process-effective organizations are often well prescribed. The tasks and goals are clear. Teams in these types of organizations need far less facilitation around making decisions because the alternatives are obviously in line with the culture or not. There is not a lot of discussion or conflict around setting goals or other major issues. However, process-effective organizations must have strong controls around procedures. Teams in these organizations are much more likely to need the types of roles traditionally associated with management to be clear and present. So what are these important manager roles for the team leader?

Table 8.1 asks eight questions that provide some insight about the extent to which the management leadership role is being carried out in a team. Like the previous chapter, these questions stem from the studies outlined in chapter 6. The next section of this chapter describes each of the manager roles in more detail and provides ideas about how to strengthen those roles within your teams.

✦ THE MANAGER ROLES

✧ Team Goals Aligned With Organizational Goals

Teams in process-effective organizations usually know what the overall goal of the organization is supposed to be. If a team wants to take on a new initiative, or suggests a change to an existing process, there will un-

TABLE 8.1
Manager Capabilities

Rate these items on a scale of 1 to 5 with 1 meaning they are not carried out at all, 3 meaning they are carried out somewhat, and 5 meaning they are carried out regularly. Scores range from 8 to 40, with 8–16 indicating low, 17–28 indicating average, and 29–40 indicating high levels of the facilitative role being executed in the team.

1. My team's goals are clearly aligned with the organization's goals.

2. The resources needed by my team are available.

3. My team receives feedback about its performance.

4. My team's performance is evaluated fairly and accurately.

5. My team is recognized and rewarded for its efforts.

6. My team's work is coordinated with other work going on in the organization.

7. My team's work is "championed" in the organization.

8. My team is "protected" from outsiders.

doubtedly be ramifications to other units. The manager must ensure that these changes will not be disruptive. If they are disruptive, then approval needs to be sought from the rest of the organization.

Similarly, if the organization shifts its priorities, this information must be filtered down to, for instance, the shop-floor teams. If the result will be a change in policy or procedure, those affected on a daily basis need to know how to change their tasks to align with the new goals. In both situations, the manager role has to be executed or the organization will be adversely affected.

✧ Ensuring Adequate Team Resources

Teams are often formed without giving thought from where the physical, financial, or human resources they need to get the job done will come. This is likely to be particularly true in process-effective organizations made up of standing teams. Teams are created using members of work units that may not be accustomed to working on a project basis. For those who work in project-type environments, it is often inaccurately assumed that everyone knows how to figure out what resources need to be in place before embarking on the project.

Instead, the working assumption should be that the team does not know how to determine its resource needs. Thus, the work needs to be broken down into its units (formally called a task analysis) and the physical, financial, and human resources tied to each task need to be articulated. In one workshop I was involved in, a team had been assigned to complete a specific task for their manager. The team knew it did not have the resources needed to do the work by the deadline imposed. As part of the workshop, we went through the task analysis with the team. In the end, it was obvious that the team did not have the resources to do the job adequately. However, the team took this analysis and put together an argument to take to the manager in order to secure more resources (in this case a temporary personnel increase). The team was successful in arguing its case.

Teams without this kind of leadership expertise are very common. They need an individual to assist them in determining those resources they have at their disposal and those they do not. They also need to have the gaps filled or else they need to ensure that the clients/customers are willing to settle for a less than high-quality product, or a product or service delivered late.

✧ Providing Performance Feedback

Everyone needs performance feedback to determine if they are doing things as expected as well as to develop their skills. Teams are no different. Members need to know how they are doing and whether or not they are on the right track. Team members left to fend for themselves will likely not get the feedback they need and as a result perform inappropriately or inadequately. The more honest and constructive the feedback the better. The more sources that provide the feedback the better. In the present context, "feedback" is presented as a formative phenomenon. That is, its purpose is developmental.

The team manager's role is to help in identifying the various constituent groups that should be providing feedback to the team. The manager should work to secure the feedback and review it with the team. The manager should also enable this feedback to be provided on a regular and frequent basis. When this role is exercised well, it ensures that what the team works on and how it works on it is consistent with the expectations of those who are affected by the team's work.

In examining the feedback, courses of action for improving performance on those dimensions where there is room for improvement and maintaining a high standard on those dimensions where it presently exists is a final stage in the developmental process.

✧ Team Performance Evaluation

Performance appraisal has long been considered to be a standard managerial duty in traditional workplaces. When organizations switched to team-based structures, the performance appraisal and the accompanying performance feedback often disappeared. Although this may initially have been perceived to be a boon to teams, insofar as they now did not have to worry about those awful performance appraisal meetings, this loss turned out to be detrimental, as one of the more enduring complaints of teams is the lack of performance feedback provided to them.

When the feedback takes on an evaluative tenor, it becomes a summative exercise. Teams need summative evaluations as well as formative ones. In other words, not only do they need developmental feedback for team improvement using an internal standard, they also need feedback using an external referent. The referent performance source may come from other teams' performances (norm referenced) or from an absolute performance standard (criterion referenced). Both approaches are useful and both may be provided to teams. Regardless, some sense of how the team is doing must be provided to the team.

The manager role here is obvious. In the end, someone has to be accountable for ensuring that the team delivers the organization's product or service at a level of quality expected by the customer. At the bare minimum, the manager provides his or her own perspective to the team members about how well they are meeting expectations. In addition, as the manager role includes being the primary point of contact between the team and the rest of the organization, it is expected that the manager also secures organization-wide summative performance feedback for the team. The manager should also then be expected to work with the team in sifting through the performance feedback and determining what must change and what must remain the same in order for customer expectations to be met.

✧ Team Recognition and Rewards

Far too frequently teams are so busy performing their work that recognition for their accomplishments goes unexpressed. This is truly unfortunate. Though it is possible for teams to "pat themselves on the back" if they know they did an excellent job, this cannot replace recognition by a superior of a job well done. It is as simple as that. A traditional manager responsibility, which again seemed to get lost in the rush to form team-based structures, was that of recognizing and rewarding performance. Teams have too frequently been left to their own devices to congratulate themselves and to make time on their own for doing exceptionally good work.

The manager role is to determine what will be recognized and rewarded, and then to ensure that mechanisms are set up to actually follow through with those rewards. It no longer suffices to explain away an organization's inability to recognize team performance by blaming the personnel accounting systems. References (e.g., Parker et al., 2000) are now available that provide lots of ideas about how to reward team performance. Someone needs to take ownership of this role of team leadership and execute it effectively. Teams are highly aware of who recognizes their contributions. Hopefully this person will be their manager.

✧ Coordinate the Team's Work With Others Teams' Work

This issue arose as an unintended consequence of the hierarchical flattening that was pursued with vigor during the 1980s and 1990s. Clearly one of the negative outcomes of the downsizing effort was that individuals whose responsibility included a "coordination component" disappeared. This is an impossible situation for teams. Team members are often busy and feel overworked as it is. No member will make sure that the team's work is coordinated with that of the rest of the organization unless that role specifically falls to him or her.

We have inadvertently created a series of extremely efficient silo organizations where one group doesn't talk to another group, not because they wouldn't like to, but because no one has the time to do so. The manager role of ensuring coordination is particularly important in process-effective organizations. Teams in these organizations tend to be functionally divided and thus, teams in one department may have no clue about what is going on in another department. When is comes time to deliver the product or service, the possibility for slippage is huge as a result of the loss of the managerial role of coordination.

✧ Be a Team Champion

Extending on the points noted previously, which relate specifically to reward and recognition for the team, the champion role "toots the team's horn." This manager role takes the outputs of a team and brings them to the attention of senior managers, the rest of the organization, and outside stakeholders. In carrying out this role the manager gets to tell stories about how great the teams are that work in their organization.

Excellent venues for doing this champion work are trade shows and trade magazines, annual general meetings, and professional conferences. At a local level, newspapers and radio shows are good outlets for sharing the work of the organization's best team efforts. The time and effort taken to publicize the good work of your teams will not go unnoticed by them. In fact, it may prove to be an exceptionally good recruiting strategy to use in getting new team members on board in your organization. Though some individuals may shy away from the limelight, as a collective, teams have not been in the limelight to the degree they should be.

Being a champion for a team does take time and effort and both commodities are in seriously short supply in organizations these days. However, from a team leadership perspective, this role cannot be ignored or put aside as being less important than completing the day-to-day tasks.

✧ Protect the Team

Sometimes teams need to be protected from external forces. For these occasions, manager can be a very powerful role for the team leadership to assume. For example, say a team has expectations put upon it without the needed resources. This scenario is more common than one would like to believe. One way the team manager could protect the team is to buffer it from the inevitable negative fallout from such an untenable situation. A more proactive team manager would go about trying to secure the resources needed so that the product or service is not compromised. Finally, again as a proactive measure, the team manager can protect a team by interacting with the external agents regarding their expectations, say, specifically indicating that an inferior product or service will result from unrealistic expectation.

A team leader that engages actively in this manager role will be respected by and secure the loyalty of the team members. On the flip side, team leaders who do not diligently exercise this role are perceived by their teams as "hanging them out to dry" or "leaving them out on a limb." The upshot is that the team leader has no credibility with the team that they are supposed to be leading.

CASE STUDY EXAMPLES

The next section of this chapter describes several cases of when a managerial leader was reported to be an important figure in the success or nonsuccess of a team. These are cases based on actual teams facing real problems.

Successful Examples

Case 1. A team leader who led the best-performing team in an organization was transferred to being in charge of the worst-performing unit in the same organization. Within a year, the worst-performing team had become the best-performing team. The team members ascribed the change to the leader and how he carried out his role.

The first thing the leader did was to immediately set out high expectations for team performance. The leader basically operated under the assumption that people perform up to expectations. By setting challenging goals the team was motivated to perform. In addition to setting high expectations, the leader also provided support to the team. Some of the support was moral support—a feeling of being on the team's side and wanting them to succeed. The leader lobbied for the team in meetings with senior management to secure the resources needed to be successful. He held regular meetings with the team to provide the members honest feedback about what was happening in the organization and how well the team was doing.

At an interpersonal level the leader was trusted. He met with individuals who were experiencing difficulty and they worked out the problems together. Individual members felt that the leader actually cared about them as people—not just as workers to accomplish a task. The leader's behavior was predictable. He was consistent in the messages he provided to the team and to the rest of the organization, and he was consistent over situations. He provided a lot of positive feedback—particularly at the initial stages of the team's work. Any promises made by the leader were followed through on. Clearly a leader who exhibits these types of behaviors is likely to end up with a team who wants to perform well for him or her.

Case 2. A small company was formed as a result of a merger between two parts of two large companies. A new leader was appointed and a leadership team was formed. It comprised members representing both former organizations and the leader came from one of the original organizations. There was a high probability that there would be a severe fracture in the team and the organization. However, because of the leader's personal style, he was able to get the team up and running and functioning well, and the organization was profitable within the first year of operation.

His personal style was to listen actively to both sides of the table on issues. He ensured that there was balanced input from the various perspectives. These were critical steps to demonstrating that he was not going to adopt a partisan approach to running the new business. He also said that he was going to take a nonhierarchical, nonauthoritarian approach to making decisions. When he was forced to make a decision after hearing input from the stakeholders, he referred constantly to the goals of the organization. Thus, key decisions were perceived to be fair and in alignment with the organization's goals.

He followed through on his promise of being accessible by moving from his cloistered office to his secretary's desk. This put him literally out on the shop floor in the middle of the workers. This way, although he did have authority over the team, it was obvious that he was with them as they carried out their daily work.

He then adopted some new ways of interacting at team meetings. There was no tolerance for statements such as "this is the way we have always done things" or "this is the way things used to be." Pretty soon the team members began to shed their need for tribalism by virtue of having belonged to one of the former organizations. They started to think, talk, and act in a manner consistent with that of being a member of a single, new organization. This forced members to be future-oriented rather than past-focused. The result was that they brought the fledgling organization to financial success within a year.

Unsuccessful Examples

Case 3.   A team leader who led the worst-performing team in an organization was transferred to the best-performing team in the same organization. Within a year, the best-performing team had become the worst-performing team. Team members ascribed the change to the leader.

This team leader motivated the team by fear; either the team performed or the members would be fired. Although a high standard of performance was expected of the team members, he did not apply the same standard to his own performance. He frequently was absent and was caught telling lies. The leader would belittle individual members in front of the team or in front of other members of the organization. He also attempted to use his position to intimidate individuals. No effort was made on his part to secure needed resources for the team.

It was obvious to the team that this leader cared nothing about them either as individuals or as a team. The members began to withdraw from the organization—they did not care about their work and it showed. Quality of the team's service suffered, and as a direct result customers complained. Eventually this individual was replaced, but the damage done to the team was irreparable. The most talented individuals did leave the organization as opportunities arose for them to do so.

Case 4. A leader called together a meeting of a task force. The leader proceeded to distribute the workload for accomplishing a particular task. One member of the task force on receiving his duty responded by saying: "I don't do that kind of work." The leader lost his temper and openly engaged the member in a verbal fight. The result was that the leader lost the ability to work with that individual for the rest of his tenure at the organization.

In addition, though, the leader lost credibility with the rest of the team. Other members now did not want to cross him and began to withdraw their input for fear of being publicly berated. As well, the leader became gun-shy about asking any of the task force members to take on work. The leader found himself making decisions without the input of the rest of the team, which was problematic not only in terms of the lack of input for making the decisions, but also in terms of securing buy-in for implementing those decisions. The team was reconstituted over a period of 6 months, and the leader—fully aware of what his actions had done previously—actively sought out and praised members for critically providing input into decisions.

Case 5. In this case a group of professionals worked together on architectural projects. They had different interpersonal styles, but worse, they had different work ethics, norms for performance, and philosophical backgrounds. Although this group was called a team within the organizational framework, they were clearly fractionalized and didn't like each other at all. There was a high degree of tension in the workplace so that even the secretarial and clerical staff knew they had to behave differently around different individuals. Camps started to develop. From a customer perspective, this mode of operating was devastating, as the members would often engage in debates in client meetings. They simply were unable to present a unified front on any issue.

The leader did not care. In fact, his rude and abrasive style of interacting with others—both with the team as well as other members of the organization—provided a ready role model for the rest of the team to emulate. All of the team members knew that the leader had no interpersonal skills. His saving grace was his ability to manage outside clients and bring in lots of money. More senior members of the organization refused to do anything about this person because of his ability to bring in business. The work environment for the team was miserable. Members were prepared to tolerate it only until a better offer came along. Unfortunately, what they "learned" about team management they would take with them to their new organizations.

Case 6.   In an organization made up of work teams, there was one team that willfully violated the organizational norms. They came late to meetings, did not follow normal procedures, and just generally made it clear that the rules were made for other teams—not them. The leader of this team made it clear that the individual members worked for him—not for the team or the organization as a collective. He used his position of power to coerce the members into doing what he wanted, not what was necessarily the right thing for the team or organization.

When this leader, who was a senior manager in the company, discussed the issue of teams with his superiors, he "said all the right team things." In other words he said one thing and did the opposite. This leader completely sabotaged the team initiative in his department. Anyone who had anything to do with this team pointed to it as an example of why teams don't work.

Months later the issue remained unresolved. The team from his department continued to go against the norms to which the rest of the organizational teams adhered. The team was viewed as different from the rest of the organization. Other teams did not like to interact with this group and avoided doing so. Although the cost to the organization did not surface for a while, eventually this negative interaction between teams proved to be very expensive, costing the company in lost customers and lost good employees.

Case 7.   A group of teams had everything they needed to be successful. They were part of a new start-up company. The company had lots of resources in terms of money and talented personnel. These talented team members were highly motivated to succeed. The problem was the leader. Her overly controlling style ensured that the teams never felt autonomous. All decisions made by the teams had to be screened by her. All communications between teams had to be first filtered through her. As a result, political game playing took the place of honest communications between the work teams. Misinformation was sent out. No attempt was made to ensure that the teams were working together. No common set of values was adhered to and no common organizational goals were adopted. Clearly barriers between the teams were being built. Paranoia and withdrawal became the typical team member response.

In the end the work environment became very negative. Many people left the organization, preferring to damage their careers rather than stay. On the organizational side it was also a failure. Productivity was lost and shareholders lost their investment.

Lessons From the Cases

Valuable lessons can be taken from these case studies, both the successful and the unsuccessful ones. Following are several:

1. First, there were far more examples of team leadership roles that were not carried out than examples where the role was carried out effectively. This is not surprising given that the manager roles have been perceived by many to be replaced by being on a team. This is simply not true. Teams need the manager roles carried out at least as much as in traditional organizational environments.

2. The interpersonal style of the team manager is critical. Team members are looking to the leader for examples of the expected behaviors. The ones modeled by the leaders will be the ones picked up on by the team.

3. The team leader role carries with it the responsibilities of helping to set goals and ensuring that the resources are available to do the work.

4. Norms and values can't be just rhetoric. Leaders who want their teams to act like teams have to operate using a set of principles that value and respect team members.

5. Interpersonal damage is easy to cause and repairing that damage takes a long time—it may even be irreparable.

6. The team manager is the go-between for the team and the rest of the organization. These coordinating and communicating roles are ones that if not carried out will not be done.

7. Team managers should be assessed on their ability to effectively manage teams. Those who are not able to do so should not be allowed to manage teams or should be provided the training to upgrade their team management skills.

9

The Coach

Individuals and teams who thrive in customer service-focused organizations are usually social creatures. They typically enjoy environments where they interact with people and like solving other people's problems. They expect to be treated with a high degree of interpersonal skill, as that is the model that is expected of them in their interactions with customers. The organizational structure in which they operate is highly dependent on other team members. These individuals have to be prepared to contribute quickly to ensure that a customer is satisfied, and to be willing to take on more than their fair share of duties if needed—again to ensure that the customer has a seamlessly enjoyable experience while interacting with the organization.

The kinds of individuals who comprise these teams, and the customer service-oriented environment in which they tend to operate, will likely benefit most from the coach type of leadership. Figure 9.1 highlights that the rest of this chapter focuses on the role of the leader as coach.

✦ THE LEADER AS COACH

Team coaches need to be most concerned with how to complete the day-to-day work of the team. They are often in the work trenches themselves and have little time to worry about the facilitative role or the man-

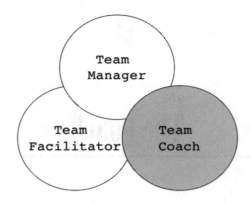

FIG. 9.1.   Team leadership roles: Team coach.

agement role of the team leader. It is enough to make sure that a high-quality product or service is delivered on time and within budget. These individuals may well have no positional power over the rest of the team members. Instead they operate from the authority that comes from being the most expert, or the most senior, or the most knowledgeable for a particular task. In fact, this position may well be that of a "chair," where the willingness of the rest of the team to follow the coach must come from an interest in being part of the team rather than by the coach having authority over the team.

The unique role of the team coach over and above other team leadership roles has been described by others, albeit not using the same framework as that presented in this book. For example, Katz (2001) convincingly argued that the coach role is distinctive from the management role in team performance. The context of her discussion was her concern over using sports teams as analogous to workplace teams. She claimed that although it is tempting to view today's "managers" as "coaches," it is dangerous to do so. Specifically, in the sports world coaches have a high degree of influence on the success of their teams, whereas the sports team managers have comparatively little. The opposite is the case in the workplace.

The reason for the reduced impact of the team manager role for sports teams is that the design of the teams (i.e., what positions are needed), design of the teams' task (i.e., the rules of the game), and other contextual issues do not differ much from team to team and thus do not have much of an impact on the team's performance. Thus, for sports teams, the role of the manager is minimal whereas the coaching role becomes very important. However, in the workplace, the design of the team, design of the task, and other contextual issues are highly variable. Providing the team with support in these areas is the responsibility of the team manager and is extremely important to team success. The coach in a workplace operates from a very different place than on a sports team.

There is an exception I have found in the sports world literature, however. Specifically, Krzyzewski and Phillips (2000) provided a perspective in their book about coaching basketball that distinguishes the coaching role from the facilitating role. Though they did not use the same terms I have, they did argue that the role of the coach is distinct from that of the person who provides the team with "heart." They noted that the term *heart* is not easy to define. It is, though, imperative to the team's success that at least one member of the team has it. The team member with heart is usually not the most talented or gifted player. Instead, this team member inspires the rest of the team by bringing out the best in everybody else. Krzyzewski viewed part of his role as coach as finding the team's heart and using it to the team's advantage.

Bennis (1989) separated the role of the leader from the role of the manager. Though he did not use the term *coach*, what is relevant to the present discussion is that he viewed leadership as something separate from "managership." In this particular work, Bennis discussed his perceptions about leadership in general. Many of his examples came from university settings. I found this very interesting insofar as leading in a university setting largely involves skills I believe are similar to those in coaching. That is, university leaders have lesser expertise than the professors whom they are supposed to lead. These professors are not about to follow just anyone—they need a compelling reason to do so. Bennis argued that when leadership is effective people feel significant, learning and competence matter, people feel part of a community, and work is exciting. From the role perspective, these are the hallmarks of an exceptional team coach.

Table 9.1 asks eight questions that provide a metric on the extent to which the coaching leadership role is being carried out in a team. Again, these items are based on the studies reported on in chapter 6. The next section describes each of the coaching roles in more detail and provides ideas about how to strengthen those roles within your team.

✦ THE COACHING ROLES

✧ Team Goal Understanding

This role emphasizes the importance that each and every team member understands and adopts the short-, mid-, and long-term team goals.

TABLE 9.1
Coach Capabilities

Rate these items on a scale of 1 to 5 with 1 meaning they are not carried out at all, 3 meaning they are carried out somewhat, and 5 meaning they are carried out regularly. Scores range from 8 to 40, with 8–16 indicating low, 17–28 indicating average, and 29–40 indicating high levels of the coach role being executed in the team.

1. Team goals are known and understood by all members.

2. Everyone on my team knows his or her role in getting work accomplished.

3. Milestones and timelines are set for our team.

4. Team members deliver high-quality work.

5. Our leader models the behaviors expected by the team.

6. Our team members' talents are developed.

7. Our team members are encouraged to respect one another and their needs.

8. Our team has open and honest communication.

Whether this is done through a team meeting, or in meetings with individual members, it is the first step in ensuring that the team will work together. Without common goals, the team cannot function effectively—the activities of the members will be disjointed and their energies will be expended on activities that the organization does not value. As an added incentive, the team should be able to see how its goals fit into the organization's goals.

Sometimes teams have to set up their own goals—particularly if the project they happen to be working on is ill-defined. This does not have to be a problem, but it often turns out to be one because if nothing is done about it then the lack of common purpose surfaces after activities have been completed. This is not a useful way for team members to spend their time. So as a general rule it is safe to assume that the purpose of the team and its goals should be reviewed on a regular basis. It helps to keep the team members' "eyes on the ball."

✧ Member Role Clarity

The next important task of the coach is to ensure that the tasks to achieve the goals are divided up in a fair, equitable, and effective manner. This means that the coach has to know what kinds of skills and talents the team members bring to the work. Team members appreciate it when their leader remembers that they have a particular area of expertise to contribute to the team. It is important that the coach demonstrates how each member's work contributes to the larger whole and thus is valued.

In addition to providing clear direction at the individual level, this process ensures that individuals are held accountable for their part of the work load. When "who is responsible for what" is public knowledge, this becomes a powerful social motivator for members to act in a conscientious manner.

✧ Setting Milestones and Timelines

Coaches are the ones who set the expected team milestones and ensure that the project keeps moving toward them. Timelines for when specific activities are to be completed are also the coach's job. Breaking down the long-term goals into observable weekly (and even daily) accomplishments is encouraging for the team. They see themselves moving forward. If the team gets behind, the coach can intervene to determine what the problem might be and resolve it before it gets out of hand and before the team loses face to outsiders. If milestones and timelines are not set and someone does not take on the role of ensuring that they are being adhered to, then there is the real possibility that the team will not detect that their performance is lacking until it is too late.

✧ Delivering High-Quality Work

In the end the product or service has to be delivered to the customer in a timely manner. The coach is the one who is the closest to the interface between the work and the customer. It is up to the coach, then, to keep tabs on where the work is at in terms of completion, and to keep the customer informed about any possible delays.

Norms for expected performance on a day-to-day basis are largely the responsibility of the coach. The coach should expect all the team members to pull their weight, and if they are not, to do something about it. If the coach does not have the authority to intervene then the individual who does needs to be contacted.

✧ Be a Role Model

The coach is the individual closest to the team in terms of a leader. The members will observe the coach's actions and emulate them. On the other hand, if the coach has an "I don't really care" attitude about the team or its work then the team adopts this approach as well. If the coach demonstrates through their actions that they do care about the team members as individuals as well as the team's work, then the members will adopt this attitude.

Teams in customer service organizations really do take their cues about personal interactions from the behaviors of their coach. Members of these teams have to deal with customers all the time—many of whom have complaints or problems. Frequently the coach may be called over for assistance—particularly if the team member is new and does not have a lot of experience dealing with various customer complaints. Thus, coaches have to be able to model the behavior expected of the team members when dealing with customers who have concerns.

✦ Develop Team Member Skills

Because coaches know each and every member of their teams, they are in an excellent position to determine what skills members need to develop. Those members wanting to develop specific skills should be provided the opportunity to do so. Those who need the skills but do not realize it yet, also need to be provided the opportunity to improve.

Particularly in some customer service industries, career development opportunities are minimal. An organization that expects their coaches to identify and satisfy the career development aspirations of their teams is an organization that people will want to work for. This particular benefit should be adopted more frequently and with more intensity than is current practice.

✦ Develop a Culture of Respect

Customer respect by employees comes at the end of a chain reaction. In other words, to respect and value others, first you need to respect and value yourself. Coaches have a major role to play in demonstrating that respect. Coaches who respect and value the contributions of each and every team member, demonstrate to them the value that they have for the team. A coach who does not tolerate disrespect between team members and instead leads them to appreciate each other will have created a team. The team members then have the capacity go out and show each and every customer they come into contact with that they too are to be valued.

✦ Open and Honest Communication

It is somewhat troubling that open and honest communication should even be an issue. It should be taken for granted. Perhaps the many breaches of psychological contracts that occurred in the 1980s and 1990s have resulted in these communication problems. In any case, trust has to be earned. Coaches play a key linking-pin role in developing trust in the organization. The first step in doing so involves being open and honest in communicating with team members. They need to know what is going on, why, and how it will affect them. To do less is simply unfair.

CASE STUDY EXAMPLES

The next section of this chapter describes several cases of when a coaching leader was reported to be an important figure in the success or nonsuccess of a team. These are cases based on actual teams facing real problems.

Successful Examples

Case 1.   A government agency was charged with making a decision on a politically charged issue. Because the agency had no credibility with the public, it announced that it was obtaining an independent assessment and recommendation before making a decision. Thus, the individual charged with coming up with the decision was scrutinized quite heavily. There were many different stakeholder groups with vested interests in the outcome.

It was determined at the outset that this was going to be a long process. Because of the vested interests and the completely divergent expectations of the parties involved, the individual in charge had to use all of his coaching abilities to ensure that the process was deemed to be fair and the decision appropriate. He also had no direct power and the stakeholders knew it; in the end he was only going to make a recommendation to the decision makers. He could also secure the input of the stakeholders only so long as a sense of goodwill prevailed. Thus, his role was that of a coach.

As part of the exercise, the coach had the team of various stakeholders meet with many different professional, community, and administrative groups. This made the team come to form a common frame of reference regarding other groups' interests. They also came to depend on each other for sharing information, and they learned from each other. For example, how to most effectively obtain useful input from the stakeholder groups was a skill that not all the team members had at the beginning of the project. The less skilled members counted on two of their teammates for assistance in developing this skill. Other skill sets that team members shared and appreciated in each other included the ability to effectively deal with the government, how to carefully craft public announcements regarding the status of the project, and how to manage a budget. The tenor of the interactions between the team members shifted from animosity to respect, and the coach played a pivotal role in making sure that member contributions were valued.

All of the team members clearly had adopted the goal and were willing to collaborate to ensure that it happened. Each member of the team contributed greatly to the success of the project. Team members let down barriers between one another in the common interest of the end goal as communication systems, data-gathering, data analysis, and data synthesis tasks unfolded.

In the end the team actually exceeded the agency's expectations. They were surprised. A decision that was reached collaboratively and consensually had been rendered. The leader's role was nothing short of critical to the success of this team. Though he had no position power, there was a job to do and a timeline to be met and both were achieved through his coaching skills.

Case 2. This team example involves the strategic planning meeting of an executive board of directors for a professional association. The team's task was to set the strategy and goals for the following year, plan for their completion, and assign tasks accordingly.

The leader had prepared himself excellently for the first meeting. All members of the board had been asked for their input on agenda items, that is, ideas to be discussed at the meeting, beforehand. The agenda was sent out for review and thus, before the team had met for the first time, there was a clear, agreed upon agenda. The meeting began on time and the time limits of discussion for each idea were strictly adhered to.

While each idea was debated, the leader remained detached from any decisions. He never got irritated or lost his cool; this set the tenor for the rest of the team to do the same. He moved through the different ideas in an affirming manner, that, is showing respect for the individual who had made the suggestion as well as summarizing both the positive and negative aspects associated with each idea. Although the agenda had been set, he also ensured that there was enough flexibility to add new ideas as they came up during the meeting.

Before the meeting, the leader had also solicited information about each member's skills and interests. He used this information to ensure that tasks were allocated appropriately—using members' skills to the team's advantage. At the end of the meeting he summarized what had been accomplished and then worked with the members to set action steps and assign roles and responsibilities. All members ended up with similar-size work loads, and all felt that their skills were being used well. Afterward he followed up on each of the action steps with the team member responsible.

He ran his whole chairmanship in this manner. As a result, the process was viewed very positively by all the team members. His approach removed from the process any competitive elements the team members may have had to start with.

Case 3. This team leader was the head of a human resources (HR) department in a large organization currently shifting its organizational structure. Specifically, it was going from a traditional functionally based hierarchy to a team-based cross-functional structure. This meant that the department was going to have to completely change both the types of services it delivered to the rest of the organization and how the services were delivered.

The members of the HR team had no idea where to even start. The leader assisted the team in making the changes. First the team determined that because the department was no longer a just functional arm, but instead a free-standing business unit, it had to figure out not only who its customers were but also how to determine if their service expectations had been met. Team members actually had to go out and talk to the customers that they had known for years, realizing that those customers' HR service needs had changed drastically.

The HR team could have just hunkered down and hoped the changes would all blow over, but the leader was able to make a case for why it would be fun and interesting to actually be closer to their direct customers rather than to always be working through administrative assistants and managers. The team adopted the new approach, worked to set their expectations, and reevaluated their work roles. The change proved to be invigorating rather than frightening.

The leader was a key player in making this team successful by playing up the positive aspects of the opportunity and moving the team forward. She kept it from wallowing in the hope that things would go back to the way they always had been. Members could see their progress on the goals and changes they had set for themselves. Other units in the organization began to go to the HR team to find out what they had done to make the transition so smoothly. This, of course, made the team feel very proud of its accomplishments. The leader was quick to always give praise to the members rather than take it for herself when events like this occurred.

Unsuccessful Examples

Case 4. This team of a dozen individuals had been together for a couple of years. The team leader had come from a self-directed team environment and so had experienced a "hands-off" approach to teamwork. Early on, interpersonal conflicts within the team began to emerge that were not dealt with—avoidance was the way conflict was handled. The team members were unable to work as a unit and unable to organize their work. The result was that the team fell behind. Individual members were asked repeatedly to work on evenings and weekends to catch up. Members resented this infringe-ment on personal time and it exacerbated the negative feelings on the team—toward each other and toward the organization. Mem-bers began to take stress leaves. The internal customers the team was supposed to be serving found that interacting with this team was a very negative experience.

These problems finally filtered up to the senior managers of the organi-zation. To this point upper management had simply failed to deal with the leadership of the team, assuming that the leader would take care of things. Clearly the team leader's "hands-off" style was not working. His team reported that he was not good at listening to the issues the members brought to him, and that they needed far more direction than what was being provided. Members needed clearer goals, expectations (team and individual), and deadlines. Members also needed to have their career de-velopment desires looked after; the technology used in the industry changed constantly so that obsolescence was a concern of these team members. They wanted to have the time to devote to their personal lives, which had been usurped by their getting behind in their work. From all accounts, the members needed a coach to take control of a situation that was out of hand.

To the leader's credit, he wanted to improve his team leadership skills and was willing to put in the time and effort to do so. The leader began to have regular meetings with the team. They spent some time together to set goals that were consistent with the organization's goals, and worked to assign roles and responsibilities in a fair manner. Just as important, they produced a set of performance standards to which they were willing to adhere. Members began to take ownership not only in their part of the team's work but in the work as a whole. Members actively began to fol-low up with customers about their satisfaction with the service the team had provided. The team now was an effective entity.

Several key things happened in this particular case. First, the leader was willing to acknowledge his ownership in the problems the team had experienced. He then demonstrated, by putting forth the time and effort, that he was committed to doing better himself and he expected the other team members to do the same. He showed that he was willing to listen to individual members' personal and professional needs and to try to ac-commodate them. The team members had no reason to not trust the leader and so were willing to give him a second chance.

Case 5.   In this example, a team was set up at a postsecondary ed-ucational institution. They were assigned the task of putting a new pro-gram of teacher instruction into place. This program was deemed necessary, as some concerns about teaching had been consistently raised by one of the institution's key customer groups—the under-graduate students.

The team had no designated leader. In fact, the members of the team vehemently opposed any efforts by the upper administration to put into place a leader. All members of the team felt that they were committed to the purpose of the team, that they were professional enough, and that they were willing to work hard enough so that they did not need a leader. Instead, all members were to share the team's responsibilities including setting meetings, assigning roles and responsibilities, collating relevant information, meeting with all the right stakeholder groups, and setting timelines and deliverables. A year later the program had not gotten off the ground. The team was leaderless and rudderless. Although this particular group clearly did not want or need a manager, they did need a coach. An effective coach would have taken on the drudgery roles of setting timelines, taking minutes of meetings, finding out what the goals were for the team, and getting other members to agree to the goals.

By this time, the previous team members had completely soured on the whole idea, and knew their team was perceived to be a failure by both the upper administration and their colleagues. Finally, the upper administration intervened and named a new leader and secured a new team to work on the project. The new leader ensured the team members at the outset that their role was that of a coach and not a manager. This may have placated some of the team members' concerns about being "overly managed."

Case 6. This organization wanted to change how the information systems (IS) service was delivered to the rest of the organization. Unfortunately for the members of the IS team, the team leader made a conscious decision to cope with this change by ignoring it. Her presumption was that if she ignored it long enough, the initiative would go away. Because she knew that her skills were valued by the organization, she felt she could do this with impunity.

The IS team was in a shambles. They received conflicting messages from the team leader and the organization. The IS team was made up of highly skilled individuals who worked together well. They had ideas about how to be better at delivering their service, and the team could certainly have risen to the challenge. Instead, there was constant conflict about what to work on, how to prioritize tasks, and how to do the work. Clear goals, clear roles, clear expectations for performance, and no measured outcomes undermined the effectiveness of the team.

Case 7. An individual in a work group of professional engineers was assigned to be a project leader in delivering a product to a customer. This individual had been assigned the task because he had excellent contacts with the customer firm. There was immediate negative reaction by the team he was leading. They felt that he did not have as much expertise as the rest of them. This negativity was passed on to the leader.

Instead of using it to his favor by touting the importance of the members' skills and clarifying his role as the coach rather than the expert, he preferred to ignore the problem. He also felt that he was not competent. So the tasks that should have fallen to him as leader, such as ensuring that the customer's expectations were clear, the tasks were assigned appropriately, any skills needed were secured, and the project was generally kept on track, he was unwilling to take on. Unfortunately, no one else did either.

Clearly he should have used his time and energy to build bridges between team members and between his organization and the customer. He should have found a way to use and celebrate the skills and expertise of the team. Instead he preferred to withdraw from his coach role. In the end the product never was completed. The customer was lost to the organization for good, as were many other potential customers as word got around fast about the firm's inability to deliver.

Lessons From the Cases

1. Teams need a coach. The members are often so busy that one individual needs to take ownership of ensuring the goals are set, the roles are assigned, and the work moves forward. If an individual is not assigned to this role, these are likely not going to happen by chance alone.

2. Coaches motivate at an emotional level. The manager role carries with it the opportunity to hand out tangible external rewards and recognition. This is often not the case of those who find themselves in a coach role. They must be able to win the hearts of their members.

3. Coaches are not necessarily the best and brightest members of a team. Instead, the skills that they bring to the team are those of taking on the important, and often behind-the-scenes, roles associated with the day-to-day operations of the team.

4. Coaches are highly familiar with the tasks of the team. They have to have that much credibility. But more important, they have to be able to see how to best use the skills and talents of the various members.

5. Coaches play a developmental role for members. The skill and expertise gaps that the team has need to be closed. This means ensuring the team has sufficient training to do the work.

6. Coaches make sure that all members of the team see value in one another. Just as the coach makes it clear that he or she does not have all the skills to carry out the work, neither do any of the other members alone.

7. Coaches take a personal interest in the members. They are the ones in the best position to see that a member is under undue stress and work with that member in trying to solve the problem.

III

Top-Team Actions

T he next four chapters are about executive teams and how they function. There is actually very little literature that has focused exclusively on the processes of executive teams. However, in chapter 10, a review of what the extant literature does have to say, as well as some of my own research, begins to put some structure to the phenomenon of executive team functioning. In chapter 11, a series of cases and examples of ineffective executive team functioning are presented. In chapter 12, on a more positive note, a series of cases and examples of effective executive team functioning are described. Chapter 13 summarizes the information from these chapters, highlighting the lessons learned about executive teams.

10

Executive Teams: An Overview

This part of the book speaks to the importance of the executive team, or top-management group (TMG). The executive team carries the responsibility for ensuring that (a) a market focus is adopted, (b) organizational systems are aligned with the market focus, and (c) members model the behaviors they expect from the rest of the organizational members. The degree to which the decision-making processes and outcomes of this particular team are consistent with a market-focused, team-based organization plays a critical role in ensuring that team performance at all levels of the organization occurs (see Fig. 10.1). Unfortunately, too often executive teams do not function as well as they should.

This chapter is devoted to reviewing the executive team literature. The two chapters following this one pick up the threads flowing throughout this book on linking organizational systems to organizational strategy. Specifically, they focus on how executive teams are an important part of the overall picture. Chapter 11 does this using ineffective team examples (based on the premise that we can learn through understanding the mistakes of others) and chapter 12 uses effective executive team examples (based on the premise that we can learn through understanding the successes of others).

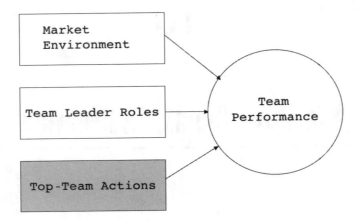

FIG. 10.1.   Aspects of team leadership: Top-team actions.

✦ EXECUTIVE TEAMS: A DEMOGRAPHIC VIEW

The literature on the success of TMGs has often used demographic characteristics of the group members to predict organizational performance. In a recent example, West, Patterson, and Dawson (1999) found support for age diversity, education level, and team tenure in predicting organizational outcomes. Carpenter and Fredrickson (2001) examined the relationships between TMG tenure, size, turnover, international experience, educational and functional heterogeneity, and firm tenure heterogeneity with the organization's global strategic posture. Others have found that TMGs made up of individuals with diverse backgrounds are more likely to make better strategic decisions when the environment is uncertain (e.g., Bantel & Jackson, 1989; Murray, 1989). Cohen and Bailey (1997) had concerns about using such archival data for team research. They included the degree to which these are actually "teams" and the lack of information about the tasks on which the teams are working. In their review, they pointed out the need for taking into account the industry and environmental context before coming to conclusions about TMGs.

✦ EXECUTIVE TEAMS: A ROLE VIEW

McIntyre (1998) discussed executive teams in the context of other management teams, including line management teams, staff management teams, not-for-profit management teams, and boards/councils. She concluded that management teams are unique from other types of organizational teams in that to be effective, executive teams need to attend to strategic goals, have extensive external networks, and form collaborative relationships.

Nadler (1998) argued that executive teams are different from other teams in organizations insofar as they: have more contact with the external environment, have more complex tasks, act in a more intensely political manner, compete more openly for a single position—that of the CEO, are more carefully watched by other members of the organization, are composed of individuals who have very high needs for achievement and power, have a high level of prestige and power in the organization, and have a leader (the CEO) who is likely to be distant. Although these observations, as well as others provided in this book, were interesting, I found that most of the principles and practices suggested were very consistent with other team effectiveness books (e.g., Hackman, 1988; Kline, 1999; Mohrman et al., 1995). The uniqueness of executive teams and their development was not addressed.

Leifer, O'Conner, and Rice (2001) spoke to the issue of the role of the executive team in fostering innovation. Their research led them to conclude that there are three primary roles that the executive team can play that can help to foster innovation. The first is that of executive as patron. In this role the executive team provides organizational protection, resources, and encouragement to maverick innovators. To be effective in this role, executives need to have a passion or personal liking for the project and provide their support over a sustained period of time. Another role they cited was that of provocateur, wherein the executive team sounds a cry that innovation must occur. In this role, the team stimulates a level of activity focused on innovation as well as the direction of the innovations. The third role the executives play is that of culture shapers. Here is where executives leave a legacy for innovation throughout the organization that will be sustained for the long term. Innovation becomes natural, accepted, and valued by the organization.

✦ EXECUTIVE TEAMS: A CASE STUDY VIEW

Another common approach to the study of executive teams uses a case study method. For example, Northcraft, Griffith, and Shalley (1992) found that potential members of TMGs needed to be moved around into different functional areas to develop their skills. Whereas this is now common practice at many organizations to address concerns such as career plateauing, lack of creativity, and succession planning, Northcraft et al. also pointed out that several added benefits were realized. These included loyalty by high-potential managers to stay with the firm, high-potential managers gaining a strong degree of confidence about the business, jobs being redesigned based on a fresh perspective, and development of a strong peer network within the high-potential candidate group. There was also a cultural shift that began to place value on the expertise of non-high-potential individuals in that the organization recognized that these people could actually teach their bosses something.

Katzenbach and Smith (1993) observed that executive groups need to consciously make a decision about whether they should be a working group or a team. They convincingly argued that the team route takes much more time and effort than does the work group route. After observing several executive groups and teams, they concluded that to become a real team the executives must find ways to do real work together. A pattern with six characteristics emerged in how this process of becoming a team was best facilitated. The first was that the team would assign itself very specific tasks to accomplish as a team. Additionally, the team would create subgroups to work on specific tasks. The purpose here was to have the subgroups work together and report back to the larger team. This was in contrast to the work group approach where the whole group worked on a task or reviewed the work of others. The third characteristic was that team membership was based on skill, not position. This presumes that not everyone on the executive team needs to report to the CEO; conversely, not everyone who reports to the CEO has to be on the executive team. The fourth was that all members of the team were expected to carry their full share of the "real" workload—no delegating! Nonhierarchical interactions constituted the fifth characteristic, and the sixth was that rules of behavior followed in other teams needed to also be followed by the executive team.

Eisenstat and Cohen (1990) recounted three TMG case studies and summarized what they perceived as aspects of the TMGs that were problems and those they perceived as helpful. One problem was that although the TMG was supposedly in charge, really the final decisions and authority rested with a single individual—the top executive. The other members of the TMG were only allowed to have as much power as was given to them by the top executive. In one example the top executive was perceived to have abdicated his authority in his zeal for group participation. In another example, the top executive was perceived to be "meddling" into the day-to-day operations of the other TMG's authority. Clearly a balance of power that is consistent with not only the organization's culture but also the expectations of the rest of the TMG is an important consideration for the top executive in terms of being a positive influence on the TMG.

Despite this, the TMG members did feel powerful in their own right. They were involved in setting the strategic direction for their organization and their decisions had a profound effect on their own careers as well as the careers of many other organizational members. In addition, most of the time they did have a great deal of autonomy for their functional units.

Another issue for the TMG was that their actions were closely observed by all other members of the organization. TMG members were presumed to have a large degree of control over the organization—whether that was actually true or not was irrelevant. TMG members also observed each other and were continually interested in which of their group was currently in or out of favor with the top executive. Not surprisingly, TMG members did not make waves or dissent from the views of the top executive when decisions about their own careers were imminent.

Additionally, TMGs generally are composed of very competent, bright, and ambitious individuals. Their diverse skills and interests allow for creative and innovative ways to solve problems. Their high degree of autonomy also allows them room to fall flat. Because their actions were very public, and their success or failure could be directly tied back to them, TMG members have "high risk" positions.

Managers reporting directly to TMG members sometimes were resentful of not having been chosen to be part of the TMG. Thus, another issue facing TMGs is how to appropriately mentor, reward, and deal with their direct reports.

Eisenstat and Cohen (1990) concluded that two issues characterized TMGs that did not function properly. The first was that the internal workings of the members of the TMG (outside of the top executive) began to derail. Members would show up late for meetings or not show up at all. Decisions made in one meeting were undone at the next. Conflicts between members were ignored and allowed to fester or caused explosions at meetings. The second was that the top executive saw that the TMG was not functioning and so started making decisions without TMG's input or ignored their input altogether. Sometimes the top executive would consult with some members of the TMG and not others, fostering an acute rivalry between members. This spiral of fragmentation continued to worsen.

On the upside, Eisenstat and Cohen (1990) cited several things characterizing TMGs that function well. The first is the high level of task-relevant skills the TMG members brought to the table. This allowed for a huge pool of expertise to be drawn upon in making decisions. Another was organizational stability. This allowed TMGs to have clearly defined tasks and time to develop team norms. It provided some organizational slack that tolerated some failures while the TMG members learned new top-level management skills. TMGs that performed well actively learned from their experiences. They trusted one another.

In addition, TMGs that performed well had a top executive who was consistent in treating and rewarding the TMG as a team—not showing favoritism. The degree to which the top executive also set out the boundaries of the TMG role and his or her role was critical to success. TMGs function better when they know what is expected of them by the top executive. Thus, Eisenstat and Cohen (1990) concluded that TMGs could be only as effective as the senior executive allows them to be.

◆ EXECUTIVE TEAMS: THE LEADER (CEO) VIEW

Given the importance placed on the leader of executive teams, it is not surprising that a body of literature has been written just about that individual. A brief chronological review of that literature follows. Harper (1992) surveyed 171 CEOs from small, medium, and large organizations on a variety of topics. One interesting finding from the perspective of executive team leadership was that the most rewarding areas of management reported by the CEOs, regardless of organizational size were: first, discovering and advancing new talent, and second, seeing what people are capable of accomplishing together. Clearly, there was interest on the part of these individuals to be good team leaders.

Organizations have historically been governed by the CEO, who is clearly "in charge," and a COO who is clearly "second in command." This sets the stage for tension to exist between these two individuals. Levinson (1993) provided insights into why there is often difficulty in relationships between them. These two individuals are critical players in most TMGs. An effective and smooth relationship between them positively affects other TMG activities. He provided several ideas about how to make this relationship more effective. All of the suggestions demand a strong level of communication and interpersonal skills. This theme about CEO and COO tension was picked up on by Cannella and Shen in 2001. They wrote about "heirs apparent" to the CEO position. Specifically, they found that heirs who arise from within firms are less likely to exit and that CEO power is a very important factor in the decision to promote the heir apparent.

The work of Hambrick and his colleagues (Hambrick & Abrahamson, 1995; Hambrick, Geletkanycz, & Fredrickson, 1993) primarily focused on the most senior executive. Hambrick and Abrahamson examined the degree to which a top executive actually had discretion in making decisions and found that it varied across industry types. Hambrick, Geletkanycz, and Fredrickson examined the predictors of why top executives stay committed to the status quo of the organization's strategy.

At a more psychologically unconscious level, Kets de Vries (1994) wrote about individuals who are in leadership positions. He proposed that there are several psychological pressures on individuals in positions of authority in organizations. Although these negative traits are present to lesser degrees in other organizational members, the pressure of those in positions of leadership encourages their extreme manifestation. These included: loneliness at the top, envy by others, fear of losing power, and a feeling of "what is there to do now?" In addition to these feelings by the leader, followers can also act in ways that induce negative consequences for the organization as a whole. These included: displacement of their hopes onto the leader, idealization, intolerance of perspectives other than the leader's, inducement of dependency by followers, and a general "groupthink" (Janis, 1982) phenomenon.

In a similarly negative vein, Van Velsor and Leslie (1995) cited that over several studies, converging evidence suggested that executives who derail are those who: have problems with interpersonal relationships, fail to meet business objectives, fail to build and lead a team, and are unable to change or adapt during a transition. Again, from a personality perspective, Waldman, Ramirez, House, and Puranam (2001) found that whereas charismatic leader characteristics were helpful in some environments (i.e., uncertain), they were actually detrimental in other (i.e., stable).

After working with more than 60 executive teams over many years, Nadler et al. (1998) compiled their collective wisdom about the nature of executive teams and the specific requirements of the CEO as the team leader. They started with the assumption that no one person can run an entire enterprise alone. There is simply too much pressure to demonstrate consistent corporate growth; the trend of mergers, acquisitions, and joint ventures has blurred traditional organizational boundaries; competitive and time pressures have increased the need for speedy, high-quality decisions; and technological advancements demand that diverse cultures and geographies need to be coordinated. There is too much to do alone. Thus, the need for a team approach to running the organization is an imperative.

Nadler (1998) defined an executive team as "a set of people who collectively take on the role of providing strategic, operational, and institutional leadership for the organization. Thus each member is not only responsible for his own unit or function but also explicitly wears another 'hat,' that of corporate leadership" (p. 9). He also observed that executive teams emerge under three conditions:

1. The business is so diverse a team needs to provide strategic input.
2. When new CEOs are put into office, they usually want to have a team of senior executives to assist them in leading the organization.
3. It is the end of a CEO's term, and he or she determines that the current COO is not a desired successor. The executive team then becomes an arena for finding a new successor.

In a positive vein, Dulewicz (2000) cited several studies that converge on the notion that aspects of the construct of "emotional intelligence" are important ingredients for the successful management of others. It is particularly important, therefore, in executive teams. He noted that in his opinion, sensitivity, influence, and self-awareness are aspects of emotional intelligence that can be developed. In contrast, motivation, decisiveness, resilience, conscientiousness, and integrity are acquired very early on and are difficult to change. He argued that individuals should know where they stand on these latter six dimensions and make a conscious choice to put themselves in situations that play to their strengths.

Again, from the perspective of positive leadership, Collins (2001) described "Level 5 Leadership." He used this term to characterize a few individuals (11 to be exact) who, when they occupied key executive positions, saw their good companies become great companies. The data on which he based his conclusions were gathered in a 5-year study of 1,435 Fortune 500 companies from 1965 to 1995. The criterion for going "from good to great" was: A pattern of stock returns was at or below the market average for 15 years, then at a particular point in time, the cumulative stock returns moved dramatically upward to be at least three times the market average over the next 15 years. At the transition point upwards was where he and his research team focused their attention.

His research team did not set out to look for individuals with specific personality characteristics to understand why an organization was able to make the successful transition. In fact, the team was told to specifically avoid making claims about "great leaders." Despite this, the team members came back and said that they could not ignore the critical role that the Level 5 leader played. All 11 of the firms that showed this interesting pattern of performance had a Level 5 leader in place.

So what were these Level 5 leaders like? They were able to build enduring greatness through a paradoxical combination of personal humility plus professional will. They were personally modest, calm, and acted with quiet determination. They channeled their ambitions into the company—not into self-aggrandizement. They did not blame others when things went wrong. They also created superb results, demonstrated an unwavering resolve no matter how difficult the task, set high standards for themselves and others on which they did not compromise, and ascribed the success of the company to others.

◆ SUMMARY OF THE EXECUTIVE TEAM LITERATURE

The literature on executive team function has typically been characterized by one of several approaches. The first uses archival information about organizational performance and demographic data about executive team members and relates the two. A second focuses on the supposedly unique context and roles of the executive team. A third observes or works in depth with executive teams and provides a narrative recounting of the findings in case studies. Yet another examines how the rest of the team relates to its leader. Another important line of inquiry zeroes in directly on the leader of the executive team.

An exception to these approaches is a study by Longenecker and Gioia (1992), who reported the findings of a study that examined the team as a whole. Their data were obtained from semistructured interviews with 84 executives from 11 different organizations. They found that although members of executive teams should be (indeed wanted to be) supplied with effective feedback about their performance, just the opposite was the case. They pointed out that members of executive teams have the most important, unstructured, and ill-defined work of the organization. But several myths preclude executives from being provided the feedback they need. These myths included: Executives neither want nor need structured performance reviews; formal reviews are beneath the dignity of the executive; top-level executives are too busy to conduct appraisals; lack of feedback fosters autonomy and creativity; results are the only way to really assess executive performance; and formal performance appraisals simply cannot capture executive job performance.

In support of the notion that executive teams should be examined from more perspectives than has been the case, Clark, Collins, Smith, and Stevens (1999) proposed that research be conducted to examine the role of the social network of the executive team (which included links within the organization, actors outside the organization, and between the members of the team itself) in terms of impact on organizational performance. Although they provided several propositions for examination, empirical support for them has yet to be forthcoming.

Yukl (1998) summarized the sentiments of several researchers who have made the claim that executive teams can offer a large number of potential advantages for a company, such as good strategic decision making, representation of diverse organizational interests, strong communication and cooperation between units, and clear understanding of how decisions will be implemented. The caveat is that there is no guarantee that these advantages will be realized. Executive team success seems to be dependent on several factors including the trust between members, the skills and ability of the leader to get the members to work as a team, and the situation. Some situations, such as where there are scarce resources, divergent goals across subunits of the organization, or competition to be the successor to the leader, will lessen the chances for an executive team to be successful. Thus, although many speculations have been put forward about executive teams, many questions remain unanswered in this literature.

✦ AN ADDITIONAL STUDY ON EXECUTIVE TEAM FUNCTION

Next I present the findings from a study I conducted, the purpose of which was to describe and understand executive team functioning. As noted, there exists very little empirical literature that brings together a common frame of reference on this very important topic. Thus, the methodology used in this study served to fill this gap insofar as a variety of perspectives was sought to shed light on why executive teams function well and why they do not.

A structured interview format was used to collect the data, which enabled a fulsome discussion of the participants' comments. In addition, a predetermined set of questions allowed common themes on certain issues to be developed.

✧ Participants

A total of 28 participants (22 men and 6 women), all from different organizations, were interviewed in this study. They represented several industry sectors including: oil and gas, information technology, transportation, executive search, health care, and education. The participants provided a variety of "lenses" through which they viewed executive teams. Participants' most recent, primary relationship to executive teams were as follows:

1. Nine were executive team members (experience ranging from 2 to 16 years with a mean average of 10 years).
2. Eight were executive team leaders (experience ranging from 4 to 30 years with a mean average of 21 years).
3. Six were executive team facilitators (experience ranging from 5 to 18 years with a mean average of 9 years).
4. Five were executive search specialists (experience ranging from 10 to 20 years with a mean average of 16 years).

In addition to these primary roles, many participants had experienced more than one role. Finally, six of the participants also had experience serving as members of boards of directors.

✧ Measure

A common set of questions was used in a structured interview format with each participant. The questions reported in this summary were as follows:

1. What do you believe is/are the role(s) of executive teams?
2. What motivates executive team members to "play like a team"?
3. What is the role of the leader of the executive team?

4. What are some of the barriers to carrying out the mandate of executive teams?
5. Who is responsible for executive team decisions/actions?
6. What are the characteristics of excellent executive team members?
7. What are the characteristics of excellent executive team leaders?
8. What should organizations be doing to prepare "up-and-coming organizational members" to become part of executive teams?

✧ Results

Content analysis was used to examine the data. Each question, as well as the frequency of responses to the question, is presented in the following tables. Note that the response categories include a variety of ways of "saying the same thing." The frequencies represent the number of participants who included that response category in their own answer. Therefore, for any response category there were no more than 28 in the "frequency counts." However, many participants made several responses to each question (e.g., when asked what characteristics make excellent executive team members, most participants indicated several characteristics). Only responses that were made by at least five of the participants are noted in the tables. Thus, what you will see are comments made by between 15% and 20% of the participants.

Table 10.1 shows the responses to the question about the role of the executive team. The first category indicates that the primary role for the executive team is to set strategy. To do this effectively they need to bring their considerable expertise and talent to the decision-making table. They need to be held accountable for the organization's performance—which will include setting the criteria for success. The roles that follow ensure that the strategy can actually be carried out—making sure the resources are there, marshaling the talents of the rest of the organizational members, and communicating with stakeholder groups about the strategy.

Table 10.2 clearly indicates that the leader plays a critical role in motivating the rest of the executive team to be team players. The leader can do this by creating an environment (including his or her own actions) that indicates a respect for teams and team process. The executive team members need to be emotionally, cognitively, and attitudinally aligned with what the organization is doing to really be effective as a team. In addition to the usual "shared vision/mission" and "shared success/failure," there does need to be a clear sense of what the individuals on the team are getting out of the process.

Table 10.3 illustrates that several other important roles are expected of the executive team leader. This individual must keep the organization's strategy "front and center" at all times. In terms of directly relating to the

TABLE 10.1
What Do You Believe Is/Are the Role(s) of Executive Teams?

Response Category	Frequency
Develop a strategic plan/develop a vision/develop an organizational framework/have a future orientation/provide a sense of purpose/have the "big picture" in mind/provide leadership in moving everyone toward the strategic plan/plan ahead for growth	17
Bring complementary skills, attributes, styles, perspectives to the decision-making table/bring area of expertise to the table/sharing "intelligence"/avoiding silos of information/bounce ideas off one another/act as a pyramid for information to flow upward/point of convergence for organizational capabilities	10
Evaluate/be accountable for organizational performance/monitor organizational performance and make corrections as needed/get results	6
Ensure implementation of the strategic plan/bring the strategy to life/translate the vision into reality/execute the strategy/accomplish objectives	6
Contact with all stakeholders/ensure all stakeholders are on side/ensure the strategic plan is communicated and understood by organizational members	5

TABLE 10.2
What Motivates Executive Team Members to "Play Like a Team"?

Response Category	Frequency
An enthusiastic leader/the leader creates an honest and open culture/confidence in the leader/the leader is committed to the team concept with consequences for those who do not/the leader sets aside traditional authority role and allows for members to make decisions	11
Get the members excited about what they can accomplish/satisfaction, fun, enjoy experience, pride/belief that working together is the only way to accomplish things or get work done/recognize that working on teams leads to better solutions	11
A shared vision/common goal/set of values that are meaningful	9
What is in it for me?—career path, advancement, rewards, recognition, personal desire, being "on the inside," exposed to great mentorship	6
Set up measures of shared success/have a vested interest in the outcome/have an "open scorecard"/see that everyone benefits/see results	6

TABLE 10.3
What Is the Role of the Leader of the Executive Team?

Response Category	Frequency
Ensure the objectives of the organization are carried out/achieve the vision/total commitment/hold focus/hold the torch/be a champion for the vision/keep everyone focused on the vision/put clear targets in place and keep strategic goals in sight/remind the team of what is important	13
Make sure the executive team members are effective/hold executive team members accountable/keep executive team members focused on the organization as a whole, not on their individual needs/select, motivate, and evaluate the executive team members	12
Let the executive team members shine and excel/inspire others to do the best they can/mentor/coach/allow the executive team members to grow and lead/play to the executive team members' strengths and develop their skills as needed	11
After listening, make decisions if needed/be the tie breaker/lead but don't direct/know where the final authority rests/develop collaborative, collegial decision-making process/tie the decisions together/facilitate the team by drawing people out	11
Inspire/integrate/be a model for the behaviors you are wanting to see/be fair/show respect/be honest/be open/be an example	10
Articulate the vision/tell how each individual contributes to the vision/know where the strategic ability is in the executive team/be strategically focused/paint a clear picture of where we are going and how we are going to get there	7
Be a good chairman/run effective meetings/provide tools as needed/get conflicts out on the table/be a coordinator/be a facilitator/hear all the ideas/don't waste people's time	7
Be the "glue"/keep all the ducks herded in the same direction/keep the horses reined together/keep team harmony	5
Create a culture of success/create an environment for participation/create an environment for good corporate citizenry/create a culture of achievement/establish appropriate conditions for honest and open communication	5

executive team members, the leader must hold all members accountable for their part of the organization's success. On the other hand, the leader needs to be a mentor and allow for team members to grow. The leader also has a decision-making role to play if necessary. He or she must be a role model and be able to tell people where they "fit" in the overall organizational strategy. The leader must also be an excellent "chairman" and have good facilitation skills. He or she needs to be the one who keeps everyone together and moving in the same direction, even if that direction is not clear to everyone all the time. Finally, the leader needs to be able to create a culture of honest and open communication.

The most prominent barrier to executive team success is the members themselves, as highlighted in Table 10.4. If members act out of self-interest rather than the organization's interest, then the team will not work. Several factors are, however, beyond the team's control. For example, leaders who are not capable of modeling team behavior and rewarding it will not likely get a fully functioning executive team. If the vision is unclear, conflicting, or not meaningful, then team members will not be likely to be interested in working toward it. If the skills are not present on the team to do the work, then it simply won't get done. If the overall organizational culture does not embrace a team philosophy, then neither will the executive team.

Clearly the leader is ultimately responsible for the actions of the team (see Table 10.5). There is no abdicating that responsibility. However, in

TABLE 10.4
What Are Some of the Barriers to Carrying out the Mandate of Executive Teams?

Response Category	Frequency
Personality/themselves/jealousy/rivalry/egos/competitiveness/individual objectives are more important than organizational objectives/self-interest/achievement/ambition/no trust/no confidence/no respect/used to being a star/politics/dishonesty/weak "team players"/power plays	16
Unskilled leader/leaders who won't let go of authority or command-and-control style/dictatorship/board of directors that won't let go of authority	10
Not having a common goal/lack of vision/conflicting mandates/nothing special to accomplish/not having a legitimate mandate/goal misalignment/not sharing the "big picture"/ structures—particularly rewards—set up for inappropriate outcomes	9
Lack of skills/incompetence/lack of cross-functional skills/no appreciation of others' skills/lack of diversity/gap in skills/skills not represented at the table	7
A culture or a tradition of a traditional bureaucracy/not embracing a team philosophy/resistance to change toward working as a team/not enough sharing/unwilling to delegate	6

TABLE 10.5
Who Is Responsible for Executive Team Decisions/Actions?

Response Category	Frequency
The leader/CEO/president	22
The team should be collectively responsible in highly functional teams, but when they are not then it falls on the leader.	19

well-functioning teams the executive team plays a large role in advising the leader about what decision to make.

Table 10.6 indicates that to be an excellent executive team member you must first be highly capable in your own discipline. Then you have to have strong interpersonal skills, be able to think strategically, and be driven toward your goals. In addition, a need for being flexible and seeing other perspectives is important, as is being a good team player. Finally, a host of "good character" items are listed as important for team members.

The question articulated in Table 10.7 frequently prompted a response of "everything in the previous question plus ..." by almost all the participants. Therefore Table 10.7 contains the characteristics that need to be embodied in the leader of the executive team in addition to those characteristics listed in the previous question. Most prominent is the need for creating and articulating a vision. This individual is the one who is looked to when times get tough in terms of "what do we do now?" This individual needs to be visible to all members of the organization as well as to outsiders.

Respondents clearly indicated a need to keep potential members of executive teams around by providing challenging, growth-oriented, leadership-building, meaningful, and interesting work (see Table 10.8). To do this likely means sending them off to various places to immerse themselves in different aspects of the organization or industry, as well as

TABLE 10.6
What Are the Characteristics of Excellent Executive Team Members?

Response Category	Frequency
Bright/intelligent/common sense/industry knowledge/expertise/critical thinking/very competent	19
Communicate effectively/interpersonal skills/diplomacy/listening skills/ negotiation skills/people skills/social skills/be able to challenge ideas and not people	16
See the organization as a whole/have a global perspective/have a strategic perspective/see how the pieces go together/commitment to the organization as a whole/organizational goals are in mind/organizational goals over personal goals	13
Confident/ambitious/courage of conviction/decisive/not compliant/drive/ deliver/results oriented/lead when needed	12
Open to new ideas/tolerate differences/open to change/embrace change/ see others' perspectives/flexible	11
Be a team player/share/cooperate/deal effectively with peers	8
Good character/integrity/humanity/do what is right	7
Candid/open/honest/direct/trusting	5

TABLE 10.7
What Are the Characteristics of Excellent Executive Team Leaders?

Response Category	Frequency
Think strategically/clear vision/keep your eye on the ball/keep what is important in focus	10
Visionary/inspiring/conviction	10
Warmth/personal caring/compassion/take a real interest in people/care about people/make the human connection	7
Have the respect of others/others like and want to be like them/seen as competent by others	7
Articulate a vision/outline the position of the organization	6
Make decisions when needed	5
Action oriented/results oriented	5
Charismatic	5

TABLE 10.8
What Should Organizations Be Doing to Prepare "Up-and-Coming Organizational Members" to Become Part of Executive Teams?

Response Category	Frequency
Provide leadership and growth opportunities/develop their strategic skills/challenge them/make their work meaningful/keep their work interesting	19
Broad, diverse, cross-functional, cross-organizational experiences/rotate jobs	16
Know the organizational needs and identify up-and-coming members who will be able to contribute/identify them by their skills, interpersonal skills, enthusiasm, performance, self-awareness, strategic thinking, interest in the organization, ability to coordinate with others	11
Open up the executive team process experience to them/put people on task forces or executive team committees working on projects/bring them along to meetings/expose them to the board of directors	9
Good team training/exposure to teams that work well	6
Formal education/formal training	5

allowing them access to the executive team and the work in which they are engaged. Try to ensure that these individuals have good "team" experiences so that they are prepared to work as members of a team and not just as a group of individuals. Interestingly, formal training and education was rather a long way down on the list.

✧ Conclusions

Though executive teams do not always function well, this study has provided some clues as to why this may occur. On the positive side, it has also provided insights as to why teams do function well.

The last question I asked of the participants was whether they had any other thoughts about executive teams. There were very idiosyncratic responses to this question, but one thing did come out—that is, the executive team models the way for the rest of the organization. If it functions well as a team, then it sets the tone for the rest of the organization. Executive team members are closely watched by other organizational members as to how they act. As such, it is very important for them to evaluate how they are perceived by others on a regular basis.

✦ EXECUTIVE TEAM DEVELOPMENT

Executive teams are important in any organization. They are particularly important in organizations intent on capitalizing on teams to assist in market leadership. If the executive teams function well as a unit, then this trickles down into the rest of the organization.

McCall, Lombardo, and Morrison (1988) found through their research on executives, that effective executives learn how to do what they do by doing it, by observing others doing it, and by learning what not to do by not doing things right. That is, they make decisions, observe the consequences of those decisions, and then learn from them.

McCall (1998) provided excellent insights, consistent with his earlier findings, into the development of leaders. He made the argument that the perspective taken by most organizations is that leaders can be selected from a pool of identified "high-performers." These individuals are identified via first determining what attributes to look for, second assuming those attributes are largely fixed, and third setting up some mechanisms whereby to test for those attributes. This, he said, is short-sighted and simply wrong. The alternative assumption is that leaders are developed.

This assumption presumes that attributes of leaders are highly complex and many different types of leaders are possible and desirable in different contexts. It also presumes that the characteristics of successful leaders can be learned. Another assumption then is that the best way to learn these characteristics is through learning experiences. The search then is not for "high-potentials" as measured solely by achievements to date, but instead is for those individuals who learn from their experiences. These people are often not the stars who have all sorts of achievements ascribed to them. Instead, these are people who actively put themselves into challenging positions, and are willing to say that things did not work out well if they did not and then to learn from those experiences.

How to best to develop effective teams of leaders is an elusive, yet intriguing problem to solve. The next chapters translate and use the information gained in my own research as well as that of other scholars to provide a road map to executive team development.

✧ Back to Markets

At the beginning of this chapter I made the following knowledge claim: The degree to which the decision-making processes and outcomes of this particular team (i.e., the executive team) are consistent with a market-focused, team-based organization plays a critical role in ensuring that team performance at all levels of the organization occurs. In reviewing the literature, it is obvious that this specific issue has not been addressed. Therefore, in addition to attending to executive team development concerns in the following two chapters, I also begin to tackle the matter of market strategy alignment, organizational effectiveness, and how the executive team plays a pivotal role in this process. These are integrated into the overall conclusions about executive teams found in chapter 13.

11

Ineffective Executive Teams

If we adopt the approach that those who will be good members of an executive team are those who are willing to learn, then we have to have something to teach them. Over the course of the next two chapters, I go over the findings of two particular questions I asked my subject matter experts in their capacity of providing a lens onto executive team functioning. The first question asked them to describe an incident where an executive team was exceptionally ineffective. The second asked them to recount an incident where an executive team was particularly effective. The latter findings are described in the next chapter.

These cases can be used as either a teaching device in formal settings or when working with an executive team to get them to learn more about what to do and what not to do in certain situations. After each case, I summarize what I believe made the team most effective.

Case 1: Off-Site Meeting

In this case, planning meetings were being held "off-site" with about 25 senior managers of a large oil and gas service company. The senior managers arrived and that day had an excellent series of meetings that clearly identified areas of concern to them that they thought the company needed to address over the course of the next 3 to 5 years.

The next day these managers were to be joined by six members of the executive team. The managers had been led to believe that the executive team's roles during the second day of the planning session were to answer questions, build linkages between departments in terms of longer-term plans, prioritize issues of concern, and generally get all of the senior management communicating and working together. Much time and expense had been spent to organize and hold the meetings, and the managers felt positive about the work they'd accomplished the first day.

Meanwhile, back at the head office, the executive team had received some negative news about the company's performance. They had been given this news and their marching orders were to improve the situation by the next quarter. The executive team members wanted to get together as soon as possible to formulate a plan of action. Instead, they all headed off to the off-site meeting where their attention was supposed to be focused on the senior managers.

Not surprisingly, the executive team came in "flat" and highly distracted. They all demonstrated negative affectivity, showed no enthusiasm to the rest of the managers for what they had accomplished the previous day, were preoccupied, and responded to the managers' questions curtly and incompletely. When the executive team members were challenged by the managers about their behavior, the team became defensive. The meeting continued to go downhill from there. Nothing else was accomplished. In fact, emotional bridges were burned that would take time to repair. Everyone felt resentful about the time they had wasted.

The executive team in this situation was responding in very human terms to negative information. What they should have realized was that their emotions were going to carry over into the off-site meeting. A couple of options were open to them. They could have sent information about what was occurring to the managers, indicated that they felt they would not be very constructive at the meeting at this time, and then rearranged the meeting. They could also have met together and recognized that their emotions might get the better of them at the meeting and to "watch out" for each other to ensure that no negative feelings poisoned the atmosphere of the meetings. The team did neither. Instead, they thought themselves to be above such human frailties and as a result alienated their senior managers for months to come.

Case 2: Technical Change For Culture Change

In this software development firm, the manufacturing, marketing, and delivery units had been operating independently of one another for several years. The organizational structure fostered this independence as the hierarchy was clearly a functionally based one. In fact, there was a rivalry between the functional units. Unhealthy competition between the units meant that they would not share information or help each other out.

As a result of the nonintegration of the product system, customers were unhappy with how their orders were being handled. The orders were late or not of high enough quality. The executive team members decided that they needed to take action and deal with the customer complaints. Action was taken to adopt a new technological procedure that was supposed to deal with the integration issues. That is, a technological solution was being mounted to solve a cultural problem. The executive team had no overall consensus about what the technology was supposed to do—only that they expected customer complaints to drop. How the technology was going to achieve this purpose was not clear to anyone.

The executive team chose a senior manager to head the implementation of this new technology. He took on the job to increase his profile to the rest of the executive team, and he believed he had the right to move forward based on the executive team having given the go-ahead. No one, however, other than this particular individual was consulted on the scope of the problem, its sources, or its possible solution. Thus, the needs of the individuals who were going to use the technology remained unknown to the executive team and to the project leader. Because he did not rectify this himself, he proceeded without broad-based support from the operating core to carry out the mandate given to him by the executive team.

The project drifted. Anyone involved with project implementation became frustrated as they felt their time was being wasted. The executive team blamed the project leader. He, in turn, felt frustrated and left the company. The project hit a low point when he left. No one else could be persuaded to pick up the project.

Several problems occurred at the executive team level. First, the problem was not specified correctly. The organization had developed a culture such that departments did not communicate with one another. Instead, a technological problem was incorrectly pointed to as the root cause. Not surprisingly, then, a technological solution was applied. Second, even when the solution was identified, when the problem was going to be solved and by what criteria was the success of the solution to be evaluated were not understood by anyone in the organization. Third, the executive team did not confirm that the needs of the shop floor workers were being met with the new technology. Their needs were never considered. Fourth, the executive team abdicated all responsibility for the project's success. They placed it on the project leader, when in the end the executive team should have borne the brunt of the complaints.

Case 3: Successful Past

The 10-member executive team of this large utility company had been together for many years. The company had been created to address a public need and operated within the context of a highly regulated monopoly. It had prided itself over the years in delivering a high-quality product to the customer at a reasonable price.

The public began to be more aware of the company, and questioned the need for the monopoly. In response, several small companies got together to set up an alternative arrangement for delivery of this service. The start-up process took a long time to come together. Government regulations, legal ramifications, operational costs, and a whole host of other factors made it seem like these "upstarts" were not going to get anywhere. So, the executive team in the monopoly sat on their laurels, anticipating that their future market position would be the same as it had been in the past.

Instead of dealing with the fact that they would eventually be working in a deregulated environment, the monopoly tried everything it could to stop the upstarts from making any headway. They spent countless hours plotting ways to tie them up in legal knots and government entanglements. In the end the upstarts won out. There was now a competitive marketplace for the service and the monopoly's former customer base had left in droves to the new upstart group.

The executive team members decided that they had better change their market strategy. Exactly what that was going to be and how to execute it was not clear to them. To their credit the organization used its considerable resources to engage in market surveys and gather data on delivery systems. In the end, though, when they finally went into action, it was a case of "too little too late."

This executive team was made up of a group of individuals who did not do their jobs of scanning the environment. Trying to preserve and protect the past never works. The executives should have seen this coming, and during the time when the upstarts were marshaling their resources, worked on changing the entire company. They simply ran out of time. The team also failed to see that their market strategy was going to need to change from a process-oriented one (I don't call it process effectiveness because of the monopoly the organization held) to a customer service one.

Case 4: Unconscious Nonalignment With Strategy

In this midsize electronics production firm, a group of six executive team members were faced with a decision regarding how to increase their market share. Recently, a wholesale giant had moved into the market and this smaller firm was now faced with a set of new issues around pricing and customer service. They believed that they had a bit of time to consider alternative strategies, but it was expected that they could not continue with "business as usual" for much longer.

The CEO had proposed an alternative model of service delivery that was unique in the marketplace. All the other executive team members were unfamiliar with the approach. They did not understand how the change would fit into their functional units nor did they understand how this approach would increase market share. However, none of them had come up with any other plausible alternatives for the company to pursue.

So, it was decided that the approach proposed by the CEO would be tried. This meant many changes in personnel training as well as retooling current production lines. Unfortunately, there was a strong undercurrent throughout the organization that there was not a consistent understanding or buy-in of the new business strategy by all members of the executive team. Although they thought they agreed with each other at the surface level, when it came to retooling their functional areas of responsibility, the lack of cohesion was quite evident.

Inconsistencies in the implementation of the strategy occurred with regular frequency and the employees became confused about what was supposed to happen. The result was chaotic and poor performance at the organizational level. This phenomenon did not happen due to any malicious intent on the parts of the executive team members. Instead, something very wrong occurred in the decision-making process.

In analyzing this team and how they interacted, it is clear that they consciously avoided conflict in their meetings. None of the members of the team knew how to actively manage constructive conflict. They were afraid to challenge one another and ask pointed questions, believing that this was confrontational. As a result, the various alternative courses of action and the consequences thereof were not fully discussed. So, a decision was reached that seemed to be consensual on the surface. However, it really had no strong support at its foundation. Clearly this team needed to learn how to engage in active, participative, strategic decision making. The well-being of the organization was at stake and needed to take precedence over personal concerns about problem-solving techniques.

Case 5: Acquisition Problems

A very large financial conglomerate was created by the acquisition of one institution by another. The new executive team was made up of members from both of the original organizations. The new CEO was very assertive. He clearly stated what his views were on each and every decision. Although he had discussions with his vice presidents (the others on the executive team) about the issues, at the end of the day it was "his way or the highway." The CEO would actually publicly chastise people for not being "on his side" if they disagreed with him.

Thus, the new executive team members, although very technically skilled, did not function as a team. They quickly learned that it was politically expedient not to express their opinions. Instead, they focused on what they could control—their functional units. They spent much of their time involved in the daily operations of the business and made very little use of their own subordinates' skills. Members tried to protect their own turf and held onto their own positions quite strongly in any discussions and with regard to decisions that might affect their functional units.

The executive team was quite simply driven by the fear that their positions and functional units would be dismantled. As a result, they spent much of their time and energy acting in ways that were self-promoting and face-saving. They acted not for the betterment of the organization but for themselves as individuals.

The results for the organization were devastating. The integration between departments was poor to nonexistent. There were disputes in the executive team that were never resolved to anyone's satisfaction. None of the team members trusted one another. As soon as the opportunity arose, members began to leave the organization. The whole climate of noncooperation filtered to the lower levels of the organization. Camps of employees began to form that were based on their allegiances to the two former organizations. Again, these camps evolved to serve the purpose of self-preservation. No one acted in the interest of the organization as a whole. Following the example set in the executive suite, those employees who could leave the organization (usually the best and brightest) did so.

The CEO got back exactly what he had cultivated. He got people to say "yes" to him immediately and experienced a heady sense of power. Those who were interested in furthering their own careers rather than making the new organization work were rewarded handsomely. The consequences included a dysfunctional huge organization that was headed for failure. The cure for this problem was going to have to come directly from the CEO. To turn the situation around, he would have to modify his own behavior to create an environment where the vice presidents actually acted as an executive team. Once that was accomplished, then expectations of the other employees to follow would be credible. Whether the CEO would be capable of making the personal change or not was unknown. However, the board of directors needed to monitor the situation closely to determine if the present CEO had changed his approach or whether a new one would need to be found.

Case 6: Founder Problems

The owner and original founder was the president of a 20-year-old firm that enjoyed a small, but lucrative market. The firm provided unique solutions for organizations. Their products not only were expensive to create but because they sold only a few of them, they in turn were very expensive to purchase. They worked very closely with their clients throughout the production process.

The founder was careful in selecting only individuals with very high levels of expertise to join the firm. Thus, the products were of excellent quality and very few companies had the technology and expertise to compete effectively with the firm. The company grew and the members of the executive team were made up of longtime employees who had risen through the ranks of the organization.

The problem was that they did not act like a team. The members had all come into the organization with different professional backgrounds that did not prepare them to work in teams. They were all highly educated individuals who had been trained in their own way of doing things. Unfortunately, these experiences did not include an appreciation for the contributions or perspectives of other professions. The reward and recognition systems in the organization reinforced the value that individual achievement was the road to success. Indeed, they were recognized and promoted for their outstanding individual contributions to the organization.

This set of conditions worked well for a long time. However, eventually conditions changed. New providers arrived on the market, and the firm faced stiff competition. A new way of doing business needed to be developed that dealt with the expense of creating only small batches of product serving single customers. The members of the executive team did not know what to do. They assumed that if they just kept doing more of the same their firm would prosper—they just had to keep working harder at what they always had done. They did want the firm to survive.

Despite their good intentions, the executive members could not figure out how to work as a unit to face this strategic change. They simply ended up solving the daily problems and not focusing on the larger issue of market strategy because it was perceived as intractable. Every time the subject was broached, there was such dissent among all members of the executive team about how to solve the problems that nothing constructive came from the discussions. In fact, the opposite happened: Individual members came away feeling that their contributions were not valued. As a result, the preferred way to deal with the concerns was to not deal with them at all.

There was also a high degree of frustration with the president by the team members, as he did not demonstrate a willingness to lead any change either. There was a sense that something drastic needed to be done but no one was going to champion a change. The executive members had never had to develop trust between each other because they had operated in such isolated functional units for so long. They had never been in situations where they had to depend on one another. Thus, there was no need for them to assist each other in times of crisis.

As the company started to unravel and do more and more poorly financially, the president sensed that he needed to keep the team members on board. Instead of engaging them in work that would make them learn to trust each other, he began "cutting side deals" with some of the members. Those members who were not in the "inner circle" of the president did not get such deals and so left as soon as they could. Eventually the company was sold.

What had started as a good approach for a niche market did not last in the long term. Whereas highly trained employees were strong assets to the organization as individual contributors, there were no opportunities for them to learn how to be part of a team nor were they recognized or rewarded for being team players. Organizational members who are individualists to begin with, and are then placed in an environment that encourages only personal achievements, are not surprisingly highly individualistic by the time they reach the pinnacle of the organization. There were no opportunities to learn to be team players in this particular company and team behavior was not rewarded. When the pressure was on to solve an acute problem, they did not have any team skills on which to draw for solving it collectively. Despite the ingredients of talented people and a good product, the company could not make the mix work without developing their team skills.

Case 7: Feedback Fear Concerns

This midsized retail firm was experiencing success and growth. The executive team felt very positive about the firm and how business was doing. In fact, they were considered the "industry darling." Everyone felt happy to be part of such a great place to work. The climate was upbeat and exciting. Members of the executive team discussed the virtues of sending out an extensive employee attitude and perception survey for input on improving the organization.

The assumption of the utility of gathering the survey data was that the information could be used to increase employee satisfaction. If the company could increase employee satisfaction above its current levels, then this would lead to increased customer satisfaction. Given that customer satisfaction was the focus of this particular firm, this assumption seemed quite reasonable. Presumably, if customers were happier then this would lead to increased sales and then to increased shareholder satisfaction. This would directly affect the financial well-being of the executive team members, as they held stock options as part of their compensation packages. All the members of the executive team, including the CEO, were on board with the idea.

Then the market changed drastically downward for the company. A host of other retailers came on the market and the market share of the company plummeted. The executive team revisited several earlier decisions, including the idea of the employee attitude survey. A debate ensued with one group of the executive team arguing that morale was not very good right now and to send out a survey was to invite criticism. These members did not want to hear about the fears of employees and the griping. They did not want to try to "fix" things with no resources. The other executive team members argued that now was the best time to do the survey. Employees could be counted on to provide constructive ideas as well as express concerns about the firm. By allowing them the opportunity to voice their fears, they would feel that someone cared about them.

A discussion began about the merits of the idea. Fruitful arguments for both positions were put forward in a rational manner. However, after a short time, individual members' insecurities emerged. The CEO was closely watching the activities, but was not partaking in the discussions. Members felt as though they were being watched and the discussion became less open and frank. The team's attention was no longer focused on the issue at hand, but on how the CEO was reacting (through body language) to every statement made. Finally, the CEO did contribute to the discussion, making it clear which option she favored. Two of the executive team members who had previously been in favor of the survey "jumped ship" to show solidarity with the CEO. Others followed and the survey was ditched.

This is ineffective teamwork. The CEO should have steered clear of any position until all the arguments had been presented. If she could not do so, then she should have exited herself from the discussions until the rest of the team had come to some firm conclusions about their respective positions, advised her of the content of the discussions, and come up with a single recommendation for action. Instead, the team members feared for their own futures at the organization, given that layoffs were going to be discussed soon. They believed any decisions about their continued employment prospects would be heavily influenced by whether or not they agreed with the CEO. Any hope of a decision based on open and rational communication was dashed.

This was not an effective leadership model. Members needed to feel that even when they dissented, if they did so in a constructive and noninflammatory manner, their positions at the firm would not be at risk. There should have been a culture developed in the team that encouraged constructive debate, and where contributions to effective decisions were the basis for determining value to the organization. This did not happen. In the days of the organization's success this was not a problem; however, it did not take long for the problem to surface when times got tough.

Case 8: Professional Implosion

This professional firm of six industrial designers was very successful. They had built the organization themselves by partnering together many years ago. Basically, they had pooled their respective expertise areas together to bid on bigger and more complicated projects. By working in partnership they also were able to share office space and support staff. They were successful enough to be able to hire new junior partners and associates as well. Thus, they were individual professionals who had a common need to come together and share expertise and resources.

As time passed they worked more and more collaboratively such that the viability of the partnership was collective—they either sank or swam together. These people were highly trained and rather artistic by nature. They were also assertive—bordering on aggressive—in their interactions with one another, their staff, and clients, particularly on design issues. Although they were used to being pretty aggressive with each other, eventually some of the interactions became downright hostile.

When this started, no one had any ideas about how to turn things around. Instead, the partners became more interested in "getting even" with each other than with resolving the problem. Withholding information on projects in the bidding as well as in the execution stages was common. Even though there were only six partners involved in this team, alliances had formed. The climate at the organization became very tense and the employees became unhappy. Turnover became a concern. Overall in the organization, the skills and abilities to carry out the work were present, the supportive infrastructure was in place, and a solid reputation had been built. Despite all this, the firm was ready to implode.

The partners needed to clarify how they were going to communicate with one another. Common interpersonal skills such as showing respect for one another, actively listening to different perspectives, inclusiveness in making decisions, and reminding each other when they were reverting back to the "old way" were all missing.

Case 9: Undermining Success Via Structure

In this example, one company (Company A) purchased another competing organization (Company B). The CEO of the Company A was selected to move to the newly acquired organization. As a stipulation of the purchase, the companies were not allowed to merge. This was done because Company B wanted to maintain financial autonomy from Company A. So, right from the get-go the employees and managers at Company B did not want the parent company to succeed—a very unusual and almost impossible situation.

The executive team at Company B was made up of three members from Company A and five from Company B. One of the three members from Company A was the individual who'd been selected to be the CEO of Company B. The team never worked properly. There was so much animosity on the team that nothing could be accomplished. A common vision could not be found. Although the CEO wanted to replace the members on the team, no one wanted to fill the positions because this particular purchase was known throughout the industry as being a disaster, and no one wanted to come into such a negative situation.

The "team" (in name only) struggled for 3 years to bring some alignment to the enterprise. The environment for all the workers in the organization was very negative. The executive team members from Company B fostered the same animosity they felt toward Company A in the employees from their respective functional units. After much time and effort, it was apparent that people were not prepared to work together. By then half of the executive team had left the organization. Company B lost 3 years of momentum and productivity.

The situation was hopeless. The business principles and values held by the team members were divergent. No common goals could be identified behind which all of the team was willing to rally. The CEO was unable to resolve the problems by using his interpersonal skills. The team had to "agree to disagree" on fundamental issues, which was unworkable. The strange organizational structure had been inherited by this team, and the members were never able to function properly within the boundaries that had been erected.

Case 10: Strategic Planning That Never Started

The executive team of an organization planned to get together on a retreat to set out an action plan and the objectives for the next year of operations. A facilitator had been brought in to assist in keeping the retreat meetings moving and to ensure that communication protocols were observed. In addition, the facilitator was to objectively summarize the outcomes and reiterate action steps and accountabilities.

The team members arrived at the retreat one evening and were to start work early the next day. The team members had just been through several weeks of being under a lot of pressure. They had been putting in long hours and were under a great deal of stress. So, not too surprisingly, but still unfortunately, they used the occasion to let off steam. Most of the participants stayed up too late, had too much to drink, and arrived at the meetings the next morning unable to fully participate in the discussions.

The CEO did not intervene in any of this. Although he might have been able to model appropriate behavior the evening before, he chose not to do so. The rest of the team followed suit. The next day the CEO again did not step forward to reiterate the tasks for the day and the active participation expected of the members. Instead, the CEO and several members of the executive team began to debate the issues that were going to be addressed.

The team could not get away from generating new items to be added to the agenda, then debating whether they should be on it, and then defeating the items one by one. At the end of the day, the only things that the team agreed to discuss and come to conclusions on were issues that were relatively unimportant. No one wanted to bring up the major concerns that the company was facing. The analogy of the ostrich with his head in the sand comes to mind here. They had missed an opportunity to work together to come out of a problem situation, and because it was not handled properly, the opportunity was lost.

ABBREVIATED EXAMPLES

In addition to the lengthier cases described previously, following are some other examples of ineffective top teams in action.

Example 1: A New Venture.   This company was in the midst of making a decision about whether or not to go into a new market abroad. The executive team believed that it had all the relevant information to make a decision. Much data had been marshaled to substantiate the "yes" alternative. The data that suggested a more cautious approach were not provided to all members of the team, resulting in serious information "gaps." And in fact, the decision to go ahead was incorrect. No one on the team suggested that there might be problems that were not being raised. In retrospect, critical issues had not been dealt with—only the most salient ones such as the financial investment and operational considerations were examined in detail. The potential political and cultural problems were not even raised.

Example 2: Postsecondary Education.   This example comes from a postsecondary educational institution. The president as well as the deans of three faculties made up the members of this executive team. Despite many efforts by the president to ensure that the deans wore their "organizational hats," they inevitably were political in their fights for their respective faculties. Student needs and the needs of the organization as a whole were irrelevant. There was no recognition that there were clients to serve. There was no respect and appreciation of the expertise and skills of the other team members. Of course, they all had to be replaced eventually.

Example 3: Leader Domination.   In this organization the CEO was a dominant person. He was a respected member of the industry and a well-liked individual. He was an active participant in the community and so he was always given positive media attention. The problem was that the members of his executive team felt impotent. They were not a team, nor were they active contributors to the organizational strategy. Instead, the organization was run as a kingdom under a benevolent monarchy. There was no point in having a team; in fact, being called a "team" did more harm than good in that it raised the cynicism level of the vice presidents.

Example 4: Ineffective Merger. In this example, one company acquired another. The CEO was incapable of acting as the leader of the two different organizations. He rarely held team meetings with the rest of the executive team members. He believed that any decisions that had to be made must be solely financially driven. This was not surprising as financial accounting was his background. To get the team members to comply with his decisions, he would cut deals on the side with each member. The team never benefited from the potential of having a group of seven bright, motivated people from different functional backgrounds contributing to the decision making. Eventually the board brought in a new CEO.

Example 5: Lack of Trust. This CEO ran executive meetings in the following manner. The CEO stated his perspective on any issue immediately. This approach ensured that the members would not actively dissent from his view. In a few instances members got together beforehand to discuss how they could deal as a team with the CEO. A couple of members would agree to disagree with the CEO. When push came to shove though, the members did not back one another up, so they did not trust one another. Challenging or dissent of the CEO's ideas was not tolerated. The members told the CEO what he wanted to hear. As a result, the decisions did not reflect input from the various team members' expertise.

Example 6: Burying Heads. This organization was facing financial hardship. However, there was a very low level of communication between the members of the executive team. There was no sense of urgency and the dire consequences of the problems were not discussed openly. Instead, each member of the team buried their heads in their respective business units and hoped that it would all work out in the end. Much time and energy was spent on showing why their respective units were the most important ones in the organization. There was no sense that if they worked together as a team, the organization would come out of this problem.

Example 7: Leadership Vacuum. In this company the CEO was well liked by all members of the executive team and respected by all members of the organization. The board of directors, however, decided that they did not want him, let him go, and hired someone with a very different style to come in and make changes. The executive team fell apart. The former CEO had for so many years been a driving force behind the team that they had developed no strong vision for themselves.

At executive team meetings, it was clear that all members were going off into different directions—the new CEO complained that he felt like he was trying to herd ducks. Because the members felt useless as a team, they reverted to being successful in leading their respective functional units. The executive team, which had previously always focused on long-term strategy, was now bogged down in the day-to-day decisions of the departments and managers felt that their territory was now being stepped on.

Example 8: Playing Games. In this merger there were clear "wins" for each of the two firms. Expertise that was complementary was now housed in the same organization. The boards of directors that had initiated the deal were anticipating a success story. However, personal agendas of each member of the executive team became of primary importance.

As the executives fought battles over who was redundant, the organization as a whole suffered. Territorial attitudes prevailed, and no one acted with honesty or openness with each other. There was absolutely zero alignment between what the units were doing and where the organization was going. So much time was spent on garnering alliances and creating coalitions over various issues that the merger was a complete failure. The problems that had started in the executive suite were played out throughout the entire organization.

Example 9: One Side. The executive team of a very large national conglomerate demanded that all of their units put into place strict health and safety programs. Members of the team were responsible for various units across the country. The larger units complied in implementing the program. However, many of the smaller units did not, as they were constrained by financial resources, time, and the lack of resident expertise. These smaller units made up two thirds of the workforce. They were viewed as "freeloaders" by those units who were moving ahead with procedures, processes, and so on. The safety records for the organization as a whole reflected those smaller units that had not as yet complied. The large units were not getting credit for doing all the work and paying the expense. Instead, they felt their image suffered due to the smaller units' noncompliance.

The problem was that, in theory, all members of the executive team agreed with the need for the new programs, but in practice the members applied different standards to their respective units. Much friction and bad feelings occurred throughout the organization as this had not been thought of in advance and dealt with then.

Example 10: Change in Size and Culture.   In this company, the founders had a high degree of energy when they started out. As the company got larger and more successful, the entrepreneurial drive and zeal no longer fit as the dominant culture. That is, people were hired later who did not have the same feelings of being attached to the company as did the founders. The founders made up the executive team. The executive team did not understand why these new people did not show the same level of commitment to the company as did they. In fact, they became resentful of the time and energy that were needed to be spent on personnel issues. Why couldn't everybody else just be like them?

Example 11: Creating Silos.   This executive team was composed of five senior vice presidents and one president. They were all very intelligent individuals. However, they had serious communication and political problems. In their meetings they would always try to "one-up" each other in front of the president. The president unwittingly encouraged this behavior by not calling the members on it when it occurred. The result was that each vice president became more and more insular. The perspective of putting the good of the overall company first was held by no one on the team except the president. The members were involved in the day-to-day operations of their business units, as this is where they felt most powerful.

Example 12: Owner-Made Issue.   Two individuals owned this small oil field supply firm for more than 25 years. It had fewer than 50 employees. The problem was that there was continuous turnover in the sales department. The owners were blame-driven, and had poor self-images. This negativity permeated all interactions with the rest of the employees.

Communication workshops had been provided to the owners. Coaching exercises for those on the executive team who directly reported to the owners had been conducted. These were to no avail. The executive team was really not a team at all. They, and everyone else in the organization, knew it. The company was expected to continue to limp along until the owners decided to sell it. This was too bad, as the company had the potential to be much more successful than it was at present.

✧ Concluding Remarks

Clearly, there is no shortage of examples of executive teams failing to live up to expectations. However, the next chapter contains several positive executive team experiences, providing hope that real team functioning is possible.

12

Effective Executive Teams

The focus of this chapter is on the response to the question I put to executive team subject matter experts about effective top-team actions. The first 10 cases are fairly detailed in describing how executive teams have responded to crisis situations. The fact that they are in a crisis is their common feature. I found it very interesting from a researcher perspective that when asked to provide an example of when an executive team was particularly effective, many respondents selected a crisis to describe. Anyway, here are their stories. After each one, I summarize what I believe made the team most effective.

Case 1: A Crisis Situation Abroad

This large, publicly traded oil company had one of its operations located in another country. Although there had always been some difficulties associated with working in the country, these were dealt with on an as-needed basis. The real crunch came when civil war broke out in the country. Not only were the lives of the company workers at stake, so too were the company's extremely valuable assets. If the company were to lose these assets, it would likely go under.

Three issues arose in trying to deal effectively with this situation. One was the short-term concern of securing the valuable human and physical assets of the organization. A second was that the firm had not seen this civil war crisis coming and so ended up reacting to the situation rather than taking proactive measures. A third was that the firm had been on precarious footing in the country to start with—an issue that should have been dealt with on an ongoing basis and resolved earlier.

Regarding the first issue, the executive team showed a clear sense of purpose and was extremely effective. Members were brought together immediately for a briefing session and then were assigned their roles (e.g., operations, media relations, evacuation) based on their unique skill sets. All members accepted the role that was given to them without question. Members had to carry out their roles quickly, as the employees were facing life or death and the viability of the firm was at stake. Clearly everyone viewed this as a high-priority crisis. Their communications were focused on the issue at hand and everything else in their lives became of secondary or tertiary importance.

The circumstances ensured that several things happened from a team perspective. First, a clear, common goal was shared by all members. They had to save their employees and the company. Next, the priority of that goal was shared by all members. Nothing else was as relevant; all members acted in a manner consistent with this issue being the highest priority. Third, whatever their previous differences might have been, the members of the executive team were willing to do whatever they were assigned to do to get the job done. No one role was viewed as more important or more of a "plum" than any other role. Fourth, all team members knew that the rest of the organization, as well as much of the external community (e.g., government, industry players, media), were closely observing all of their actions.

In the end the crisis was dealt with effectively because the members of the executive team pulled together and did so very quickly. The other issues, however, speak to a problem that the executive team was having up to that point and remain unresolved. Unfortunately, if these issues are not resolved another similar crisis is likely to occur.

Case 2: A Financial Crisis

In this case, a high-technology firm involved in telecommunications had been operating since its inception 10 years ago in fairly stable marketplace. Technological changes were incremental and could easily be accommodated by the current production lines. However, a drastic change in one area of the technology rendered the product virtually useless. Clearly, changes were going to be needed in what was produced and how it was produced or the company would face bankruptcy.

The executive team in this firm was made up of 10 individuals, each representing a functional unit. Of these 10, four were realistic in making the market call that the company was on the brink of financial failure and that drastic changes to the company's strategy were now needed. The other six team members assumed that the standard production facilities would be able to handle the new technological change. The CEO of the company was part of the latter group in his thinking. If the four had not persevered in their push for radical change, nothing would have happened.

Instead, the four team members decided that they would need to present their case to the board of directors, along with their vision of what the new production facilities, new production process, new organizational structure, and new personnel should be like. They had only a week to prepare for this meeting. Given the proclivity of people to not change unless pushed to do so, the four knew that they had to present an exceptional case. They met as a foursome, divided up the tasks, and went to work. A week later they made their presentation and convinced the board of the need to change.

Within 6 weeks the company was overhauled; half the staff was laid off, and two members of the executive team left the organization. The company then became involved in producing a vastly different product than it had been before and is currently doing very well.

In examining this case, this is a good news–bad news story. On the good-news side of the ledger, a financial crisis was averted. The company did not go under and thus saved millions of shareholder dollars. Let's first take a look at the four mavericks, as I call them. They had a single, common goal: to reposition the company to take advantage of a new technology, realizing that the old technology would not be viable in the very near term. They then put their collective energies together to make a convincing case to the board. They were willing to risk their careers at the firm, as they clearly held the minority view on the executive team. However, each was so convinced that this was the right thing to do that they were willing to risk their individual careers for the sake of the organization.

On the bad-news side of the ledger, this crisis was averted at the expense of many organizational members, as half the staff were laid off. In addition, the executive team as it had been constituted no longer existed. With the loss of two members, and the good will of the CEO, there was now a lot of repairing to be done.

Case 3: A Recruiting Crisis

A government agency is the focus of this example. The executive team faced the crisis of being unable to hire the personnel needed to provide the expected level of service. This was an impossible situation, as the public deemed the service as essential. The organization was under heavy media, government, and community scrutiny in terms of how they were going to respond.

The CEO called the executive team together in what was termed an "emergency meeting," setting the tone immediately to get all members' keen attention. He then took the lead role in defining what needed to be done and by when. Thus, the short-term goal was clearly defined. The members of the executive team recognized that everyone's efforts were necessary and that long hours over the next few weeks were going to be in order.

The next task of the team was to divide up the work, which was done efficiently, using people's strengths and their time appropriately. There was simply no time for quibbles or individual agendas to take precedence over this situation. Members of the team communicated clearly when they had completed their tasks and when they needed assistance. The CEO took the lead in ensuring that the additional resources were deployed accordingly.

The team was able to effectively come up with a workable plan within 2 weeks to present to the board of directors. The CEO complimented the members and the team for an exceptionally well carried out task.

Several things are notable about the success of this exercise. The first was that a common goal was defined and adopted by all members as being of highest priority. Another was that historically this team had faced crises and dealt with them successfully, and thus had learned to be a team. They had also learned that they could cope effectively with difficult situations and that coming together as a team was a good coping strategy in dealing with crises. Another ingredient in their success was the assistance provided by the CEO, initially in helping to define the goal and then securing the needed resources for getting the work done. He then gave credit to the team and its individual members for doing the work rather than taking it for himself. The executive team members had come to know that this would occur.

Case 4: An Environmental Crisis

In this situation, a large mining company with several mines in operation encountered an environmental disaster. The water supply to nearby towns was at risk due to mechanical malfunctions at one of the major mining sites.

The executive team was called together by the CEO and the outline of the crisis was put forward. There were several fronts on which the crisis needed attention. There was the obvious one of the operation of the mine itself. There were concerns over the welfare of the company's employees. There were concerns about dealing with the towns' water supplies. Media coverage ensured that government regulatory agencies would be contacted and environmental groups would be alerted.

What to do and in what priority was an issue. The team worked smoothly to diffuse what could have been a calamity for the organization.

This particular team had been together as an intact unit for several years. The CEO over that time had consciously tried to develop a collegial value system. All members of the team felt that they were valued not just as functional unit leaders, but also as human beings. All members had learned that listening to one another's perspectives before making decisions (even those that were not crisis-driven) provided a full picture of the issue at hand.

The CEO had a history with the team of making decisions after all input from the members was secured. They had learned to trust one another insofar as members conscientiously followed through on what they promised to do. Each member of the team acted with integrity with the other team members as well as within their functional units of the organization; they did not try to compete with each other, which was valued by the organization. Thus, before this particular crisis came along, an entire system had been set up beforehand in terms of how the members interacted with one another, and their commitment to the organization's survival was apparent. The rest of the employees were also aware that the executive team operated in such a fashion. As a result, they were willing to assist in whatever manner possible.

Clearly, this team had lots of things going for it before the crisis struck. To develop such a culture takes time and effort. The CEO had realized this years before, and he had taken steps to carefully manage a culture of cooperativeness and openness. The executive team's ability to work together had been picked up by the rest of the organization as well. As noted earlier, many executive teams are not as aware as they should be about the impact their interactions have on the rest of the organization. In this case the impact was positive.

Case 5: An Employee Crisis

This example focuses on a very large technology company. The newly retired CEO, who had been with the company for 15 years, was replaced by a new CEO from outside the company ranks. The new CEO had a command-and-control style of operation. His interactions with the rest of the executive team were characterized as being dictatorial. The company was facing financial difficulties that, although not at crisis stage, needed to be dealt with soon.

The CEO asked the executive team members to implement a large downsizing program that would affect 17% of employees. This was his way of coping with the current financial situation. The executive team disagreed and said that a layoff approach was not prudent in the long term and the financial stress the organization currently faced could be handled in alternative ways. The CEO disagreed and insisted the downsizing effort be implemented as soon as possible.

The executive team members met with each other clandestinely in order to ensure that the best severance packages were secured for those employees facing layoffs. The members also agreed that some of them should meet with members of the board of directors and express their concerns about the decision. They hung together, ensuring that no one was reprimanded by the CEO.

Several issues emerged from this whole exercise, some of them positive and some negative. On the positive side, the executive team members became a force in and of themselves. They had learned that they could work together toward a common goal. In this case it was buffering the employees as much as possible from a decision over which they had no control. The members became much more powerful operating as a united team in confronting the board with their concerns. On the negative side, the culture of the organization changed from being collaborative to being suspicious. The company had never been a union shop, but after the downsizing the employees unionized and a rift between the employees and management developed.

On the positive side again, the board of directors began to have much more confidence in the executive team and took notice of what they had to say. On the negative side, the board showed their displeasure with the CEO quite openly. He soon recognized this, but by then his critical decision had been made and acted on, and he felt he could not back down. He left after another year had passed, putting the organization at risk due to internal turmoil.

Case 6: A Culture-Shift Crisis

This medium-size publicly traded insurance firm had been around for 75 years. It had a bureaucratic structure and was slow to make changes. The industry simply did not change very quickly and so the company was not used to developing any new ways of doing business, exploiting new technologies, or developing new markets. The company had been slowly losing money over the past 10 years; the amounts were never enough to make anyone overly concerned on an annual basis. However, at the 10-year mark an epiphany occurred with at the annual general meeting; the company was in a downturn from which they were not going to recover unless something drastic took place.

Realizing that they needed assistance, the board of directors formed a new executive team. Some of the members were long-term senior employees and some were brought in from the outside. The task assigned to the team was to turn the company around. Although the goal was clear, how to get there was not. Luckily for them, the company was not in a financial crisis, so they had some time to think and reflect rather than acting immediately. The team used the time effectively; they carefully identified what they believed were the problems that needed to be solved, and set out a plan to deal with them.

They immediately identified three priority problems. First, the employees were generally dispirited and low morale in the company was rampant. The team realized that in this atmosphere it would be very difficult to get people excited about their work. Second, the relationships with the various brokers the firm dealt with were poor. In the past, the company's responses to the brokers and their clients were slow and relatively ineffective. Because of its size, market share, and the type of industry in which it operated, the organization was never really held accountable to its customers. Third, the CEO was one of the new members of the executive team. Because he was new he had no track record of success with the other members of the executive team, or with the rest of the employees.

The team decided that a whole new organization needed to be built. Old technology, old ways of dealing with brokers and clients, and old processes and procedures were not viable. To deal with these very major issues one at a time within a culture that would not tolerate change was not going to work; instead major changes on all fronts were planned. All members of the executive team agreed with the radical change approach. They team estimated that it would take about 3 years to turn the company around. They enthusiastically and uniformly presented this to the board and were assured of the board's support for 3 years.

The team then got to work. Each of the members took on large areas of responsibility including everything from exploiting new technology, to customer relations training, to new personnel policies that would support the new culture. A new model of mutual interest with the brokers was developed. This helped the company in that better clients were brought to the company because the appropriate risk analyses had been carried out, which in turn helped the brokers in that the company responded to them much more quickly. The CEO constantly preached the new approach to everyone in the company. Pretty soon everyone knew that the organization was changing, in what direction it was going, and what changes they had to make in their day-to-day work to stay aligned with the new direction.

In the end, 75% of the top management of the organization changed. The executive team had clearly articulated what it needed its senior managers to do and kept only those who were willing to carry it out. They hired replacements who were willing to be involved with the new approach. This meant that the executive team did not necessarily hire the best-known experts in the various fields. Instead, they focused on finding people with mind-sets that were consistent with where the organization was moving toward, and who had enough energy and drive to be part of the process.

In 3 years the company had changed from being in slow but steady decline to being profitable. All employees who had been part of the process felt a sense of ownership in the change, which meant its effects had filtered throughout the entire organization. Morale was at an all-time high. The executive team had set their goal, taken the time to decide on their preferred strategy to attain that goal, and were fully aware of the time and resources needed to bring it to fruition. Because it had been so carefully thought through, and because all members of the team were excited to be a part of the change, it was easy to get employees on board with the new approach. The new strategy was consistent with all of the team members' personal values. Although there were tough times over the 3 years, the team members were able to provide leadership through the change to the other members of the organization.

Case 7: A Shareholder-Induced Crisis

A major shareholder decided to sell his interest in a publicly traded company. In essence, what this meant was that he put the company up for sale. The executive team had been aware for some time that this was a distinct possibility and had prepared itself for the eventuality. Within the hour of the announcement being made, the board of directors advised the executive team to deal with the issue so as to save the company from takeover.

The first thing the team did was to meet with legal advisers to set up a shareholder rights plan. Up to this point the team had not been legally able to actually meet with the advisers. Still the team had identified with whom they would speak when they were allowed to do so, and so these contacts were made swiftly. Contingency plans were set up so that both small and large shareholders would be protected.

In 6 weeks the team had created a plan that was ready to go to the shareholders for a vote. It was passed. In the meantime, the team spent many hours working with potential purchasers. Two were able to pick up the outstanding shares put up for sale by the major shareholder. As a result, the company did not go up for sale. The entire episode was watched closely by other industry players and was well received. Members of the executive team were seen as heroes.

Several positive things assisted in this situation. First, the team was not taken by surprise. There was sufficient understanding among all members that something catastrophic could happen and that plans needed to be in place to deal with it. If the team had tried to hide from the fact that the shareholder was going to sell, hoping that the problem would never arise, then it would not have had the time needed to deal with the issue. Second, all members of the executive team were committed to finding a solution to the problem. They all ensured that their time and energy could be spent on this issue for several weeks and were not distracted by the day-to-day functional operations of the company. Each executive played a critical role, as there was much work to do over a short period of time and no one had a more important role than anyone else. Third, the needs of the shareholders—including all the small ones—were put ahead of those of the executive team. That is, members were willing to set aside their own concerns for the good of the organization. This resulted in a favorable reception of their actions by the industry.

Case 8: A Deregulation Crisis

This company found itself moving from a regulated to a deregulated environment. The new rules of the game had to be learned by every player. The executive team had to learn to do business in a completely different way, which meant that each team member was faced with a steep learning curve. The team members had been primarily concerned about effectively leading their own line function duties. To begin to act more as a team and to think in a strategic marketplace was something foreign to them.

They helped each other. In an initial meeting, the consequences of the deregulation were laid out. The areas that would be most affected were identified. Resources that they were going to need to meet the new demands were reallocated. All members had to agree to this approach. If there had been turf wars between team members at the initial stages rather than the cooperative approach taken, then the company most likely would have been bought due to its tumultuous internal environment.

The strengths of each team member had not been fully realized in the previous environment. This actually gave an opportunity for members to show they had strengths in areas not previously tapped. When questions and issues arose, no one felt that they had jurisdiction over the problem. It was a company problem, and input and assistance from any source were welcome. Small problems that might have been covered up were placed on the table immediately for action. As a result, issues that could have become major problems were dealt with quickly and with input from the entire team.

This experience made the executives grow as a team. The company not only survived, but did well in the new environment. The supportive nature of the team made it possible for the members to grow professionally, be open to admitting they needed help, and actively participate and help others. This optimism and spirit of collaboration filtered through the rest of the organization. This was beneficial as all of the employees needed to change their job focus.

Case 9: A Growing Pains Crisis

In this example, a company experienced massive and uncontrolled growth. In a 2-year period, gross sales increased fourfold and the number of employees increased fivefold. The owner of the company was very charismatic, had lots of energy and drive, and was well liked by the members of the organization. With the increased value of the company, the company was bought by a mutual fund company that was highly board-driven in its decision making. The former owner was kept on as the CEO and the executive team remained intact.

Problems started to occur. There was a drop in the quality of the product. Customers were returning the product and repairs were constant. Deadlines to meet the distributor's demands were not being met. Communication between departments was sporadic and inconsistent. Technological systems that were supposed to streamline production were unreliable. All members of the organization started to feel under pressure to perform and when the executive team met tempers would flare.

Clearly, something had gone wrong both in the high-growth phase as well as in the change from an owner-operated environment to a board-driven, executive team-run firm. The executive team decided to take some time out to think about what had happened and, more important, what they were going to do about it.

The team decided that the problems were coming from so many directions that common problems with common solutions needed to be correctly identified. This meant that the team had to get connected to the shop floor. The leaders of each functional division met with carefully identified individuals. These people were willing to speak their minds and be critical, but they were also willing to provide constructive solutions to their pressing problems. Ongoing communication links with these key individuals were set up, which ensured that the executive team didn't become disconnected from the business of the firm.

These important first meetings went on for about 2 weeks. Each member of the executive team shared with the others the findings that they had garnered over that period of time. Once the many issues and ideas were set out on the table, the team had to sift through and decide what needed action, what type of action was needed, and what resources were going to be needed to deal quickly with the concern. The team also was committed to monitoring the changes that occurred as a result of their actions. That is, when initiatives were taken, expected results were determined and the degree to which the expectations had been met was shared with the rest of the team.

This highly data-driven approach to dealing with corporate issues and involving staff at all levels of the organization in problem solving is not a new technique. It has, though, been underutilized. For this particular team, the approach worked extremely well. This case also highlights that crises can come from financial success as well as financial insolvency. No matter what, the executive team needs to be in touch with the organization.

As with the other cases presented thus far, this team of individuals had a common goal. An interesting aspect of this story was the identification of the goal. It was not just to become financially solvent. Instead, each member of the executive team knew what it was like to feel successful. As they had all been part of the organization in its early years, they had been part of the heady process of rapid and exciting growth. The members wanted to have that feeling of success back. Their common goal then was to revive the feeling of being part of a success story. None of them wanted to be in the stewardship of a company that was known to be a poor performer.

Case 10: A New-Venture Crisis

In this situation the company had to make a decision about whether or not to go into a new line of business. If the company did not invest the needed capital and operational resources into the new venture now, the company would miss the opportunity to be a leader in the field. Because this venture was new, there were the usual concerns about it not being part of the business plan and the risk of investing in an idea that may or may not pan out.

The executive team members had been together for many years when this situation arose. One member of the team really believed in the virtue of the idea and she had a few like-minded colleagues—I call them the "championing team." They were, however, in the minority. The championing team had a common, short-term goal. They had to convince the rest of the executive team of the urgency of taking advantage of this opportunity. The members of the championing team had to work overtime to put together their arguments. Not only did they have functional duties to perform as managers of their respective units, but they also had to find time to make their case. Thus, all of them had to be strongly committed to the goal to put in such long hours.

Because of the executive team's long history together, the championing team knew where support for the idea would come from, where opposition would come from, and what the arguments on both sides would be. The championing team did its homework. The questions that would inevitably be raised were dealt with before the presentation. In addition, they had carefully thought through the question of "What is in it for me?" as it related to each executive team member. They designed the presentation so that the personal benefits for each member would be readily apparent. They also were clear that the benefits would be not only to the members of the championing team's units. The focus was always that the primary reason for getting involved in the venture was so that the organization would not be left behind in the industry.

After their presentation at an executive team meeting where the decision was going to occur, they were peppered with questions. Those executive team members who had previously been unconvinced, but were open to the idea, voiced their support for the new venture. Two members of the executive team remained opposed to the idea. However, it became clear to the rest of the team that these members were opposed because the new venture would erode their power base in the organization. The questions and concerns they raised reflected this obvious bias. To the CEO's credit, he did not show any inclination one way or the other throughout the presentation or subsequent conversation. He wanted to hear all of the arguments without anyone being afraid to say what they felt was necessary. In the end when he was asked his opinion, he said "let's go with it." The idea turned out to be a great one for the organization.

For this team, their crisis was not one of reacting to an oncoming problem, but the resistance to take up an opportunity. Fortunately for them, a process was in place for making decisions of this magnitude. The length of time the team had been together was both a positive and negative factor in the situation. On the positive side, the championing team members knew what to expect and how to make the opportunity attractive to each member. On the negative side, the inertia factor was something that needed to be circumvented. A sense of "we have always done things this way" is a hard thing to overcome. The CEO was helpful here. By not playing partisan politics, he remained an unbiased observer to the end. He never allowed his perceptions about the idea to influence any executive team member's questions.

ABBREVIATED EXAMPLES

In addition to the lengthier cases described previously, here are some other examples of effective top-team stories. These are not characterized by crisis or urgency as were the lengthier cases just described. However, I present them because it is important to know that effective top-team action does not have to show itself only during a crisis.

Example 1: A Hostile Takeover.   In this example, a company was subjected to a hostile takeover bid. The members of the executive team believed that the offer being made was unfair to the stockholders, whereas the offers to the executive team members were quite attractive. The executive team worked to ensure that a better deal was made for the stockholders at their expense.

Example 2: Making a Huge Investment.   The decision was before the executive team whether or not to purchase a billion dollars worth of aircraft. The team members all did their parts in gathering the relevant information. All information, positive or negative, was laid out on the table. All members of the executive team then participated actively in helping to make the decision.

Example 3: Venturing Into a New Country.   This executive team had to decide whether or not to go into a foreign country. The political, cultural, and economic impact on the head office operations all were carefully thought through and dealt with before a decision was rendered. Each executive team member was assigned a particular area in which to gather data, then present the data to the rest of the team, and advise them as to the positive and negative points to consider. The information was collected at various points in the organizational hierarchy and fed upward. The information had been compressed properly, so that all members of the executive team were able to make an informed choice. It really was a team decision in the end.

Example 4: Selling a Company.   This executive team was charged with selling the company. Because it was 100% employee owned, there was a need for everyone to work together to get the best results for those who had worked hardest to build the company. All eyes were on the executive team. Not only was the team accountable, but it also had complete authority in the deal making. The team adopted the common goal of doing the best possible for all stakeholders, rather than favoring one group over another. Each member felt responsible for the entire deal.

Example 5: Merging Two Companies.   Here, the executive team was charged with making a merger happen. The team acted very decisively. Roles were allocated quickly and individuals moved very fast to carry out their respective work loads. Not only were the financial aspects deemed important, but the human issues around building a common culture were dealt with appropriately. The two companies were integrated quickly. People in the two organizations were not left wondering for weeks on end about what was happening. A common set of goals and an executive team that modeled respect and cooperation for each other all assisted in making the merger a success. As a result, work started up again rapidly by most merger standards.

Example 6: Strategic Planning.   In this situation there were eight players at the executive team table. All the functional areas were represented, including HR, legal, finance, and operations, not just the technical or functional "hot" areas. All members of the team fully participated in the discussion. They were not just wearing their functional hats.

Prior to the meeting the CEO had asked that they each take the perspective of their area of expertise and the good of the entire organization. He reminded them of their obligation to the corporation as a whole, and that they had to think about the good of the entire company.

The members knew they needed to get all the issues on the table and discussed at that meeting, not later after the decisions had been made. It was made clear that they would not be allowed to say "I told you so" or ascribe the decisions to the other team members. When the new strategy was rolled out to the organization, all members of the executive team were going to be tied to it.

Example 7: Hiring a New CEO.   The executive team realized that their team was deficient in a particular area of expertise: someone with very strong people skills. They knew that they had to go out and hire this person. To entice the individual they were hoping to secure, the team had to offer him the CEO position. This was an issue because the team had a CEO. However, they worked together to solve the problem.

The members changed their portfolios and one individual was willing to step down as CEO to a vice president position in order to make the needed hire. The members communicated openly with one another and relied on each other for details and support. They clearly were all on the "same wavelength" in terms of what the company needed.

Example 8: Starting a New Business.   This new venture was very small. It was the first entry of a foreign company into the marketplace. The founders were five individuals, who eventually made up the executive team. They had to build the entire organization. Although the members had a head-office model to work from, there was a conscious effort to do things in a manner consistent with the country into which the company was now branching. All members of the team had the same vision for success. It was very exciting for them. There were lots of challenges that needed to be met, opportunities that needed to be capitalized on, situations that arose causing excitement, and accomplishments to be shared. Whenever an issue came up that needed the input of all members, they were willing participants in the process. All of the important decisions for the company were made together. It provided the opportunity for young people to "make their mark."

Example 9: Internal Challenge. There was conflict on the executive team. Members used the team as a way of advancing their own functional area's needs. There was no evidence from this group that the organization as a whole was important, which was reflected in the rest of the organization where people in different departments had little to do with each other, and in fact openly competed for resources.

Two members of the executive team were uncomfortable with this situation. They had seen the fallout of this noncooperation in their departments and saw it as destructive. These two challenged the rest of the executive team to look at what was happening in their own units to see if they observed similar negative interactions. Although the executive team knew that they acted in a nonunified manner in their own meetings, they were not aware of how it affected the organization. To their credit, they made a conscious effort to make changes in how they interacted with one another and provided new expectations within their respective departments for all employees to do the same. The morale of the organization improved immensely with the stress of internal competition removed.

Example 10: Purchasing a Company. The executive team was deciding whether or not to acquire a new company. Two members of the team discreetly assessed the company and brought their findings to the board of directors. These two members were completely different from each other. Professionally, they had different educational backgrounds, functional specialties, personality styles, and approaches to problems. Personally, they differed in terms of age, career stage, and personal interests.

Despite their differences, the two members worked very well together. The team had always valued the differences that their members brought to the table. Thus, they had grown to appreciate that they each brought complementary skill sets to the problem of assessing the value of this particular company. They did excellent work and the executive team was able to bring to the board a well thought through and unanimous recommendation.

Example 11: Setting and Implementing Goals. The board of directors challenged the executive team to move the organization in a new strategic direction. The team members spent time coming to a full and consensual understanding of exactly where they were going and why. How to get the organization there became the next issue. However, the team members did not find this to be a big problem, and worked through it themselves. They articulated all the changes that were going to be required and set up appropriate time frames for completing them. They set criterion measures along the way to check frequently on how well they were progressing and to identify problems early on that needed attention. The team also talked about how to get other people engaged in and excited about the change. The members understood that the other organizational members would need to get on board to make the changes happen. To address this, each member made time to go out to their respective constituents to answer questions and champion the change.

Example 12: Passing Along Excitement. This company decided to go into a market where they currently had no market share. The executive team determined that they were going to be the number one player in that market. Within 3 years the company realized this goal. The executive team's actions played a critical role in its success. The team members had a crystal-clear sense of purpose that was communicated clearly and frequently throughout the rest of the organization by the members of the executive team—not just members' immediate supervisors. Team members made themselves accessible by having a truly open-door policy. They believed their role was to be supportive and to be the cheerleaders for those on the shop floor.

The connection between the executive suites and the shop floor was incredibly strong. The executives realized that they had to set up a clear line of sight between the activities on the shop floor and the company's success. So on the shop floor there was up-to-the minute feedback to everyone about how well they were attaining this goal. All members of the organization had their compensation closely tied to the company's market share and how well the company was doing financially. Members took initiatives to make sure that this information was in front of everyone all the time. The excitement of building a successful enterprise was thus shared by all organizational members.

✧ Concluding Remarks

These examples demonstrate that it is possible to have executive teams functioning well. The final chapter about executive teams summarizes the findings of my own research, coupled with that of the existing literature. It should assist executive teams in determining their level of functioning and also provide some ideas about how to perform better.

13

Executive Teams: Lessons Learned

This chapter includes a series of summary statements about executive teams. In the next pages I cover four topics in this regard:

1. What makes executive teams unique from other types of teams?
2. What are the characteristics of executive teams that do not function very well?
3. What are the characteristics of executive teams that do function effectively?
4. What is the role of the executive team in market strategy?

◆ EXECUTIVE TEAMS: WHAT MAKES THEM UNIQUE?

Turning to the first question, what makes an executive team uniquely different from other types of teams? In all the research and readings about executive teams, much of the advice that is provided to executive teams is similar to that provided to other teams. In fact, Katzenbach and Smith (1993) said that teams that run things must meet the same criteria as do other teams. They did point out, though, that they found far fewer real teams at the top than elsewhere in the organizational hierarchy. I won't cover those criteria as they have been dealt with in many other venues.

The other cautionary note is that these things are characteristic of well-functioning executive teams, not dysfunctional ones.

First, executive teams are primarily outwardly focused. The individuals on this team are asked to be accountable to people external to the organization. Up to this point, these team members have been accountable to the next person above them in the hierarchy. Now there is no one else. It is to shareholders, customers, government agencies, regulatory bodies, and the media that the executive team is accountable for its actions. The environment that needs to be paid attention to exists outside the organization. Industry changes, technological changes, demographic shifts, and cultural shifts all have to be observed and taken into account when the executive team meets to make decisions. It is no one else's job, only the executive team's, to make sure that this kind of constant environmental scanning and integrating is done on a regular basis.

Second, the accountability is for the entire organization, not the functional unit. Whereas effectiveness and efficiencies at the unit level have been of great concern to these individuals in past work, the present demands that the organization as a whole be effective and efficient. The entire tree, not just each branch, is the unit of analysis. Working with this type of data and information can be very disconcerting for many people. It is much simpler to deal with budgets and accounting for a single unit to determine its particular effectiveness, but how do you know if the organization as a whole is working properly? These are the types of metrics now needing to be employed by the executive team.

Third, the need for achievement can be a hindrance. Those people who have spent their lives in the limelight and being singled out for excellent individual performance will have difficulty making the transition to team-based accountability and rewards. To work properly, the members must act as a team—there is not room, nor time, for individual self-aggrandizement. Pulling together, appreciating alternative perspectives, trusting, and being trustworthy are imperatives for effective executive teams. These are the attributes most often looked for when hunting for new CEOs. This is because if the individual has learned how to do these things on previous executive teams, then they can carry the learning forward into the CEO position.

Fourth, the executive team members change from being the most mentored to doing the most mentoring of their more junior colleagues. Delegation to senior-level managers and constructive feedback on their performance is crucial to the long-term success of the organization. No one else can groom the new leaders of the organization as effectively as can the present leaders.

Fifth, personal integrity plays a critical role in the long-term success of the individual member. Political intrigue is not valued by any organization for very long. Any short-term gains are lost in the long term with this kind of behavior. Being brutally honest with oneself about one's own strengths and weaknesses, and being able to live comfortably with the results of such self-analysis, will free up the member to become an excellent team player. It takes some people a long time to come to the straightforward realization that you can't be an expert at everything. The interesting revelation that also eventually accompanies this realization is that no one expects you to be, and even more revealing is that no one ever did. When these two notions converge, you are then able to effectively appreciate the skills and use the expertise of your colleagues appropriately. You can do so without worrying about what everyone thinks. They will also appreciate what you uniquely bring to the table.

✦ EXECUTIVE TEAMS: WHAT MAKES THEM INEFFECTIVE?

After reviewing the cases and examples from chapter 11, some themes about what makes an executive team unsuccessful begin to crystallize. I provide here a listing of what I consider to be a set of indicators or signals that an executive team either is, or soon will be, running into trouble. The degree to which the teams exhibit these characteristics is then directly related to their chances of not succeeding. So what are these signposts that we should be concerned about?

    1.   The members of the executive team have no confidence in the team's leader. In most of the examples provided, the individual with formal authority over the team had a large role to play in the team's problems. The interpersonal skills of this individual need to be very finely honed. The team members should be able to look to this person as a model of behavior. This person needs to be very careful about showing favoritism toward individual or an idea.

    2.   Individual or functional needs are put ahead of the organization's welfare. Again, many of the examples demonstrated how easy it is for executive team members to wear their functional unit hat rather than their organizational one. It is not surprising, given that most of the members come from a functional specialty and this specialty area will be perceived to be of greater importance than any of the other areas by its leader. Still, it is something that will have to be continually addressed, whether openly or as part of the culture of the team. In addition to the primacy of the functional needs of the departments, members who are "looking out for number one" are usually not going to be looking out for the best interests of the organization.

    3.   The real issues are "covered up." Some of the examples demonstrated that it is easy for executive team to not deal with fundamental issues facing the organization. It is much simpler to deal with the

symptoms of or fallout from the problems, as they tend to be less contentious. This does not excuse the team, though, for engaging in this
type of behavior.

4. The team exhibits a sense of power and moral righteousness.
Because of the power that this team wields in the organization, some
of this is understandable. What is problematic is when the team re-
fuses to acknowledge various perspectives because they are different
from what is normally done. It is also problematic because large problems may be looming but, because the executive team's attention is
directed elsewhere, the problem overcomes the organization because it does not have time to respond.

5. The executive team members bring no team skills to the table.
The most senior executives have a history of being singled out as
contributors. If they had not been, then they would likely not be
where they are. This brings with it a problem insofar as the members
of the team may never have been asked to be good team players before. They have reached an age and a career stage where that is unin-
teresting to them. Too often basic communication and interpersonal skills are lacking in these individuals. The organization
needs to try to ensure that being a good team player is a prerequisite
to being on the executive team. Demonstrated capability in this regard is very important.

6. The executive team leader is a dominant leader. Perhaps out of
a sense that they have to show dominance or out of common practice, the person on the authority position in the executive team makes
decisions. The executive team needs to have the opportunity to make
decisions as a team, to be accountable to the rest of the organization
for those decisions as a team, and to excel as a team. The leader (usually the CEO) can prevent this from happening—even inadvertently.

7. The need to protect the past stops the team from moving forward. The literature is clear on this problem, and it occurs at every
level in the organization. The way we have always done things around
here is a convenient way to make decisions. What it stops is the ability
of the organization to grasp new opportunities, and it puts blinders on
them with regard to what is going on in the environment. Executive
teams need to be extraordinarily vigilant in terms of making sure that
they do not fall prey to this problem.

8. The executive team makes poor use of conflict. For numerous
reasons, people in general don't like conflict. Most of us do not handle conflict well. We avoid it, we are aggressive about it, we take criticism personally even when it is not meant that way, and we are not
very good about being constructively critical, that is, debating the
merits of an idea while maintaining the dignity of the person who
made the suggestion. If conflict management skills are not present on

the executive team, then they need to be built into it with training and/or facilitative help or some combination thereof. Much of the work of executive teams is about debating the merits of ideas and examining alternatives to decisions, and conflict is an inevitable part of these discussions. To make this process productive, it needs to be managed properly.

9.   There is no trust among the executive team members. Much has been written about the construct of organizational trust in the past several years. Members of all teams have to trust one another. The importance of this is magnified in teams where the stakes are so high—those are executive teams. Following through on promises made, being honest, and taking responsibility for team actions all build trust. Just as an aside, trust cannot be developed in a short period of time, but only after a group has gone through many experiences together and has experienced support from the other team members, particularly in stressful situations.

10.   Members are too involved in their business units. One of the individuals I interviewed had this to say about this issue: He believed that executive team members needed to spend 70% of their time involved in executive team activities and 30% of their time involved in the functional unit of which they are usually the head. In practice, the reverse usually occurs. The team needs to make sure that a commitment to organization-level concerns is the primary expectation of those in executive team roles. The day-to-day management of the unit functions should be delegated. Team members should view delegation as an opportunity to mentor up-and-coming members of the organization rather than as a relinquishing of power. It is also important that the team members recognize that getting involved in the day-to-day running of the unit may be symptomatic of a larger problem such as an unwillingness to deal with broader issues, work with other members of the executive team, or make and be accountable for difficult decisions.

✦ EXECUTIVE TEAMS: WHAT MAKES THEM EFFECTIVE?

After reviewing the cases and examples from chapter 12, some reflection and summarizing regarding successful executive teams is warranted. The following list should be viewed as a set of indicators or signals about executive team functioning. The degree to which they exhibit these characteristics is directly related to their degree of success. So what are these special things?

1.   Create a common goal. This goal may be imposed on the team from outside or come from the team itself. Sometimes these goals

present crisis situations due to either the time constraints being operated under or the consequences of the actions. However, the goals don't have to be crises. The propensity for the members of this team to wear their functional hats needs to be overcome. Members have to come to the table with a perspective that places primary importance on the viability of the entire organization. Team members need a common purpose or they cannot be a team.

2.   Ensure a personal stake in the outcomes of the team's actions. They must be held personally accountable to the board and the rest of the organization for the consequences of their behavior.

3.   Value a variety of different experiences. Members who have had exposure to many of the functional areas in the organization and various types of industry experience bring a broad perspective to the executive team table. These broad perspectives are important for this team.

4.   Provide a clear notion of what is in it for them. The members of the executive team are usually very strong and capable people. Their time is a valuable resource. To get them to see the value in pursuing a particular course of action, the "what is in it for me?" question needs to be answered.

5.   Show respect for expertise. There is simply no way that any one person can possess all of the expertise needed to operate a complex organization anymore. Respect, appreciation, and utilization of all of the executive team members' skills are not just niceties, they are necessities.

6.   Show respect for individuals. It is essential for executive team members to have interpersonal skills. Interacting with each other (as well as everyone else!) in a manner that demonstrates dignity and respect is a hallmark of excellent executive teams. Criticism needs to be constructive and leveled at the idea, not at the individual who is championing the idea.

7.   Have a high level of energy. These positions are tough to hold. Operating under time constraints, responding to crises, and experiencing high levels of stress are part of the typical job description for these individuals. It is not for the faint of heart nor for those who cannot commit the vast amount of time and energy required for the job.

8.   Recognize that you are being watched. I have mentioned this before, but it deserves to be said again. The rest of the organization observes closely how the executive team interacts and what it does. Their behaviors will be emulated throughout the organization, so executive teams must model the behavior they expect from the rest of the organization.

9.   Hold common values and principles. Find out and exploit frequently those values and principles that the members hold near and

dear. Knowing that they are all in this together and have the same values will help them to get through tough times.

10. Be conscientious. What each member says they will do has to be followed through on. By doing so, trust will begin to develop in the team.

Developing these characteristics in top teams may not be an easy task. There is no magic here. Unfortunately, a 3-day workshop is not going to create these characteristics in any lasting fashion. The team as a whole has to be willing to try, to put the effort in, and to take the feedback on a regular basis about how well they are doing these things. Eventually these attributes will simply become part of the culture of how the team operates. However, the journey may very well be a long one.

✦ EXECUTIVE TEAMS: WHAT IS THEIR ROLE IN MARKET STRATEGY?

The evidence is clear that the executive team plays an absolutely critical role in setting market strategy. Regardless of the strategy adopted, almost all the respondents in my executive team study indicated that setting a clear strategy for the organization was job one for the executive team. This makes sense, as all other aspects of the organization—its structure, processes, human management systems, information management systems—have to be aligned with the strategy or the organization does not function properly.

Over and over in the examples of ineffective and effective executive teams, the issues of having common goals based on a well-articulated and widely adopted strategy came up. A couple of examples help to support this assertion. In the ineffective team case where the successful past kept the organization moving to a successful future, the executive team was unable to bring about the needed strategic market change from a process effectiveness one to a customer service one. Also, the case of the founder problems demonstrated that this executive team could not change the market strategy from a customer service one to a more process-efficient one. In both cases the organizations suffered immensely.

From a more positive perspective, the case of a financial crisis drove a small group of executives to change a process-effectiveness mass-production-focused organization to one where mass customization was needed. In this case there was not a market strategy shift between strategies, but a very real change within the process effectiveness approach. The culture-shift crisis case showed that a determined executive team could successfully change an entire organization from being process effective focused to customer service focused.

Obviously a market strategy must come from the executive suite. No other individuals in the organization have the time, clout, or resources to direct change of that magnitude. In my interviews with individuals involved with executive teams, the leadership that they expected in this domain is palpable. The rest of the employees in the organization want to know where the organization is going, why they should want to be part of the journey, what they need to do in their day-to-day work that will assist in getting them there, and that the structures, processes, information, and other resources are available to them so they can be an effective part of the process.

14

Conclusions

This book has amply demonstrated that the art and science of leading teams is a complex and dynamic enterprise. The payoffs can be tremendous for those organizations that are willing to invest the time and other resources into making teams effective. However, what is clear is that there are no silver bullets regarding making teams effective. This is not a simple undertaking where an organization can decide it is going to embark on using teams as its building block and that is all that needs to happen.

The argument presented here is that from a leadership perspective at least three domains need to be adequately addressed for teams to function well. The first is that teams need to be an integral part of the overall organizational strategy. That strategy is outwardly focused and thus I have called it a market-focused strategy. This does not let not-for-profit or public institutions off the hook. These organizations have to engage in the market strategy focus as much as the for-profits do. In fact, the competition for grants and dollars as well as the need for public accountability have forced the not-for-profits and public agencies to be much more proactive in the past 10 years than ever before.

I have used the typology suggested by Treacy and Wiersema (1995a) as the jumping-off point for my discussion of market-focus. This should be thought of as an exemplar. Whether you choose their model or another model is not as relevant as the fact that you are choosing and using a model of organizational strategy as the starting point for devising a team-based organization. Regardless, the structure, personnel strategies, and performance management techniques all need to be aligned with the organizational strategy. Teams have been all but ignored in this literature. It is time we paid attention to this aspect of teams as leaders.

The second domain of team leadership discussed was to differentiate the primary roles of team leaders. Up to this point, there have been unrealistic expectations of team leaders. Team leader training has been hit-and-miss or nonexistent. The three roles discussed at length here include the leader as manager, coach, and facilitator. Rather than thinking about this as the final word on team leadership typologies, it is better to think of it as a beginning. That is, the better we are able to understand what it is that teams in our organization with our specific issues are expected to do, then we can select, develop, and support our team leaders appropriately.

The third domain of team leadership was that of the executive team. This team should be the exemplar of team activity throughout the organization. It is disheartening to read so frequently about executive teams that do not function as well as they should. The perspective taken in this book has been twofold. First, executive teams are made up of members who need to be developed over the course of a career to work on teams. Second, executive teams must deal with unique sorts of issues and have unique problems, inherent in their composition, to overcome. Learning by engaging the team in cases and examples is one of the best ways to learn how to deal with similar issues that an executive team might face in the future.

So, with that as a set of summary statements, what are some of the lessons in each of these domains that we can take home?

◆ TAKE-HOME MESSAGES ABOUT MARKET STRATEGY

The three market strategies are product/service innovation, process effectiveness, and customer service. If the organization's strategy is product or service innovation, teams will need to be creative and excellent problem solvers. If the organization's strategy is process effectiveness, teams need to constantly monitor their systems to optimize product or service delivery so that it is faster and/or cheaper than anyone else's. If the organization's strategy is customer service the interpersonal skills of team members are their trademark.

The innovation strategy demands that the organization do the following:

- Have a future-driven strategy.

- Continually scan the environment.
- Create loosely coupled, dynamic work groups.
- Have a transparent and valid process for making decisions about what ideas survive.
- Manage by facilitating.
- Ensure that all stakeholders share in the success or failure of the idea.
- Secure technically competent individuals.
- Provide opportunities for sharing ideas.
- Encourage constructive criticism by all organizational members.
- Foster a culture that encourages learning—celebrating success and tolerating failure.

The process effectiveness strategy demands the following from the organization:

- Have an inward focus on processes.
- Determine how to mass customize.
- Form teams based on delivery criteria.
- Create a depth of specialized expertise.
- Focus management to assist in communication links.
- Ensure that management staff rise through the ranks.
- Create a culture of "urgency."
- Have centralized decision making and highly formalized policies and procedures.
- Foster a dedicated work force.
- Develop extensive training/mentoring programs.

The customer service strategy demands that the organization do the following:

- Narrow the scope of the market and serve those customers exceptionally well.
- Recognize that the emotional demands on your front line are heavy.
- Assume the contact point of customer to organization is the most important in the organization.
- Create expertise teams as well as cross-functional teams.
- Entrust the front-line personnel with decision-making autonomy.
- Manage by supporting.
- Foster a customer-first culture.
- Secure personnel who like people and dealing with their problems.
- Be prepared for the fallout when things don't go as expected.
- Have "high-touch" reward and recognition systems.

✦ TAKE-HOME MESSAGES ABOUT LEADERSHIP ROLES

The three leadership roles described are manager, coach, and facilitator. Although each of the roles is important in and of itself, one of the roles is more important for each market strategy. If the organization's strategy is product or service innovation, the role of leader as facilitator is most important. If the strategy is process effectiveness, the role of manager is most important. If the strategy is customer service, then the most important role of the leader is that of coach. This way of dividing up the area of team leadership into manageable pieces that make practical as well as theoretical sense is an important contribution to the area of inquiry. For too long team leaders have been left without the training or understanding needed to be exceptional leaders of their teams. I don't think this has been malicious on their parts, but stems from a nonunderstanding of the construct.

As you read through the next set of lists, you will likely say to yourself that all of these characteristics are important. They are. What has been problematic is that not everyone is good at all of them and no training programs can be built around developing all these skills at once. It is up to the organization as well as to the team leader to determine what characteristics are needed most and needed most urgently. This decision should be driven by the market strategy of the organization and the type of teams that the leader is asked to deal with.

Leaders as managers must do the following:

- Ensure alignment of team goals with organizational goals.
- Secure the needed resources for the team.
- Provide the team feedback from multiple sources about performance.
- Fairly and effectively evaluate team performance.
- Reward and recognize team efforts.
- Coordinate the work of the team with other teams and units.
- Be a spokesperson and champion for the team.
- Ensure that the team is not unduly or unfairly treated in the organization.

The following need to be done by leaders as coaches:

- Ensure that all team members understand and accept the team's goals.
- Make explicit everyone's role in the team's performance.
- Work with the team to set milestones and timelines for tasks.
- Ensure that all members adhere to acceptable standards of performance.

- Act as role models for the behaviors they expect of the team.
- Develop members' skills and abilities in anticipation of future organizational needs.
- Expect all members to treat one another with respect and dignity.
- Set up the mechanisms and norms for open and honest communication.

Leaders as facilitators should do the following:

- Encourage the team to take time to learn.
- Engage in exercises that foster new ideas in the team.
- Provide mechanisms for lots of constructive feedback to members.
- Assist the team in continuous self-assessment techniques.
- Encourage reflection on successes.
- Role-model and expect effective meetings.
- Be a source of team process expertise.
- Be an objective voice to comment and work with the team on how they operate.

✦ TAKE-HOME MESSAGES ABOUT TOP-MANAGEMENT TEAMS

Top-management teams, or executive teams, are a particularly interesting group. They make very important decisions and, when they do not function properly, it is apparent to everyone else in the organization. Developing team skills in the members of these teams is sometimes a very difficult task. However, if this team acts in unison and in accord with the strategy of the organization, they have a substantial effect on how teams are adopted throughout the organization. It is helpful to know a bit about these teams, as it will provide the researcher or practitioner with some insights about why the other teams in the organization are flourishing or floundering.

Top-management teams are unique because:

- They are more outwardly focused than all other teams in the organization.
- They are accountable for the performance of the entire organization, not just themselves or their functional unit.
- Members have achieved their status largely by acting autonomously and being singled out. They are now required to act as part of a group.
- Their role changes from being mentored to mentoring others.

- Personal integrity becomes very salient as these individuals are closely observed.

Top-management teams fail because:

- There is no confidence in the leader.
- Individual or functional needs are placed ahead of organizational needs.
- The real issues are covered up and not dealt with.
- The team has an overconfident view of its power and moral righteousness.
- Team skills have not been developed in the members.
- The leader is too dominant and does not allow the team to act as a single unified force.
- Members invested in past ways of doing business do not allow new ideas to develop.
- Conflict is not constructive.
- Members do not trust one another.
- Members are too involved in the daily operations of their functional units at the expense of the organization.

Top-management teams succeed because:

- A common goal is clear.
- Members have a personal stake in the success of an outcome.
- Members value and utilize each other's backgrounds and experiences.
- There is a clear idea of "What is in it for me?"
- They have respect for areas of expertise.
- Individual members are respected as human beings.
- They have a high level of energy.
- They recognize that the team is being closely observed.
- They hold common values and principles in business and personal life.
- Members act conscientiously in delivering on their promises.

✧ Top Management Teams Are Part of the Strategy

The evidence is clear that executives are expected to lead any charge in strategic change. Cases and examples amply showed that the executive team was expected to show leadership in the organizational strategy. If they abdicated this responsibility, they violated the expectations of all other members of the organization.

✦ CONCLUDING REMARKS

Teams are with us to stay. Except in sole proprietorships or very small businesses (e.g., partnerships), teams need to be formed to cope with the information, customer demands, the changing environment, and a whole host of other variables. I believe that organizations have not attended to the needs of teams to the degree that they should have, which has given rise to a cynicism about teams that is misplaced. In my first book, *Remaking Teams*, I provided a model for team performance for teams in general. In this book, I have taken a much closer look at the role of leadership in team performance. One premise has been that the market strategy of the organization must be present and be a driver of all organizational activities including team use. Another has been that team leadership needs to be developed in light of the market strategy. Finally, the role modeling provided by top-management teams is critical to team success as an organization-wide phenomenon.

References

Amabile, T. M. (1983). Social psychology of creativity: A componential conceptualization. *Journal of Personality and Social Psychology, 45,* 357–377.

Amabile, T. M. (1998, September–October). How to kill creativity. *Harvard Business Review, 76,* 76–87.

Amabile, T. M., Conti, R., Coon, H., Lazenby, J., & Herron, M. (1996). Assessing the work environment for creativity. *Academy of Management Journal, 39,* 1154–1184.

Bantel, K., & Jackson, S. (1989). Top management and innovations in banking: Does the composition of the top team make a difference? *Strategic Management Journal, 10,* 107–124.

Barry, D. (1991, Summer). Managing the bossless team: Lessons in distributed leadership. *Organizational Dynamics,* pp. 31–47.

Bass, B. M. (1990). *Bass and Stogdill's handbook of leadership: Theories, research, and managerial applications* (3rd ed.). New York: Free Press.

Bennis, W. (1989). *Why leaders can't lead: The unconscious conspiracy continues.* San Francisco: Jossey-Bass.

Berggren, E., & Nacher, T. (2001). Introducing new products can be hazardous to your company: Use the right new-solutions delivery tools. *Academy of Management Executive, 15,* 92–101.

Brown, S. A. (1992). *Total quality service: How organizations use it to a competitive advantage.* Scarborough, Ontario: Prentice-Hall Canada.

Burns, T., & Stalker, G. M. (1961). *The management of innovation.* New York: Barnes & Noble.

Campion, M. A., Medsker, G. J., & Higgs, A. C. (1993). Relations between work group characteristics and effectiveness: Implications for designing effective work groups. *Personnel Psychology, 46,* 823–850.

Cannella, A. A., Jr., & Shen, W. (2001). So close and yet so far: Promotion versus exit for CEO heir apparent. *Academy of Management Journal, 44*, 252–270.

Carpenter, M. A., & Fredrickson, J. W. (2001). Top management teams, global strategic posture, and the moderating role of uncertainty. *Academy of Management Journal, 44*, 533–545.

Carr, C. (1990). *Front-line customer service: 15 keys to customer satisfaction*. New York: Wiley.

Christensen, C. M. (1997). *The innovator's dilemma: When new technologies cause great firms to fail*. Boston: Harvard Business School Press.

Clark, K. D., Collins, C. J., Smith, K. G., & Stevens, C. K. (1999, April–May). *A relational approach to top management teams: Social capital, information processing, co-optation, and efficiency*. Paper presented at the meeting of the Society for Industrial and Organizational Psychology, Atlanta, GA.

Cohen, S. G. (1994). Designing effective self-managing work teams. In M. M. Beyerlein & D. A. Johnson (Eds.), *Advances in interdisciplinary studies of work teams: Theories of self-managed work teams* (pp. 67–102). London: JAI.

Cohen, S. G., & Bailey, D. E. (1997). What makes teams work: Group effectiveness research from the shop floor to the executive suite. *Journal of Management, 23*, 239–290.

Cohen, S. G., Ledford, G. E., Jr., & Spreitzer, G. M. (1996). A predictive model of self-managing work team effectiveness. *Human Relations, 249*, 643–676.

Collins, J. (2001, January). Level 5 leadership: The triumph of humility and fierce resolve. *Harvard Business Review, 79*, 66–76.

Cottle, D. W. (1990). *Client-centered service: How to keep them coming back for more*. New York: Wiley.

Coyne, W. E. (1997). 3M (Minnesota Mining and Manufacturing Company). In R. M. Kanter, J. Kao, & F. Wiersema (Eds.), *Innovation: Breakthrough thinking at 3M, DuPont, GE, Pfizer, and Rubbermaid* (pp. 43–63). New York: HarperCollins.

Davidow, W. H., & Uttal, B. (1989). *Total customer service: The ultimate weapon*. New York: HarperCollins.

Diller, H. (2000). Customer loyalty: Fata morgana or realistic goal? Managing relationships with customers. In T. Hennig-Thurau & U. Hansen (Eds.), *Relationship marketing: Gaining competitive advantage through customer satisfaction and customer retention* (pp. 29–48). Berlin, Germany: Springer.

Dilts, J. C., & Prough, G. E. (2001). Environmental change, strategic choice and entreprenuerial orientation: The case of the travel services industry. *Services Marketing Quarterly, 22*, 21–38.

Disend, J. E. (1991). *How to provide excellent service in any organization: A blueprint for making all the theories work*. Radnor, PA: Chilton Book Co.

Drury, C. (1994). *Cost and management accounting* (3rd ed.). London: Chapman & Hall.

Druskat, V. U., & Wolff, S. B. (2001). Building the emotional intelligence of groups. *Harvard Business Review, 79*, 80–90.

Dulewicz, V. (2000). Emotional intelligence: The key to future successful corporate leadership? *Journal of General Management, 25*, 1–14.

Edelheit, L. S. (1997). General Electric Company. In R. M. Kanter, J. Kao, & F. Wiersema (Eds.), *Innovation: Breakthrough thinking at 3M, DuPont, GE, Pfizer, and Rubbermaid* (pp. 97–121). New York: HarperCollins.

Eisenstat, R. A., & Cohen, S. G. (1990). Summary: Top management groups. In J. R. Hackman (Ed.), *Groups that work (and those that don't)* (pp. 78–86). San Francisco: Jossey-Bass.

Finkelstein, S., & Hambrick, D. (1990). Top-management team tenure and organizational outcomes. *Administrative Science Quarterly, 35,* 484–503.

Fisher, K. (2000). *Leading self-directed work teams: A guide to developing new team leadership skills.* New York: McGraw-Hill.

Fisher, K., Rayner, S., & Belgard, W. (1995). *Tips for teams: A ready reference for solving common team problems.* New York: McGraw-Hill.

Ford, R. C., & Randolph, W. A. (1992). Cross-functional structures: A review and integration of matrix organizations and project management. *Journal of Management, 18,* 267–294.

Foxhall, G. R. (1984). *Corporate innovation: Marketing and strategy.* London: Croom Helm.

Frost, P. J., & Egri, C. P. (1992). The political nature of innovation. In P. Frost, V. Mitchell, & W. Nord (Eds.), *Organizational reality: Reports from the firing line* (pp. 449–460). New York: HarperCollins.

Gladstein, D. (1984). Groups in context: A model of task group effectiveness. *Administrative Science Quarterly, 29,* 499–517.

Goleman, D. (1995). *Emotional intelligence: Why it can matter more than I.Q..* New York: Bantam.

Goodman, P. S., Rukmini, D., Griffith-Hughson, T. L. (1988). Groups and productivity: Analyzing the effectiveness of self-managing teams. In J. P. Campbell, R. J. Campbell, & Associates (Eds.), *Productivity in organizations: New perspectives from industrial and organizational psychology* (pp. 295–327). San Francisco: Jossey-Bass.

Gordon, J. (1992, October). Work teams: How far have they come? *Training,* pp. 59, 60, 62–65.

Greenberg, J. (1996). *The quest for justice on the job.* Thousand Oaks, CA: Sage.

Gretz, K. F., & Drozdeck, S. R. (1992). *Empowering innovative people.* Chicago: Probus.

Guzzo, R. A. (1995). Conclusions: Common themes amongst the diversity. In R. A. Guzzo & E. Salas (Eds.), *Team effectiveness and decision making in organizations* (pp. 381–394). San Francisco: Jossey-Bass.

Guzzo, R. A., & Shea, G. P. (1992). Group performance and intergroup relations in organizations. In M. D. Dunnette & L. M. Hough (Eds.), *Handbook of industrial & organizational psychology* (2nd ed., Vol. 3, pp. 269–313). Palo Alto, CA: Consulting Psychologists Press.

Hackman, J. R. (1988). The design of work teams. In J. W. Lorsch (Ed.), *Handbook of organizational behavior* (pp. 315–342). Englewood Cliffs, NJ: Prentice-Hall.

Hackman, J. R. (Ed.). (1990). *Groups that work (and those that don't).* San Francisco: Jossey-Bass.

Hambrick, D. C., & Abrahamson, E. (1995). Assessing managerial discretion across industries: A multimethod approach. *Academy of Management Journal, 38,* 1427–1441.

Hambrick, D. C., Geletkanycz, M. A., & Fredrickson, J. W. (1993). Top executive commitment to the status quo: Some tests of its determinants. *Strategic Management Journal, 14,* 401–418.

Harper, S. C. (1992). The challenges facing CEOs: Past, present, and future. *Academy of Management Executive, 6,* 7–25.

Harris, R. L. (1991). *The customer is king!* Milwaukee, WI: ASQC Quality Press.

Helman, D., & DeChernatony, L. (1999). Exploring the development if lifestyle retail brands. *The Service Industries Journal, 19,* 49–68.

Hennig-Thurau, T., & Hansen, U. (Eds.). (2000a). *Relationship marketing: Gaining competitive advantage though customer satisfaction and customer retention.* Berlin, Germany: Springer.

Hennig-Thurau, T., & Hansen, U. (2000b). Relationship marketing—Some reflections on the state-of-the-art of the relational concept. In T. Hennig-Thurau & U. Hansen (Eds.), *Relationship marketing: Gaining competitive advantage though customer satisfaction and customer retention* (pp. 3–27). Berlin, Germany: Springer.

Hoffman, E. J., Kinlaw, C. S., & Kinlaw, D. C. (1998). *Developing superior project teams: A study of the characteristics of high performance in project teams.* Retrieved September 10, 2001, from http://www.team-appl.com/About/findings.pdf

Hurley, R. F., & Hult, T. M. (1998). Innovation, market orientation, and organizational learning: An integration and empirical examination. *Journal of Marketing, 62*(3), 42–54.

Jacobs, R. S., Hyman, M. R., & McQuitty, S. (2001). Exchange-specific self-disclosure, social self-disclosure, and personal selling. *Journal of Marketing Theory and Practice, 9,* 48–62.

Janis, I. (1982). *Groupthink* (2nd ed.). Boston: Houghton Mifflin.

Janz, T., Hellervik, L., & Gilmore, D. C. (1986). *Behavior descriptive interviewing.* Boston: Allyn & Bacon.

Jaques, E. (1990). In praise of hierarchy. *Harvard Business Review, 68,* 127–133.

Jones, S. D., & Schilling, D. J. (2000). *Measuring team performance: A step-by-step, customizable approach for managers, facilitators, and team leaders.* San Francisco: Jossey-Bass.

Kanter, R. M., Kao, J., & Wiersema, F. (Eds.). (1997). *Innovation: Breakthrough thinking at 3M, DuPont, GE, Pfizer, and Rubbermaid.* New York: HarperCollins.

Katz, N. (2001). Sports teams as a model for workplace teams: Lessons and liabilities. *Academy of Management Executive, 15,* 56–67.

Katzenbach, J. R., & Smith, D. K. (1993). *The wisdom of teams: Creating the high-performance organization.* Boston: Harvard Business School Press.

Kets de Vries, M. F. R. (1994). The leadership mystique. *Academy of Management Executive, 8,* 73–89.

Kirkman, B. L., & Rosen, B. (1999). Beyond self-management: Antecedents and consequences of team empowerment. *Academy of Management Journal, 42,* 58–74.

Kirkman, B. L., & Rosen, B. (2000). Powering up teams. *Organizational Dynamics, 28,* 48–66.

Kirkpatrick, D. L. (1959). Techniques for evaluating training programs. *Journal of the American Society of Training Directors, 13,* 21–26.

Kirkpatrick, D. L. (1960). Techniques for evaluating training programs. *Journal of the American Society of Training Directors, 14,* 13–18, 28–32

Kline, T. J. B. (1999). *Remaking teams: The revolutionary research-based guide that puts theory into practice.* San Francisco: Jossey-Bass.

Kouzes, J. M., & Posner, B. Z. (1995). *The leadership challenge: How to keep getting extraordinary things done in organizations.* San Francisco: Jossey-Bass.

Kouzes, J. M., & Posner, B. Z. (1997). *The leadership practices inventory* (2nd ed.). San Francisco: Jossey-Bass.

Kouzes, J. M., & Posner, B. Z. (1992). *The team leadership practices inventory.* San Francisco: Jossey-Bass.

Krzyzewski, M., & Phillips, D. T. (2000). *Leading with the heart: Coach K's successful strategies for basketball, business, and life.* New York: Warner.

Kuhn, T. S. (1996). *The structure of scientific revolutions* (3rd ed.). Chicago: University of Chicago Press.

LaFasto, F., & Larson, C. (2001). *When teams work best.* Thousand Oaks, CA: Sage.

Lambert, D. M., & Lewis, M. C. (1983). Managing customer service to build market share and increase profits. *Business Quarterly, 48,* 50–57.

Lawler, E. E., III. (2000). *Rewarding excellence*: Pay strategies for the new economy. San Francisco: Jossey-Bass.

Lawrence, P., & Lorsch, J. (1967). *Organization and environment*. Cambridge, MA: Harvard University Press.

Leifer, R., O'Connor, G. C., & Rice, M. (2001). Implementing radical innovation in mature firms: The role of hubs. *Academy of Management Executive*, 15, 102–113.

Levi, D. (2001). *Group dynamics for teams*. Thousand Oaks, CA: Sage.

Levinson, H. (1993). Between CEO and COO. *Academy of Management Executive*, 7, 71–81.

Levy, P. F. (2001). The Nut Island effect: When good teams go wrong. *Harvard Business Review*, 79, 51–59.

Littlepage, G., Jones, S., Moffett, R., Cherry, T., & Senovich, S. (1999, April–May). *Relations between leadership, potency, group processes, and work group effectiveness*. Paper presented at the 14th annual meeting of the Society for Industrial and Organizational Psychology, Atlanta, GA.

Longenecker, C. O., & Gioia, D. A. (1992). The executive appraisal paradox. *Academy of Management Executive*, 6, 18–28.

Lovelace, K., Shapiro, D. L., & Weingart, L. R. (2001). Maximizing cross-functional new product teams' innovativeness and constraint adherence: A conflict communications perspective. *Academy of Management Journal*, 44, 779–793.

Lowson, B., King, R., & Hunter, A. (1999). *Quick response*: Managing the supply chain to meet customer demand. Chichester, England: Wiley.

Manz, C. C., & Sims, H. P., Jr. (1987). Leading workers to lead themselves: The external leadership of self-managing work teams. *Administrative Science Quarterly*, 32, 106–128.

Marr, N. (1980). Do managers really know what service their customers require? *International Journal of Physical Distribution and Materials Management*, 10, 433–444.

McCall, M. W., Jr. (1998). *High flyers*: Developing the next generation of leaders. Boston: Harvard Business School Press.

McCall, M. W., Jr., Lombardo, M. M., & Morrison, A. M. (1988). *The lessons of experience*. Lexington, MA: Lexington Books.

McDougall, G. (2001). Customer retention strategies: When do they pay off? *Services Marketing Quarterly*, 22, 39–55.

McGrath, J. E. (1964). *Social psychology*: A brief introduction. New York: Holt, Rinehart & Winston.

McIntyre, M. G. (1998). *The team management handbook*: Five key strategies for maximizing group performance. San Francisco: Jossey-Bass.

Miles, R. E., & Snow, C. C. (1978). *Organizational strategy, structure and process*. New York: McGraw-Hill.

Miller, J. (1997). E. I. Du Pont de Nemours and Company, Inc. In R. M. Kanter, J. Kao, & F. Wiersema (Eds.), *Innovation*: Breakthrough thinking at 3M, DuPont, GE, Pfizer, and Rubbermaid (pp. 65–95). New York: HarperCollins.

Mintzberg, H. (1979). *The structuring of organizations*: A synthesis of the research. Englewood Cliffs, NJ: Prentice-Hall.

Mohrman, S. A., Cohen, S. G., & Mohrman, A. M., Jr. (1995) *Designing team-based organizations*: New forms for knowledge work. San Francisco: Jossey-Bass.

Moore, C., Rowe, B., & Widener, S. K. (2001). HCS: Designing a balanced scorecard in a knowledge-based firm. *Issues in Accounting Education*, 16, 569–601.

Murray, A. I. (1989). Top management group heterogeneity and firm performance. *Strategic Management Journal, 10*, 125–141.

Nadler, D. A. (1998). Leading executive teams. In D. A. Nadler & J. L., Spencer (Eds.), *Executive teams* (pp. 3–20). San Francisco: Jossey-Bass.

Nadler, D. A. (1992). Organizational architecture: A metaphor for change. In D. A. Nadler, M. S. Gerstein, & R. B. Shaw (Eds.), *Organizational architecture: Designs for changing organizations* (pp. 1–8). San Francisco: Jossey-Bass.

Nadler, D. A., Spencer, J. L., & Associates. (1998). *Executive teams.* San Francisco: Jossey-Bass.

Northcraft, G. B., Griffith, T. L., & Shalley, C. E. (1992). Building top management muscle in a slow growth environment: How different is better at Greyhound Financial Corporation. *Academy of Management Executive, 6*, 32–41.

Parker, G. M. (1994). *Cross-functional teams.* San Francisco: Jossey-Bass.

Parker, G. M., McAdams, J., & Zielinski, D. (2000). *Rewarding teams: Lessons from the trenches.* San Francisco: Jossey-Bass.

Pearce, J. A., & Ravlin, E. C. (1984). The design and activation of self-regulating work groups. *Human Relations, 40*, 751–782.

Pearce, J. A., & Ravlin, E. C. (1987). The design and activation of self-regulating work groups. *Human Relations, 40*, 751–782.

Pine, B. J., II. (1993). *Mass customization: The new frontier in business competition.* Boston: Harvard Business School Press.

Porter, M. E. (1980). *Competitive strategy.* New York: The Free Press.

Ray, R. G. (1999). *The facilitative leader: Behaviors that enable success.* Upper Saddle River, NJ: Prentice-Hall.

Rees, F. (2001). *How to lead work teams* (2nd ed.). San Francisco: Jossey-Bass.

Rickards, T., & Moger, S. (1999). *Handbook for creative team leaders.* Hampshire, England: Gower.

Riechmann, D. (1998). *Team performance questionnaire.* San Francisco: Jossey-Bass.

Rynes, S. L., & Gerhart, B. (Eds.). (2000). *Compensation in organizations: Current research and practice.* San Francisco: Jossey-Bass.

Salas, E., Dickinson, T. L., Converse, S. A., & Tannenbaum, S. I. (1992). Toward an understanding of team performance and training. In R. W. Swezey & E. Salas (Eds.), *Teams: Their training and performance* (pp. 3–30). Norwood, NJ: Ablex.

Schmitt, W. (1997). Rubbermaid Inc. In R. M. Kanter, J. Kao, & F. Wiersema (Eds.), *Innovation: Breakthrough thinking at 3M, DuPont, GE, Pfizer, and Rubbermaid* (pp. 147–175). New York: HarperCollins.

Scott, S. G., & Einstein, W. O. (2001). Strategic performance appraisal in team-based organizations: One size does not fit all. *Academy of Management Executive, 15*, 107–116.

Senge, P. M. (1990). *The fifth discipline: The art and practice of the learning organization.* New York: Doubleday/Currency.

Shalley, C. E. (1991). Effects of productivity goals, creativity goals, and personal discretion on individual creativity. *Journal of Applied Psychology, 76*, 179–185.

Shalley, C. E., Gilson, L. L., & Blum, T. C. (2000). Matching creativity requirements and the work environment: Effects on satisfaction and intentions to leave. *Academy of Management Journal, 43*, 215–223.

Shepherd, C. D. (1999). Service quality and the sales force: A tool for competitive advantage. *The Journal of Personal Selling & Sales Management, 19*, 73–82.

Sizer, J. (1989). *An insight into management accounting.* London: Penguin.

Skarlicki, D. P., Latham, G. P., & Whyte, G. (1996). Utility analysis: Its evolution and tenuous role in human resource management decision making. *Canadian Journal of Administrative Sciences, 13*, 13–21.

Srivastava, R. K., Shervani, T. A., & Fahey, L. (1999). Marketing, business processes, and shareholder value: An organizationally embedded view of marketing activities and the discipline of marketing. *Journal of Marketing, 63*, 168–179.

Steere, W. C., Jr., & Niblack, J. (1997). Pfizer Inc. In R. M. Kanter, J. Kao, & F. Wiersema (Eds.), *Innovation: Breakthrough thinking at 3M, DuPont, GE, Pfizer, and Rubbermaid* (pp. 123–145). New York: HarperCollins.

Sundstrom, E., DeMeuse, K. P., & Futrell, D. (1990). Work teams: Applications and effectiveness. *American Psychologist, 45*, 120–133.

Taggar, S. (2002). Individual creativity and group ability to utilize individual creative resources: A multilevel model. *Academy of Management Journal, 45*, 315–330.

Tannenbaum, S. I., Beard, R. L., & Salas, E. (1992). Team building and its influence on team effectiveness: An examination of conceptual and empirical developments. In K. Kelly (Ed.), *Issues, theory, and research in industrial/organizational psychology* (pp. 117–153). New York: Elsevier Science.

Teal, T. (1998). The human side of management. In *Harvard Business Review on Leadership* (pp. 147–170). Boston: Harvard Business School Press.

Tjosvold, D., & Tjosvold, M. S. (1991). *Leading the team organization.* New York: Lexington Books.

Treacy, M., & Wiersema, F. (1993, January–February). Customer intimacy and other value disciplines. *Harvard Business Review, 71*, 84–93.

Treacy, M., & Wiersema, F. (1995a). *The discipline of market leaders.* Reading, MA: Addison-Wesley.

Treacy, M., & Wiersema, F. (1995b, February 6). How market leaders keep their edge. *Fortune, 131*, 88–98.

Van Velsor, E., & Leslie, J. B. (1995). Why executives derail: Perspectives across time and cultures. *Academy of Management Executive, 9*, 62–72.

Waldman, D. A., Ramirez, G. G., House, R. J., & Puranam, P. (2001). Does leadership matter? CEO leadership attributes and profitability under conditions of perceived environmental uncertainty. *Academy of Management Journal, 44*, 134–143.

Walker, A. H., & Lorsch, J. W. (1968, November–December). Organizational choice: Product versus function. *Harvard Business Review, 46*, 129–138.

Waller, M. A., Dabholkar, P. A., & Gentry, J. J. (2000). Postponement, product customization, and market-oriented supply chain management. *Journal of Business Logistics, 21*, 133–160.

Wellens, R. S., Byham, W. C., & Wilson, J. M. (1991). *Empowered teams.* San Francisco: Jossey-Bass.

West, M. A., Patterson, M. G., & Dawson, J. (1999, April–May). *The effectiveness of top management groups in manufacturing organizations.* Paper presented at the meeting of the Society for Industrial and Organizational Psychology, Atlanta, GA.

Yeatts, D. E., & Hyten, C. (1998). *High-performing self-managed work teams.* Thousand Oaks, CA: Sage.

Yukl, G. (1998). *Leadership in organizations.* Upper Saddle River, NJ: Prentice-Hall.

Zaccaro, S. J., & Marks, M. A. (1999). The roles of leaders in high performance work teams. In E. Sundstrom & Associates (Eds.), *Supporting work team effectiveness* (pp. 95–125). San Francisco: Jossey-Bass.

Zenger, J. H., Musselwhite, E., Hurson, K., & Perrin, C. (1994). *Leading teams: Mastering the new role.* Burr Ridge, IL: Irwin.

Author Index

A

Abrahamson, E., 144
Amabile, T. M., 32, 39
B
Bailey, D. E., 12, 140
Bantel, K., 4, 140
Barry, D., 76, 77
Bass, B. M., 94
Beard, R. L., 11
Belgard, W., 79
Bennis, W., 125
Berggren, E., 19
Blum, T. C., 32
Brown, S. A., 25
Burns, T., 13
Byham, W. C., 2, 77, 78C

C

Campion, M. A., 10
Carpenter, M. A., 4, 140
Carr, C., 25
Cherry, T., 82
Christensen, C. M., 18, 19, 49
Clark, K. D., 147
Cohen, S. G., 2, 10, 11, 12, 78, 81, 140, 141,
    142, 143, 144

Collins, C. J., 146, 147
Collins, J., 146
Conti, R., 32
Converse, S. A., 11
Coon, H., 32
Cottle, D. W., 26
Coyne, W. E., 19D

D

Dabholkar, P. A., 14
Davidow, W. H., 26, 27, 59
Dawson, J., 140
DeChernatony, L., 14
DeMeuse, K. P., 10
Dickinson, T. L., 11
Diller, H., 28
Dilts, J. C., 29
Disend, J. E., 27
Drozdeck, S. R., 98
Drury, C., 13
Druskat, V. U., 98
Dulewicz, V., 146E

E

Edelheit, L. S., 20
Egri, C. P., 35

Subject Index